JOACHIM OF FIORE
AND THE PROPHETIC FUTURE

CW00970724

JOACHIM OF FIORE AND THE PROPHETIC FUTURE

MARJORIE REEVES

LONDON

SPCK

First published 1976
SPCK
Holy Trinity Church
Marylebone Road
London NW1 4DU

© Marjorie Reeves 1976

Filmset in 'Monophoto' Ehrhardt 11 on 12 pt by
Richard Clay (The Chaucer Press), Ltd, Bungay, Suffolk
and printed in Great Britain by
Fletcher & Son Ltd, Norwich

ISBN 0 281 02887 7

CONTENTS

LIST OF ILLUSTRATIONS

PLATES (between pages 102–3)

Thanks are due to the Bodleian Library, Oxford, for permission to reproduce plate 1; to La Biblioteca Apostolica Vaticana for permission to reproduce plate 2; and to the President and Fellows of Corpus Christi College, Oxford, for permission to reproduce plates 3, 4, 5, 6, and 7.

PREFACE

When I began to study Joachim of Fiore only one scholar, Herbert Grundmann in Germany, had recently published a book on him and for the next ten years only a handful of Continental scholars were working on him. Now there is something of a millennialist band-wagon and the name of Joachim of Fiore (more often mis-spelt Flora) appears in many works, both on medieval history and the history of ideas. What causes those mysterious shifts of focus in historical studies of which this is a striking example? Perhaps history acts as a kind of sounding-board to pick up and throw back the preoccupations, anxieties and hopes of a generation. One of our concerns in this generation is with the meaning of history and its 'end'. The reasons are obvious. Whether the uncertainties be those of a sophisticated society contemplating a possible extinction of their civilization, or of a primitive tribe seeking refuge in millennial dreams from the intolerable impact of that supposedly advanced civilization, the future is very much part of our present today. Utopias of the future have recently been described as 'a necessary instrument of man in his attempt to understand and pattern reality creatively'. This is backed by a further comment on images of the future: 'We need utopias. . . . We need pictures of how human community might be structured so as to be peaceful, hopeful and loving, pictures that convince us by realistic analysis that we could get from here to there.'[1] That final phrase reveals a different approach from a medieval one, but the concern with the future is the same.

The term millennialism derives from the strange vision, in Revelation 20.1–3, of Satan bound for a thousand years, an image which has fascinated so many dreamers ever since. There have been two main types of millennialist: those who have placed this period within history and those who have viewed it as an extra-temporal state of bliss under the personal rule of Christ. Joachim of Fiore was certainly not a millennialist of the second category;

nor should he, I think, really be classed as a simple millennialist at all. The figure of Satan bound was only one of the clues which he found in the Scriptures and the foundations of his system were laid in his Trinitarian doctrine. Of the figures in the Apocalypse over which he pondered so much, the Book with the Seven Seals was the most important—a symbol, as he believed, of the whole of history. For Joachim was, first and foremost, a biblical scholar, intent on reading the writing of God throughout the whole time-process, rather than the prophet of an approaching climax. His later reputation as *magnus propheta* is an almost accidental consequence of his whole philosophy of history. When he was born in Celico, Calabria, *c.* 1135, Cistercianism was just making its full impact in south Italy and, as a devout young man who had been on pilgrimage to the Holy Land, it was natural that he should become a Cistercian and hence, in the great Cistercian tradition, a biblical exegete. But, as we shall see, he diverged from the Cistercian path, both in thought and in the form of religious life which he sought. With papal support he was allowed to form his own Order of St Giovanni in Fiore in 1196, yet St Bernard remained for him one of the key figures pointing to the future and in many ways he never ceased to be a Cistercian.

When he died in 1202 he left a religious congregation which seemed at first to have remarkable success in spreading its branches through south Italy and even further. Thirty-eight houses were founded in Calabria and sixty altogether.[2] Yet the Order of Fiore never became a prophetic force thrusting towards the future and, though the cult of its founder was devoutly maintained down to the seventeenth century, it steadily declined in strength after the mid-fourteenth century until in 1570 it was reunited with its parent order. Little remains today of Joachim's monastery in the town of San Giovanni in Fiore. Only one manuscript of his writings is known to have come from it.[3] Yet his books are really his monument. Cherished, as they must have been, by his first group of disciples, they were widely disseminated in the second half of the thirteenth and in the fourteenth centuries. The key manuscripts are found in Rome, Florence, Padua, Pavia, Reggio, Bamberg, Dresden, Paris and Oxford. Legends of prophetic powers, prophecies attributed to him, versions of his *figurae* and pseudo-Joachimist works, all spread his reputation and his ideas, even if in a debased form. It was the power of his idea of history and especially of his vision of the third age (or *status*) yet to come which—though often through a filter of distortion—made him a continuing force in the aspirations of succeeding centuries. When his three main works—and some of the pseudo-writings as well—were published in the sixteenth century, the printing press disseminated his influence even more widely. In the seventeenth century these works were still read, and even in the eighteenth and nineteenth centuries thinkers and dreamers could still become excited over the discovery of Joachimism. So the present-day interest has a long history behind it, and it is that history which I have endeavoured, in brief, to trace.

ACKNOWLEDGEMENTS

Thanks are due to the following for permission to quote from copyright sources:

The Baptist Times: an article by George Macleod printed on 2 May 1974.

Prentice-Hall, Inc., Englewood Cliffs, New Jersey, U.S.A.: Robert L. Herbert (ed.), *Modern Artists on Art: Ten Unabridged Essays*, © 1964.

Routledge & Kegan Paul and Princeton University Press: C. G. Jung, *Collected Works*, ed. H. Read *et al.*, tr. R. F. Hull, © Bollingen Foundation 1959 and 1968.

Thanks are also due to Oxford University Press for permission to include material previously published in *The Influence of Prophecy in the Later Middle Ages* by Marjorie Reeves.

I

JOACHIM AND THE MEANING
OF HISTORY

I

If history is the remembered past, it is also the expected future and men can no more ignore the latter than they can forget the former. The problem for medieval thinkers was how to relate the moving moments of this time-process in which they were caught to the unchanging eternal pattern of reality which was the ground of their faith. They did this by means of images. One of the commonest was the pilgrimage which took the People of God through history as aliens seeking a destination outside history. The *civitas pellegrina* confronted the *civitas terrena* in perpetual conflict. Jerusalem was for ever juxtaposed to Babylon. On the other hand, the long preparation for the Incarnation, as expressed in the genealogy of Christ, gave meaning to the time-process in a one-directional sense. It need no longer be seen as a perpetual cycle of tribulation, but rather as an organic growth, the budding, flowering and fruiting of divine seed secretly planted. This was vividly expressed in the image of the Jesse Tree. But its climax came at what was thought to be the mid-way stage in the time-process: it did not grow on into the future to the end of history. This expressed the Christian belief that history was already fulfilled in the midst of time, but it left a question-mark over the Second Dispensation, the space between the First and Second Advents. Was this a period of waiting or of growth? Was there progress in history itself, or did its significance lie solely in the two great moments of divine intervention, that already fulfilled in the Incarnation, and that to be expected in the Last Judgement? For many the time in which they lived was simply a space for waiting to which Scripture gave little meaning: 'Scripture spiritually expounded reflected the past, the present and the end of

time. The span between present and Last Things was dark.'[1]
Others, following St Augustine, saw the time-process as
positively decaying, a world grown old whose only significance lay
in the miracle of new growth in Christ happening in its moribund
carcase: 'The world is passing away, the world is losing its grip,
the world is short of breath. Do not fear, Thy youth shall be
renewed as an eagle.'[2]

Joachim of Fiore startles us by his sudden appearance and
revolutionary doctrine of history.[3] It is true that the twelfth century had been showing a quickened interest in the meaning of
history and in prophetic destiny. Two of Joachim's immediate
predecessors, Rupert of Deutz, writing in the first quarter of the
twelfth century, and Anselm of Havelberg, in the second quarter,
developed a concept of meaning within time itself by interpreting
it as a progressive revelation of the Trinity.[4] Each of them saw
progressive stages of illumination, the work of the Holy Spirit in
history, but neither clearly projected the final fruition of history
into its last age. Anxiety about the future was in the air, but
Joachim's doctrine, in his own age, seems to spring out of his own
inner experience, just as he himself first appears, unheralded,
before Pope Lucius III at Veroli in 1184.[5] Following later
legends, he was probably born in Calabria *c.* 1135 and, as a young
man, went on a formative pilgrimage to the Holy Land. But our
first real evidence is the encounter with Lucius III when he was
at once asked to interpret sibylline prophecies about the future.
By this time he must have been a well-known figure in south
Italy, a Cistercian, and Abbot of Curazzo, in Calabria. His exposition before the Pope shows that he was already absorbed in
his grand design of history. From Lucius Joachim received the
commission to work on the book which was the groundwork of all
his thought, the *Liber Concordie Novi et Veteris Testamenti.*

Why did Joachim appear at this moment? It seems impossible
to find any clear antecedents or obvious influences. His reading
was overwhelmingly in the Scriptures themselves and the Latin
Fathers.[6] He shows little knowledge of contemporary writers. His
geographical position is perhaps the most important factor to
note. He lived at the meeting-place of historical traditions. The
Greek culture of Magna Graecia was all around him and—as we
shall see—the Greek Church and its relations with the Roman
Church form significant elements in his pattern of history. Fur-

thermore, he lived in a region of many Jews and may himself have been of Jewish origin, though this has been disputed.[7] One of the few contemporaries, however, whose influence he acknowledged was Petrus Alphonsi, a Spanish Jewish convert, and it may be that Joachim's whole sense of the Godhead at work in the very stuff of history itself springs from deep Hebraic roots.[8] Finally, he lived at a point where western Europe thrusts out into a Mediterranean menaced by Saracens, where, in Messina, pilgrims, travellers and crusaders gathered and every rumour of the great conflict with the 'Beast from the Sea' was echoed. The drama of the times, the sense that events were moving to a great climax, must have impressed itself on his imagination. A dramatic view of history was perhaps a legacy from his environment.

But he needed solitude to penetrate its meaning. We learn from some vivid autobiographical hints how much the administrative duties of an abbot irked him. He tells us[9] that once, when in frustration and perplexity he could not fathom the meaning of Scripture, he turned to psalmody as the road to understanding, and learnt the meaning of the Psalmist's words: 'Blessed are those who dwell in Thy house, O Lord.' But when he longed to continue enjoying the inner peace of the supernal city, the affairs of the monastery crowded in again upon him, so that he lost the vision and was compelled to cry: 'Woe is me, that my exile is prolonged, that I dwell in the tents of Kedar. My soul hath long sojourned with him that hateth peace.' After several years he broke away in desperation and escaped to the sister house of Casamari where the Abbot loved him and where he was able to spend some time meditating and dictating to a beloved friend and scribe, Luke, later Archbishop of Cosenza. Finally, however, he broke away from Cistercian routine altogether and retired to a lonely spot in Calabria. Disciples gathered, he moved further up the mountain, and eventually was given papal permission to found his own congregation. The Cistercians were bitter about his defection, but one of the remarkable things about Joachim's career was the steady papal support he received. He called his monastery San Giovanni in Fiore, in expectancy of the new life that must come to flower, the *vita contemplativa* symbolized in St John. Yet—sadly—the Order of Fiore was quite unrevolutionary and had an undistinguished history until, in 1570, it was reunited with the Cistercian Order.

The groundwork of all Joachim's doctrine was the study of the Scriptures. The urgent task was to break through the hard surface of the Letter to the Spirit within. This required long and arduous study and meditation. Often the mind came up against immovable obstacles. Then what Joachim calls the *exercitium lectionis* was no use: repentance, prayer, recitation of psalms and waiting constituted the only approach. To such a one light was vouchsafed and a vision given which broke through the barriers and released the understanding into new creativity. Later legends[10] ascribed a first experience of this type to the time of Joachim's pilgrimage in the Holy Land, or, alternatively, to his first days as a novice at the monastery of Sambucina. Under the figure of a book, a river of oil and a draught of wine, he was credited with having received miraculous and instantaneous understanding of the Scriptures. These became stock stories and Joachim a type of those who received a special gift of spiritual intelligence. But he himself says nothing about such a youthful experience. Instead, we have two vivid pieces of autobiographical writing in which the mature thinker and experienced Abbot, baffled by intellectual barriers and terrified by doubts, battles to win through and receives illumination as his reward. The first occurs early in his *Expositio in Apocalypsim*.[11] He tells us that he had struggled in vain to interpret the text, *Fui in spiritu dominica die*, feeling himself always obstructed, until he set the passage on one side and turned to other things. Then on Easter Eve, as he lay meditating at about the hour when the Lion of Judah burst from the tomb, suddenly the stone was rolled away from his mind and he understood the concords of the Scriptures. Re-reading his former notes afterwards, the problems resolved themselves and he went ahead with speed. The second occasion was also at a high festival, the Whitsuntide during his sojourn at Casamari. This time he was actually assailed by doubts about the Trinity.[12] He went into the chapel in a state of terror (*conterritus*), seeing an abyss of unbelief opening at his feet, and despairingly turned to the discipline of repeating the set psalms. In the midst came the vision—this time in clear visual form—of a psaltery with ten strings, which utterly resolved his doubts about the Trinity. Again, creative springs were unstopped and the rush of inspiration was such that he called for extra scribes as he wrote his treatise, the *Psalterium decem chordarum*. In both these experiences what was given was not a specific answer to a specific question but an inspiration which freed his mind to work out the problems. There seems to be at work here that strange intuitive process which would later be acknowledged by so many great mathematicians and scientists as the hidden, creative source of their discoveries.

There may have been other moments of vision which set Joachim free in this way. He hints at one when, after evidences of frustration in the early pages of the *Liber Concordie*, he expounds his figure of the three-fold Tree of History and states that this is a tree such as one would never see in the natural forest.[13] It is difficult to claim that Joachim was a mystic in the full sense of passing through the successive stages recognized as the mystic way. He is too reticent about his own experience to give us enough evidence. In one short passage in the *Psalterium*, however, he describes the mystical ascent of Man, exalted into the third heaven: *Excedit homo, supergreditur angelum, requiescit in Deo. Ibi respicit mira mysteria, ibi quod oculus non vidit nec auris audivit, ibi archana verba que non licet homini loqui.*[14] This surely alludes to a moment of ecstasy which he had experienced himself. We also have one external piece of evidence from his friend Luke, who says that sometimes when he celebrated Mass his face, which usually looked like a dried leaf, was transfigured by an angelic light.[15] Thus the biblical exegete whose involved calculations and obscure interpretations we often find so difficult to read was also a visionary capable of great imaginative leaps.

To Joachim the experience of illumination was no peculiar gift, vouchsafed to him alone, but a foretaste of the Spiritual Intelligence to be poured out on all men before the end of history.[16] If it was a deep personal experience that first revealed to him the mystery of the Trinity as the sovereign key, he quickly moved on to the tremendous realization that this was the key to the destiny of all men. Just as, in the understanding of the individual mind, from meditation on the Letter of the Old and New Testaments there proceeded one Spiritual Intelligence, which gathered all truth into one comprehension, so in the history of mankind, from the work of God the Father and God the Son, there must proceed the work of God the Holy Spirit. The Trinity was built into the fabric of the time-process in such a way that its very inner relations were expressed therein. Because the

Son proceeds from the Father, the origins of His work must lie back in the Father's sphere. Because the Spirit proceeds from both Father and Son, there must be a double root to His work, one in the '*status*' of the Father and the other in that of the Son. Because the Three are One in Joachim's theology, all are active in all three spheres, even though each has its own distinctive work. The common statement on Joachim's doctrine of history is that he saw it in three successive stages—the Age or *status* of the Father, the Age of the Son and the Age of the Holy Spirit. But in fact his conception is more subtle than that of a straight progressive sequence, one after the other. Thus the accusation of tritheism levelled against him does not take into account either his insistence on history as the work of the *Unus Deus*, or the subtle inter-weaving of the three Persons in their activity throughout time. None the less, although Joachim certainly believed in the equality of the Persons, he did see the work of the Third Person as the culmination of history in the third *status*, just as in the life of the individual the Spiritual Intelligence was the crowning illumination.

Yet the two Testaments would never be abrogated: they remained immovable in authority, like the two Cherubim guarding the Ark of the Covenant. Joachim thought in terms of two coexisting patterns of history which he associated with the Alpha and Omega (Omicron), calling them the *Diffinitio* A and the *Diffinitio* ω. Here the very forms of the letters carry significance: the *diffinitio* A was the pattern of threes in which the work of the Trinity was revealed, symbolized in its triangular shape. But viewed from another standpoint, there were only two Dispensations in history, just as there were only two Covenants and two Testaments, the Old from Creation to the First Advent, and the New from the Incarnation to the Second Advent. These were like two great parallel streams each rolling on to its Advent. This pattern of twos was symbolized for Joachim in the double O of the Omega, ω. By a brilliant touch of visual imagination Joachim saw the middle stroke, the *virgula*, as representing a third part issuing from the two parts of the figure (see diagram 1). History is, in one sense, completed in its two parts, but hovering over each there is a third development, a new quality of life rather than a third set of institutions, a quasimystical state rather than a new age. It is notable that Joachim never uses the word

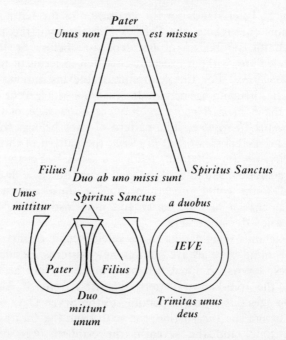

Pater

Unus non   *est missus*

Filius   *Duo ab uno missi sunt*   *Spiritus Sanctus*

Unus mittitur   *Spiritus Sanctus*   *a duobus*

IEVE

Pater   *Filius*

Duo mittunt unum   *Trinitas unus deus*

1   The Relationships of the Three Persons and the Unity of the Godhead. *IEVE* was Joachim's rendering of the Tetragrammaton

etas or *tempus* when he is thinking in terms of the pattern of threes: for this he always uses *status*. Thus 'third age' is really incorrect. Institutionally, the Latin Church will stand until the Second Advent just as the Synagogue did until the First, but its quality of life will be transformed from that of the *ecclesia activa* to that of the *ecclesia contemplativa*.

It is essential to grasp this double pattern of twos and threes with which Joachim operates since the great debate about him has always turned on the question: was he preaching a doctrine of revolution, an overturning of the existing Church and the establishing of a new authority and regime, a '*terza economia*', as the Italians call it?[17] Those who have hailed him as a revolutionary have pointed to, amongst other things, his reiterated statement that the life designated in St Peter (the active) would pass away, while that designated in St John (the contemplative) would remain to the end. But here Joachim is completely consistent:

when St Peter stands for the institution of the Latin Church he remains throughout the Second Dispensation; the passages in which the symbolism of his departure before St John is expounded are, without exception, written in terms of his *vita*, not his *auctoritas*. For the great immovable institution, the *Mater Ecclesia*, Joachim has certain designations which recur constantly: it is the *Ecclesia Romana*, *quasi altera Hierusalem*, or the *nova* or *spiritualis Hierusalem*. The pattern of twos belongs to authority: *Ille* (i.e. Peter) *maior* (*est*) *in gloria*; the pattern of threes to spirituality: *iste* (i.e. St John) *felicior in amore*.[18] Yet the distinction was a subtle one and easily missed by enthusiastic disciples. The third *status* could quickly become a third age, with a new 'testament', a new authority and new institutions. There was concealed dynamite here.

Joachim's imagination had a kaleidoscopic quality: the pieces in his mind were always forming new patterns. Besides twos and threes, sevens occupied his mind much.[19] Here he could start with the well-known pattern inherited from St Augustine of seven ages (*etates*) corresponding to the Seven Days of Creation: five before the Incarnation, the sixth from the Incarnation to his own time, and the seventh, the Sabbath Age of rest and beatitude—but when? For St Augustine and those who used this idea prior to Joachim it would seem that the Seventh Age lay beyond history, but for Joachim this Sabbath clearly coincided with and added to the understanding of the third *status*. The climax of the laborious ages would come at the end of the Sixth Age, when the tribulation of the Great Antichrist must be endured, but afterwards, *before* the Last Judgement, would be the Seventh Age. Joachim also meditated much on the Book with Seven Seals (Revelation 5.1). He saw the Seven Seals as seven periods of Old Testament history, matched by seven openings in the New Dispensation. Here the double sevens confirmed his pattern of twos, but in the seventh seal and seventh opening the pattern merged into that of threes—just as with the ω and A—for these seventh times are sabbaths. At the end of the Old Dispensation the 'sabbath' had been—in Joachim's view—the absence of history. In the New Dispensation the sabbath of the seventh seal would follow the great tribulations of the sixth and would be symbolized in the 'silence in heaven about the space of half an hour' (Revelation 8.1) at the opening of the seventh seal.

1st *Etas*	1st *Status*	Germination	Adam to Jacob	21	Old Testament } Seven Seals
2nd *Etas*	63 Generations				
3rd *Etas*		Fructification	Jacob to Ozias	21	
4th *Etas*	2nd *Status*	Germination	Ozias to Christ	21	New Testament } Seven Openings
5th *Etas*	63 Generations	Fructification	Christ to Benedict	21	
6th *Etas*	3rd *Status*	Germination	Benedict to . . .	21	
7th *Etas*		Fructification	. . . to *Consummatio Seculi*		

2 Combination of the patterns of Twos, Threes, and Sevens

The pattern of double sevens is synchronized at the end with that of over-all sevens, for the great sixth age (*aetas*) is given seven sub-divisions (*tempora*) which are the seal-openings and at the end the seventh sub-division coincides with the great Seventh Age which in turn, as we have seen, is equated with the third *status*.

There is yet another distinctive number pattern in Joachim's scheme. Twelve was, of course, a traditionally significant number, giving the concord between twelve patriarchs or tribes and twelve apostles or churches. Joachim's method of seeking clues to the meaning of history in the concrete happenings of biblical history is strikingly illustrated at this point, for, in meditating on the twelve tribes, he finds that five received their inheritance first and seven afterwards. Following his concords of twos, he then finds that five major churches, associated with St Peter, were established first and afterwards appeared the seven churches of Asia associated with St John. This division of the mystic twelve into five 'prior' and seven 'posterior' came to him as a revelation about time and its promise for the future. Then, illuminating the distinction between the numbers, came the realization that five was the number of the physical senses and seven of the Gifts of the Holy Spirit. Thus the fives represent the outer, the prior, the material, while the inheritance of the seven is inner, posterior, spiritual. There is a secret hidden within history, but mankind can only enter fully into it in the latter days. The five tribes, the five churches, the five senses represent the uncompleted inheritance of the first two *status*, while the seven tribes, seven churches of St John, seven spiritual gifts signify the final inheritance of the third *status*. Thus wherever Joachim uses this asymmetrical number pattern of $5 + 7 = 12$ he is making a prophetic statement about the future of history.

The bones of the number structures are clothed in flesh by the concords or symbolic meanings which Joachim draws continually from the material of biblical, ecclesiastical and secular history. The medieval approach to history which sought in each episode an inner meaning which linked it by concord with events of another era is, of course, quite foreign to us. It is as if each happening had a vertical point of reference, a 'thread' in the hand of God who combined threads into patterns on the inner side of history, whereas we look only for the horizontal connections and the pattern of visible cause and effect spun out along the time span. Joachim—like so many other medieval thinkers—rejoiced in looking for these inner meanings, but interpreted them, not so much in terms of the individual Christian's salvation, as in those of the destiny of the whole human race. He is endlessly ingenious and imaginative in the symbolic designs he discovers. Thus the three chief patriarchs, Abraham, Isaac and Jacob, are in concord with Zacharias, John the Baptist and Christ and, of course, typify the three Persons of the Trinity and, in consequence, the three *status* of history.[20] Isaac, prefiguring the second *status*, had two sons, Esau and Jacob. Thus in the second *status* arose the *ordo clericorum* and the *ordo monachorum*, first in the Greek Church and then in the Latin. The hairiness of Esau, in contrast to the smoothness of Jacob, signifies the Greek clergy '*quasi naturaliter pilosus*' compared with the 'smoothness' of the true monk.[21] The wives of the three patriarchs play a large part in Joachim's interpretations. Hagar, the bondwoman of Abraham, represents the Letter in contrast to Sarah, the Spiritual Intelligence, the Synagogue in contrast to the Latin Church, the Church of the second *status* in contrast to the Spiritual Church of the third.[22] Of Jacob's two wives, Leah, who conceives first, produces the spiritual children of the second *status*, but Rachel, who remains sterile until the sixth year, conceives the spiritual order of men to be born in the sixth *tempus*, that is, at the approach of the third *status*.[23] Perhaps because he sees the development of spiritual understanding in history so much in biological terms of germination and fructification, of conception and birth, Joachim returns again and again to this theme of the fertile women in the Bible.

Another favourite theme is the mysterious episode in which Jacob when blessing Joseph's sons, Ephraim and Manasseh, crosses his hands, so that the younger, Ephraim, receives the blessing which should have gone to the elder.[24] Spiritually, Manasseh represents the humanity of Christ, Ephraim, the fruit of the Spirit. Historically, that which comes last, inheritance in the Spirit, must be made first. The whole career of Elijah is fraught with meaning.[25] In general he typifies the Holy Spirit. His sojourn by the brook Cherith and with the widow at Zarephath signify that two peoples, the Greek and the Latin, will receive the Spirit when the Jews reject it.[26] Even the food offered first by ravens and then by the widow has a special meaning. The two sticks which the widow collects to make a fire figure some of the significant 'twos' that Joachim finds: Leah and Rachel, Elijah and St Benedict, Elizabeth and Mary, Peter and John, Martha and Mary. The baking of the cake by the widow typifies the Host and the two iron plates within which this is made, the two Testaments. Elijah's raising of the widow's son signifies the rise of St Benedict. Elijah's return after three and a half years to confront Ahab corresponds in the second *status* with the forty-second generation after Christ, so that the crisis on Mt Carmel can be seen as the new descent of the Spirit at the beginning of the third *status*.[27] The twelve stones of the altar are patriarchs/tribes, apostles/churches and twelve unknown in the future. The earth is the Old Testament, the water poured on by Elijah is the New, and the fire from heaven which consumes the sacrifice, the

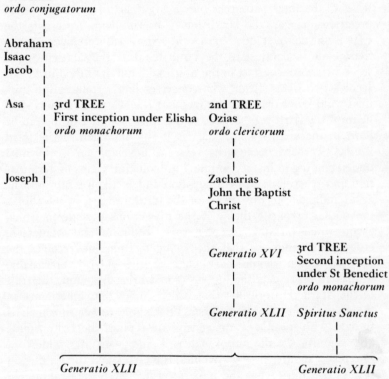

1st TREE
ordo conjugatorum

Abraham
Isaac
Jacob

Asa   3rd TREE   2nd TREE
         First inception under Elisha   Ozias
         ordo monachorum   *ordo clericorum*

Joseph   Zacharias
                                           John the Baptist
                                           Christ

                                           Generatio XVI   3rd TREE
                                                                Second inception
                                                                under St Benedict
                                                                ordo monachorum

                                           Generatio XLII   Spiritus Sanctus

            Generatio XLII   *Generatio XLII*

3   The Double Procession of the Third *Status*

stones, the water and the dust is the *Spiritualis Intellectus* about to fall on men. For as long as we see through a glass darkly these *'figurae'* are necessary to us, but when 'the Spirit of truth shall come and teach you all truth', what further need shall we have of figures? Just as the celebration of the Body of Christ superseded the Passover, so in the clarification of the Spirit the observation of all *'figurae'* will cease, for men will follow the simple truth symbolized in the fire.

In the midst of all the kaleidoscopic play with numbers, Joachim's grand design remains that of the three *status*. Each is characterized by its own order: the *status* of the Father by the *ordo conjugatorum*, that of the Son by the *ordo clericorum*, that of the Spirit by the *ordo monachorum*, or even *ordo heremitarum*. Because of the double procession of the Spirit, the *ordo monachorum* has two roots, the first in Elijah, Elisha and the sons of the prophets, the second in St Benedict and his disciples forty-two generations afterwards. The *ordo conjugatorum* is, of course, typified in the twelve Patriarchs, the second order in the twelve Apostles, and there must follow twelve religious, perhaps great Abbots, in the third *status*. Or, in institutional terms, the sequence runs: twelve tribes, twelve churches, twelve monasteries.[28] Here the five/seven symbolism comes into play, for following the pattern of the five prior tribes and churches and the seven later, Joachim is prepared to extrapolate this in terms of the third *status* by naming five great Cistercian abbeys as the first stage, but will not name the seven mystical and spiritual houses which will characterize the real age of the Spirit. To lead the Church from the second to the third *status*—out of the Wilderness and across Jordan—Joachim expects the advent of two new orders of spiritual men.[29] These are essentially transitional, intermediary orders, one of a hermit type to agonize for the Church in tribulation on the mountain top, the other a preaching order to labour in the world.[30] This prophecy is based on the many concords of 'twos' which Joachim finds in the Old and New Testaments, such as the raven and dove of Noah, two angels sent to rescue Lot from Sodom, Moses and Aaron, Paul and Barnabas. As we have seen, the authority of the Roman Church is unshakeable, but there must be a transition to a higher quality of spiritual life in the Church. This is typified, for example, in the fact that David reigned first in Hebron and then in Jerusalem. Even so for the Roman pontiffs the *ecclesia laborantium* comes first, the *ecclesia quiescentium* afterwards; first they must sweat in the *vita activa*, afterwards exult in the *vita contemplativa*.[31] But it is difficult to discover what kind of institutional change Joachim expected. Like Zorobabel at the end of the Old Dispensation there will arise a *novus dux de Babylone universalis sc. pontifex nove Hierusalem*.[32] Again, under the figure of Joseph's domination over his brethren, Joachim speaks of a final succession of Roman pontiffs who will reign from sea to sea, and he uses the figures of Mordecai and Judas Maccabaeus in the same way.[33] The Roman pontiff will be the Mount of the Lord to which all the nations will flow, for Joachim's third *status* is not only one of spiritual understanding and holy liberty, but also of ecumenism. The combination of immutability and transformation is summed up thus: the Church of Peter which is the throne of Christ cannot fail . . . but changed into greater glory it will remain unshaken for eternity.[34] It was, perhaps, too simple for Joachim to make such prophecies; his followers were faced with the problem that confronts all dedicated to change: how to revolutionize without breach of continuity and authority. As we shall see, some of them sought to solve it by the concept of the Angelic Pope.

Joachim could embody his vision of the third *status*, on the one hand, in those intellectual number patterns, and, on the other, in poetic and artistic form. In a lyrical outburst towards the end of the *Liber Concordie* he runs through sequences of imagery to express this supreme movement of history:[35] the first *status* was under the law, the second *status* under grace, the third *status*, which we expect soon, will be under a more ample grace; to the first belonged *scientia*, to the second *sapientia*, the third will be that of *plenitudo intellectus*; the first was lived in the servitude of slaves, the second in the servitude of sons, but the third will be in liberty; the first was a time of chastisings, the second of action, but the third will be the time of contemplation; the first was lived in fear, the second in faith, the third will be in love; the first was the *status* of slaves, the second of sons, but the third will be that of friends; the first of old men, the second of young men, the third of children; the first was lived in starlight, the second in the dawn, the third will be in the perfect day; the first in winter, the second in the beginning of spring, the third in summer; to the first belong nettles, to the second roses, to the third lilies; to the first grass, to the second corn, to the third wheat; to the first water, to the second wine, to the third oil; the first pertains to *septuagesima*, the second to *quadragesima*, the third to the festival of Easter. On the other hand, in the *Psalterium decem chordarum* he subjects the Eagle of St John and of contemplation to bizarre treatment by using its feathers as a schema on which to inscribe his essential number patterns of twos, threes, fives and sevens.[36] On the body are the captions Abraham, Isaac, Jacob, *Quinque patriache*; Zacharias, Johannes Baptista, Christus, *Quinque apostoli*; H.M.H., *Quinque quos Deus novit*. Correspondingly on the tail feathers are: *Septem Patriarche, Septem Apostoli, Septem quos Deus novit*. The wing feathers are arranged with five on the right and seven on the left. In the five are inscribed meanings related to Joachim's five senses of Scripture, as, for instance, *Hystorice. Abraham conjugatus, Isaac episcopi, Jacob abbates; quinque et septem filii: quinque monasteria deputati ad exteriora, septem ad interiora. Moraliter. Abraham exterior homo, Isaac interior, Jacob liberum voluntatis arbitrium; quinque et septem filii: quinque sensus exteriores et motiones septem.* This pattern is continued through the tropological, contemplative and anagogical senses. The seven feathers on the left are utilized for the seven species of the *sensus typica* which is the sense concerned with the action of the Trinity throughout history. Thus we have: *1st species (Father). Abraham patriarche, Isaac pontifices, Jacob prophete; quinque et septem filii: quinque tribus et septem.*

2nd species (Son). Abraham apostoli, Isaac episcopi, Jacob doctores; quinque et septem filii: quinque patriarchatus et septem ecclesia que fuerunt in Asia.

3rd species (Holy Spirit). Abraham abbates cassinses, Isaac alii qui venerunt post eos in alia specie, Jacob, alios qui sunt vel futuri sunt; quinque et septem filii: quinque monasteria et septem futura . . . and so on, through the other species. i.e. Father and Son, Father and Spirit, Son and Spirit, Three Persons in One.

Joachim's three main works are in many ways discursive and repetitive, although there is a kind of inner order in the *Liber Concordie* and the *Psalterium decem chordarum* which only close study reveals. In the *Expositio in Apocalypsim* the order is imposed by the text, but Joachim can go off into long disquisitions on his main themes at any moment. Ideas scattered throughout the writings will suddenly come together in a new formation. One

16

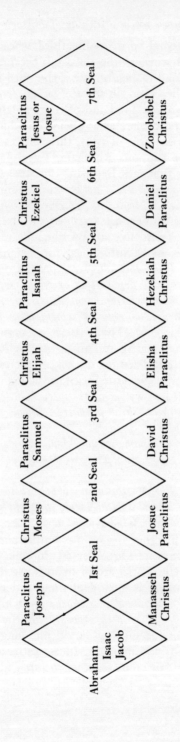

4   The *pavimentum* from the *Liber Concordie*

idea leads to another and before one realizes what is happening, Joachim is off on a new tack. There is a mobility in his thought which we shall find well expressed in his *figurae*. Only a shake of the kaleidoscope is needed for a new pattern to form. In general, however, the *Liber Concordie* makes the most intensive study of the Old Testament as prefiguring the second and third *status*, while the *Expositio* naturally centres on the Risen Christ of the Apocalypse and is deeply concerned with the second *status*, and the *Psalterium* is focused on the *Spiritualis Intellectus* of the third *status*. Around this Trinitarian sequence smaller works, sermons and poems can be grouped, using as one external criterion of authenticity their presence in a thirteenth-century manuscript now at Padua which includes none of the manifestly spurious works.[37] An interpretation of the Rule of St Benedict, a work of apologetics aimed at the Jewish faith, and an exposition of the Articles of Faith all contain characteristically Joachimist touches and have been accepted as genuine. Some short tracts are still unedited. Finally there is the larger, but unfinished, *Tractatus super Quatuor Evangelia* and the *Liber Figurarum* which—as I have argued elsewhere—seems to be an authentic embodiment in visual form of the Abbot's latest thought.[38]

Joachim's use of *figurae* shows to a striking degree the mixture of artistic and intellectual qualities in his personality. He uses *figurae* as teaching devices and some are obviously schemata for straightening out intricate patterns. Thus in the *Liber Concordie* he draws a 'pavement' of eight diamond shapes 'so that what can hardly be expressed in words can be seen at once in the figure'.[39] The first is designated in Abraham, Isaac and Jacob, and the others are assigned to the Seven Seals. Between the points of the diamonds appear pairs of great men belonging to each seal: Joseph/Manasses; Moyses/Josue; Samuel/David; Elijah/Elisha; Esechiel/Daniel; Jesus or Josue/Zorobabel, and to each pair Joachim adds *Christus* and *Paraclitus*. The three patriarchs, of course, represent the Trinity; the later leaders, appearing two by two to each seal, are seen by Joachim to typify the procession of Son and Spirit from the Father, active throughout the historical period of the Seven Seals. Twos, threes and sevens are gathered here in this double triangular form. Again, in the *Psalterium*, the use of a diagram enables Joachim to combine the Three Persons with the five 'general' Virtues, and the seven spiritual Gifts.[40]

18

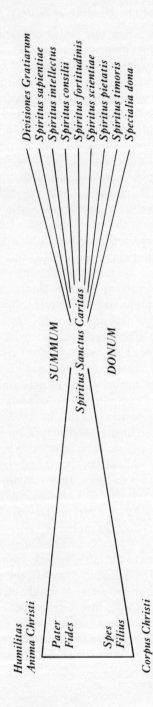

5   Diagram of Virtues and Gifts from the *Psalterium*

But Joachim's great symbols have a mystical aspect which transcends this schoolroom stuff. The Tree, for instance, had long been a powerful symbol in religious thought but Joachim's figure of a three-fold tree embodying the whole of history probably came to him, as we have seen, in a vision. He was never able to draw it properly and left instead various substitutes in the *Liber Concordie* and the *Liber Figurarum*.[41] It should have been three trees, with parallel sets of branches, the second growing out of the first, and third out of both the other two, yet still essentially one tree, with one essential life flowing through its trunks and branches. In the *Liber Figurarum* there are rich variants on this theme. One is a single tree springing from Noah.[42] Ham forms a mournful, abortive stump, but Shem and Japhet develop into the two great stems which encompass the whole of history as the *Populus Judaicus* and *Populus Gentilis*. These curve and cross, forming three great circles in the first of which the *Populus Judaicus* breaks into most leaf and flower, while in the second the *Populus Gentilis* is the more fertile, and in the third circle the tree is gloriously crowned in the leaf, flower and fruit of both Jew and Gentile. The three circles, of course, represent the Three Persons and three *status*; thus there is a subtle combination of twos and threes in this design. In a pair of trees representing the First and Second Dispensations[43] twelve branches symbolizing tribes and churches respectively are divided unevenly into five and seven instead of six and six, as in other trees. As we have seen, this five/seven division always implies the hidden inheritance of the third *status* and when we observe, first, that the trees are adorned with lilies and secondly that, reversed, they form eagles, we realize that, though only two trees appear to the eye, they carry the promise of the third which should proceed from them, that is, the third *status* whose symbols are the lily and the eagle. These are only two examples of Joachim's strange and richly coloured trees.

When Joachim sought to penetrate to the still centre of all being in the Godhead, he fastened on the geometrical figure of the circle. He wanted to represent the Godhead as Unity and Trinity at one and the same time, and he found his solution this time, not in a vision, but in a *figura* of Petrus Alphonsi, a converted Spanish Jew.[44] Alphonsi had drawn three interlaced circles for the Trinity, all enclosed within one circle for the Unity of

God. Joachim removed the outer, containing circle, because to express the Unity separately was abhorrent to him, making a quaternity. Instead he adapted the three circles to interlace in such a way that a central segment was common to all three. Thus he could demonstrate that each of the three Persons was separate, yet with a common essence which had no existence outside the three Persons. From Alphonsi he also took a parallel idea that the Trinity was already expressed in the pre-Christian Tetragrammaton. This he transliterated as *IEUE* which could be divided into three parts—IE. EU. UE.—in each of which the common element *E* occurs. Written into the Three Circles, this becomes an additional proof of the Three-are-One-ness of the Godhead. As with the Tree, Joachim can play many variants on this circle theme and in the *Liber Figurarum*[45] there is a marvellously complex page of big and little circles, with Alpha, Omega and the Tetragrammaton, in which patterns of twos, threes, fours and fives interweave in such a way as to remind one of a frozen dance.

Joachim's trees expressed in biological terms an unfolding of God's purposes through the natural time-span of history. The more spiritual movement of the Church's pilgrimage is embodied once more in a geometrical figure, a spiral.[46] Year by year the Church keeps the round of the liturgy, yet all the time she is tending towards her goal. So in a complex spiralling diagram of the religious seasons and the lectionary Joachim traces her course until it issues in the triumphant spiral which represents the time between Easter and Pentecost, or—in terms of the Church's history—the Seventh, the Sabbath Age, which is the third *status*. At Pentecost the end of the spiral takes the Church into the Eighth Day of eternal bliss. It is an ironical testimony to the subconscious associations touched off by shapes that, because this figure was coiled round in a spiral with a tail, Joachim's disciples added a wicked serpent's head and transformed it into an incongruous symbol of evil.

Two further geometrical figures sum up both Joachim's aspirations for the future and his sense of the unity of God's work in history. One, entitled *Dispositio Novi Ordinis pertinens ad tercium statum*[47] is a kind of ground plan in which four square oratories, placed on the four sides of a central oratory, represent the model of the New Jerusalem, with two dependent oratories as its 'suburbs'. Thus there are five-plus-two divisions, each of which forms a particular section of the *novus ordo* in the coming age of the Holy Spirit. These are described in notes. The five are categories of monks, but the two 'suburban' ones are orders of secular clergy and pious laymen. It is particularly interesting to find that in order to complete the seven-fold order of the third *status* the inhabitants of the suburbs must be included. Thus the pious lay people and secular clergy who represent the first and second *status* must be subsumed into the final society of the third *status*: the whole work of the Trinity in history is envisioned at one and the same time.

Finally we turn to the figure of the psaltery with ten chords which came to Joachim in the Whitsuntide vision.[48] Its shape, a triangle with a blunted top, giving two upper angles instead of one, enabled him to demonstrate visually the procession of the Spirit from Father and Son by assigning the blunted top and left side to the Father, the base to the Son, and the right side to the Spirit. In the version of the *Liber Figurarum* along the three main sides of the triangle he placed captions linking each *status* to its Person of the Trinity. The round, central *rosa* of the musical instrument represented the unity of the Godhead, though Joachim was careful to emphasize that, just as the hole in itself is nothing, so the Unity does not exist outside the three Persons. In its most developed form in the *Liber Figurarum*, the symbolism of the ten strings finally sums up Joachim's expectations for Man.[49] On the right the strings represent the seven spiritual gifts and the three theological virtues, starting at the bottom with *Timor Dei* and mounting up to *Caritas* at the top. On the left the nine hierarchies of angels similarly mount up from *angeli* to *Seraphim*. But above *Seraphim* is placed *Homo*, crowning the hierarchies and corresponding to *Caritas* on the other side. From earlier *figurae* we can follow Joachim's concept of Man's progress through the practice of the seven spiritual Gifts to that of the three Virtues, while in the *Psalterium* tract itself we get hints of his movement towards the belief that through mystical experience Man mounts up above the angels. Here Joachim was markedly departing from the angelology of the pseudo-Dionysius whom he had, in fact, quoted in the *Psalterium*. This development reaches its climax in the beautiful psaltery figure of the *Liber Figurarum*, with its unique vision of Man's place in the universal order. There were, indeed, precedents in earlier writers for placing Man above the angels, but this takes on a new meaning in the context of Joachim's doctrine of history. So the figure of the psaltery expresses in one harmony the work of the Trinity in the whole of history and the movement of Man upward to the vision of God.

One of Joachim's figures used a well-known symbol from the Apocalypse and was plain to the understanding. This probably explains why the Great Red Dragon with Seven Heads was the most popular of all.[50] The heads are named as the great persecutors of the Church—Herod, Nero, Constantius Arrianus, Cosdroe, King of Persia (sometimes Mahomet), Mesemothus (or Rex Babilon), Saladin, Antichrist to come—while the tail is labelled Gog, the final persecutor. The surrounding text expounds the tribulations of the Church. There is a contemporary urgency in the uncertainty as to Saladin's position when Joachim writes of the sixth head: *sive sit iste Salahadinus si adhuc vivet, sive alius pro eo.* This suggests that the notes were originally written when Saladin was still alive. Clearly this would be the figure on which Crusaders would fasten most eagerly and, as we shall see, this is what appears to have happened.

II

Joachim made a dramatic impact on some of his contemporaries. The most famous encounter occurred in the winter of 1190/1 at Messina, where Richard Coeur de Lion, en route for the Third Crusade, asked to see the Abbot Joachim. So Joachim was fetched down from the mountains of Calabria to stand in the eager and curious circle of English courtiers, which included Roger Howden whose first account of the meeting we have under the name of Benedict of Peterborough, as well as his later revised one.[51] Obviously the crusaders wanted a prophecy concerning the fate of Jerusalem and it is not clear if Joachim committed himself to a rash promise of victory or made an ambiguous answer. The later versions of the story postpone victory. It is clear, however, that Joachim was more interested in expounding the whole pattern of history, as it impinged on the present, than in making snap prophecies. The discussion turned largely on his exposition of the Dragon with Seven Heads as the embodiment of Antichrist: five have fallen—Herod, Nero, Constantius Arrianus,

Mahomet, Melsemutus—one is (Saladin), one is to come. So similar to the Dragon figure in the *Liber Figurarum* is this exposition that possibly Joachim had this actual figure on display. As we have seen, the accompanying text in the *Liber Figurarum* suggests that Saladin was still alive at the time of writing. The essential thing to Joachim was the inexorable working out of the pattern of tribulations. He saw his own role not as a prophet but as an expounder of the clues. Victory could not come to the crusaders until the design decreed it. Thus, in the pattern of twos, the Saracens were in concord with the Assyrians who were rampant under the Fourth Seal of the Old Dispensation, then subdued, and then revived again under the Sixth Seal. Thus, although the first onslaught of the Saracens had been stemmed, the full force of their revived power must be experienced under the Sixth Seal-opening. Moreover, after the Sixth there was still the Seventh and greatest Dragon head to come. With regard to the tribulations that must be endured Joachim's doctrine of history was deterministic and he offered little to strengthen the morale of crusaders. Rather, the signs of the times suggested to him that the crisis of history was deepening. In 1195 he was again in Messina where he encountered and questioned a man who had been imprisoned in Alexandria.[52] With a thrill of horror Joachim records the rumour which the man had gleaned from 'a certain great Saracen' that the Patarin heretics had sent envoys to them seeking peace and alliance. Here was that deadly anticipated combination of the Beast from the Sea and the Beast from the Land. Thus contemporary happenings illumined the concords of Scripture, while the study of the Testaments gave the clue to the vast events on the threshold of which Joachim believed he stood.

A fragmentary *Vita Joachimi Abbatis*,[53] probably written by a disciple, shows Joachim in a whirlwind descent on the Emperor Henry VI later in the year 1191. Henry had come to claim the kingdom of Tancred in the name of his wife, Constance, and Joachim descended like the Old Testament prophet to denounce the deeds of the invader and to pronounce political doom in the light of biblical concords. Like Tyre in the days of Nebuchadrezzar, the Norman kingdom must fall before this new king of Babylon. This fierce and sudden apparition must have made a decided impact for, it is reported, to his retreating back, Henry's marshal exclaimed: 'What a burden of evil tidings lies beneath that cowl!' So Joachim impinged dramatically on the contemporary scene as the interpreter of events in the light of God's design.

A third account of a contemporary interview which probably took place in 1198 strikes a quieter note.[54] The Cistercian Abbot, Adam of Persigny, met Joachim in Rome when, so he thought, Joachim was aged about sixty. Adam at once began to question him about the nature of his inspiration: did he foretell future events by prophecy, by conjecture or by revelation? 'By none of these', replied Joachim, 'for God who in times past endowed the prophets with the spirit of prophecy has given to me the *spiritus intelligentiae*, so that I can understand *clarissime* all the mysteries of the Scriptures.' Again we see here how contemporary interest focused on Joachim's role as prophet and the nature of his gift. This was to be his reputation in succeeding generations. There is a telling little illustration on the title-page to a sixteenth-century Joachimist edition which shows the expectant Joachim seated with pen poised and the other hand cupped round his ear to hear what God will say.[55] This is how most people thought of him: *magnus propheta*. But the interview with Adam of Persigny shows Joachim repudiating the title of prophet and claiming only the *donum spiritualis intellectus*. Again, this was interpreted in later legends as a sudden, miraculous gift of understanding to an ignorant man, but to Joachim it was illumination given at the end of arduous study and the faithful practice of psalmody, as laid down by the Benedictine Rule. The illumination itself appears to have come in the form of visual symbols and patterns concerning the meaning of history. There was no question of foretelling forthcoming events in the popular meaning of prediction.

There was one encounter which did not take place, although legend has suggested it: a meeting between Joachim and Peter Lombard. Dates, in fact, make this impossible, but it is easy to see how the legend arose, since Joachim saw in Peter Lombard his principal intellectual opponent. He wrote with passion in the *Psalterium* against the perfidy of those (*aliquorum*) who would create a quaternity in the Godhead.[56] Furthermore, in the Dresden manuscript of the *Liber Figurarum* there is a set of Trinitarian figures which was probably cut out of the Oxford and Reggio manuscripts as dangerous, but which had escaped attention here.[57] In brilliantly simple visual form Joachim here represents three heresies on the Trinity and the true Catholic doctrine. The Sabellian heresy is shown as one straight line and the Arian in three lines of diminishing length. The crucial figures are those of the *fides Catholica* juxtaposed to the *perfidia* (*Petri—* erased) thus:

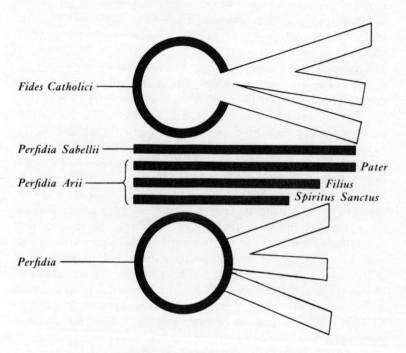

Fides Catholici

Perfidia Sabellii

Perfidia Arii

Pater
Filius
Spiritus Sanctus

Perfidia

6   Diagrams on the Doctrine of the Trinity

It is clear from the accompanying text that the circles represent water-sources, that is, the fountain-head of the Godhead, from which, in the true figure, the three channels of the three Persons flow out, as one with the source. But in the *perfidia Petri* figure the three channels are cut off from the main water-source. Peter's heresy, in Joachim's eyes, was that he had so emphasized the *una essentia* of the Godhead as to make it a separate, fourth entity, and so had fallen into the error of quarternity. Joachim used a number of images to show that the essence of the Godhead did not exist apart from the three Persons, as, for instance, that of root, stem and bark which are yet one tree.[58] The passion with which he attacked this monstrous perfidy probably sprang from his deep conviction about the way the Trinity was manifested in history: the work of each Person could be distinguished in their several *status*, but the three Persons operated together in the whole of history and there was no manifestation of the *una essentia* apart from the three Persons. Thus what might seem like an arid scholastic debate was of passionate consequence in terms of the meaning of history.

The issue in this controversy, which occupied a number of minds in the late twelfth century, was at that stage very much in doubt. There was actually a move to condemn Peter Lombard.[59] But by the time of Joachim's death Innocent III, under the influence of the Lombard, was on the papal throne and so, in 1215, at the Fourth Lateran Council, the verdict went the other way and the condemned tract was one which Joachim had specifically written against Peter Lombard. The tract was destroyed,[60] but we gather something of its content from extracts quoted in the condemnation and these fit with the evidence gathered from the *Psalterium* and the Dresden figure and text. Because he had submitted all his works to the papacy, Joachim's personal reputation was safeguarded in the condemnation, but perhaps some echoes of the emotions aroused in his disciples can be caught in the story of a double apparition which appeared to a troubled scribe, one of Joachim—*quidam senex habens in digito annulum et baculum in manu*—and one of Peter Lombard—*quandam umbram omni nigredine nigriorem, que lacertos habens pilosos et digitos ligneos ac virgam ferream in manu*.[61] Later the pseudo-Joachimist commentary on Jeremiah, known as the *Super Hieremiam*, enshrined the tradition, which probably originated at Fiore, that Joachim had been the victim of an unjust conspiracy in which the Cistercian leaders allied with Pope Innocent III to engineer the condemnation and so temporarily to extinguish the 'star' of spiritual intelligence.[62] The Order of Fiore, though lacking its founder's prophetic vision, remained faithful to his memory, even gaining permission to commemorate him in the pointed phrases of a special Antiphon to Vespers: '*Beatus Joachim, spiritu dotatus prophetico, decoratus intelligentia, errore procul haeretico, dixit futura praesentia.*'

Thus in the generation after his death Joachim of Fiore begins to appear as one with a double reputation. On the one side there stood the condemnation of his Trinitarian doctrine; on the other side he was known as the prophet of Antichrist, the recipient of the gift of spiritual understanding, the seer who laid out the pattern of history. It is difficult to know how quickly his major works circulated, but in the first decade of the thirteenth century Robert of Auxerre seems to have known a small tract[63] and an early thirteenth-century manuscript from a northern *scriptorium* includes another small tract on the Seven Seals and one of Joachim's Tables of Concords.[64] We seem to have here the beginnings of a small anthology of tracts and *figurae* which we can trace in an extended form in several later manuscripts. Since Joachim's main writings were weighty and involved works, perhaps some A.B.C. of Joachimism was required. *Figurae* must have been particularly apt for this purpose. The Oxford manuscript of the *Liber Figurarum* was made at latest, it is thought, within twenty-five years of Joachim's death, and the Dresden copy, though later, seems to derive from an early exemplar.[65] An addition to a collection of Peter of Blois's letters, probably made c. 1213, shows a knowledge of Joachim's Tables of Concords.[66]

But the revolutionary possibilities of Joachim's pattern of threes appear to have remained hidden until the 1240s. In this decade we meet the first realization that Joachim's prophecy of new spiritual men fitted the two great Mendicant Orders and the first pseudo-Joachimist work to be written from the perspective of the three *status*. The recognition of the Friars Preacher and Minor as the fulfilment of his prophecy greatly enhanced Joachim's reputation, but in the 1250s, as we shall see later, the appropriation of Joachim's concept of the three *status* by a rash and revolutionary Franciscan, named Gerard of Borgo San Donnino, suddenly highlighted the dangerous, even heretical, implications which could be drawn from the Abbot's doctrine. The scandal of the Eternal Evangel, as it was called, caused a furore in the University of Paris in 1254 and led to a papal commission and condemnation. Joachim's reputation seems again to have been somewhat protected but a provincial condemnation at Arles in 1263 made quite clear that connection between the Abbot's teaching and the pernicious Eternal Evangel. This second condemnation was more damaging than that of 1215, as the tone of the many chroniclers who record it shows.[67]

Thus Joachim emerges as a man with two reputations. On the one hand, he was *magnus propheta*, the one who interpreted the dragon with seven heads, the seven Seals and Openings, above all, the one who foretold the advent of the Mendicants. On the other hand, he was the twice-condemned. When handbooks of saints and heretics began to appear in print in the fifteenth and sixteenth centuries, he found a place in both. The discussion as to whether he was orthodox or heretic has gone on ever since.

2

NEW SPIRITUAL MEN

I

It was of the essence of Joachim's belief in the fruition of history that the agencies to bring the Church through the transition period must be human, albeit divinely commissioned and inspired. One of his favourite symbols for the perilous passage through the tribulation of the great Antichrist into the peace and beatitude of the third *status* was the passage of the River Jordan which ended the laborious journeyings of Israel in the Wilderness and brought them finally to the Promised Land. As Moses and Aaron, and after them Joshua and Caleb, led the Israelites, so two new orders of spiritual men must lead the Church of the second *status* into the third. As we have seen, Joachim found these two orders prefigured in many 'twos' of both the Old and New Testaments. Perhaps the most interesting point about his concept is that these orders have a function in relation to the whole Church. They are not 'religious' in the traditional sense of withdrawing from the world, but rather intermediaries between the life of contemplation and the active life of secular clergy and laity. He distinguishes two degrees of involvement in the world: one order will preach among the people, living an active life; the other will live the hermit life on the mountain top, interceding for the salvation of the world, but finally descending in fiery denunciation of sin. Joachim describes the intermediary position of the first order under various figures, and notably under that of the Son of Man seated upon a white cloud in Revelation 14.14.[1] This figure signifies *'quendam ordinem iustorum cui datum sit perfecte imitari vitam filii hominis'*. These men will be learned to evangelize, yet their conversation will be light and spiritual as a cloud. The cloud itself symbolizes their position midway between heaven and earth, for their life will be contemplative in comparison with those involved in earthly affairs, but not as high as that of the hermits figured in the angel who issues from the temple in heaven (Revelation 14.17). So the two orders distinguish themselves: one, the order of perfect men serving the life of Christ, the other, the order of hermits emulating the life of angels.

The idea of this new 'intermediary' function was taking shape in Joachim's mind precisely in the period—the latter part of the twelfth century—when the impulse to enter new forms of religious commitment was rising to the surface most markedly. The traditional monastic mode of a life apart from the world did not meet the aspirations of those who wished to express their commitment in terms of service within the secular order. The Humiliati, Waldenses and other groups were groping for a new concept and Joachim's vision is surely in tune with this contemporary movement. Here he was prophetic in the sense of expressing the expectations of the times. The fact that this aspiration finds its most powerful fulfilment a decade after his death, in the advent of the Friars Preacher and Minor, really confirms his intuition, although people later saw it as a great feat of foreknowledge.

Attempts have been made to trace a connection between St Francis's sense of vocation and Joachim's vision of new spiritual men. So far no firm evidence for this has been established, and, indeed, it is not inherently likely. As we have already remarked, for a full generation or more after his death Joachim was known as a prophet of Antichrist, projecting into the near future by his pattern of twos the crisis of tribulation expected at the opening of the Sixth Seal. It is not until the 1240s that we begin to see clear signs of an awakening interest in Joachim's third *status*. Did this second phase of Joachimism originate in the circle of Joachim's disciples, i.e. in the Order of Fiore itself and sympathetic Cistercian houses, or in early Franciscan houses of south Italy, particularly Naples? This point is still in debate. I have argued elsewhere[2] that the first substantial pseudo-Joachimist work, the *Super Hieremiam*, together with two somewhat later works, the *De Oneribus* and the *Super Esaiam*, was written in Calabria by Joachites of the Fiore/Cistercian group. These have been ascribed to a Franciscan source, because of their considerable emphasis on the two new orders. But only a few passages in these enigmatic prophecies seem directly to apply to the Franciscan and Dominican Orders. Others, particularly in the *Super Hieremiam*, are oriented towards a future for the Cistercian Order. There are

other points, too, which link these works with Joachim's immediate disciples. In Joachim's scheme there is a place both for
the general order of monastic contemplatives which would characterize the third *status* and for the two 'transitional' orders described above. It seems likely that the Calabrian circle of
Joachim's disciples quickly accepted the advent of the two great
Mendicant Orders as the fulfilment of the role allotted to the
transitional orders, for when the first Dominicans approached S.
Giovanni in Fiore the monks of Fiore went out to hail them as
one of the two expected orders in obedience, so they said, to the
command of their founder.[3] The pseudo-Joachimist works suggest that they still hoped for a future place in the monastic order
of the third *status*, but energy to pursue a prophetic destiny seems
to have been lacking and it is to other groups that we must look
for the assumption of this role of new spiritual men.

There may have been other encounters besides that dramatic
one outside Fiore in which Mendicants met with Joachite
enthusiasts in south Italy and caught from them the inspiration of
Joachim's vision. A prophetic role for the two Mendicant Orders,
sent to save the world *'novissime diebus istis in fine seculorum'* is
officially endorsed in a joint encyclical issued in 1255 by the two
Generals, Humbert de Romanis and John of Parma.[4] For the
Dominicans, Humbert claims the position of the order which is
novus et antiquus in his *Legenda*, and certainly not all the
Preachers could remain impervious to the power of the prophetic
role.[5] Dietrich of Apolda, for instance, writing in 1297, knew that
Joachim had foretold the coming of the Order of Preachers, and
hailed his order, in Humbert's words, as God's final messenger,
the order which is new in institution, but old in authority. An
anonymous *Brevis Historia* of the Order, dated 1367, has a prophecy purporting to be Joachim's, in which there will be twelve
leaders of the new order to illuminate the world, standing in
concord with the patriarchs and apostles. Other examples can be
adduced to show that Dominicans were interested in, read and
collected Joachimist prophecies. But the story of how St Thomas
Aquinas confiscated one of Joachim's works in a Dominican
house represents his heavy disapproval of the Abbot and his
disciples.[6] Official policy was modelled on this attitude and on the
whole the Friars Preacher steered clear of this dangerous dimension of prophecy.

It is within the Minorite Order that we must look for the first full appropriation of that role of the new spiritual men which Joachim's own order somehow let slip. Whether or not Franciscan interest in Joachimism originated at Naples, our first clear link appears at Pisa. Salimbene, the Franciscan chronicler, tells the story of a Florensian abbot from Fiore who, fleeing from the wrath of Frederick II *c*. 1240, carried the works of Joachim to the Franciscan house at Pisa.[7] There Salimbene encountered them and got his first taste of Joachimism. His chronicle is our chief source for the spread of these ideas among Franciscans, but much remains unclear.[8] When Salimbene was sent north in 1248 to study at Paris there was apparently already a Joachite circle at Hyères in Provence which drew him away from academic study. The centre of this group was Hugh de Digne whom Salimbene calls *magna Joachita*. He gives a vivid account of the enthusiastic circle—which included lawyers, doctos and *alii litterati*—and their debates on the prophecies of Joachim. Their concern, however, still seems to have been with crisis and Antichrist, rather than with the third *status* to follow. Nor in the writings of Hugh de Digne himself do we find any concept of the third *status* or the role of the Franciscans within it. Probably the key person in the process by which the group that we call the Spiritual Franciscans came to realize the implications of Joachim's doctrine for themselves was Hugh de Digne's friend, John of Parma, General of the Order from 1247–1257. Within the Order the split between the 'Spirituals' and the 'Conventuals' was already developing over the question of maintaining a rigid adherence to St Francis's Rule and Testament or allowing modifications to the ideal of absolute poverty.[9] To the Spirituals the figure of St Francis was so unique that he represented a turning-point in history and his instructions were therefore an absolute command. The concept of transition from a second to a third phase of history offered them both an eschatological basis for this deep conviction and a reason for clinging rigidly to his Rule, which became for them the key to the new age. The intense joy with which the first Zealots greeted John of Parma's election to the Generalship suggests that they expected his leadership to be crucial; Brother Giles is reported as greeting him with the prophetic words: 'Well and truly you have come, but you have come late.'[10]

Whether or not John first caused the fusion of 'Spiritual' con-

viction and Joachimist prophecy, it is a lesser figure, his companion, the fanatical Gerard of Borgo San Donnino, who gives us our
first clear evidence that this fusion had taken place. Gerard announced the advent of the third *status* in a book which was to be
the Eternal Evangel, superseding the Old and New Testaments.
This consisted of Joachim's three main works, together with a
Liber Introductorius and gloss written by Gerard himself. This
book dropped like a stone into the pool of Paris University in
1254, creating a series of ever-widening ripples.[11] The secular
masters, always hostile to the Mendicants and ready for any stick
with which to beat them, seized on it eagerly, made their own set
of excerpts and sent these to the Pope. Alexander IV appointed a
commission which met at Anagni and examined thoroughly, not
only Gerard's production, but the writings and *figurae* of Joachim
himself. No full copy of Gerard's compilation is known to have
survived[12] and our knowledge of his work derives mainly from
the Paris Masters' articles and the report of the Commission.
There seem to have been three main points in his gospel: the
proclamation of the imminent third *status* of the Holy Spirit
which would be '*sine enigmate et sine figuris*'; the declaration that
about the year 1200 the spirit of life had departed from the two
Testaments '*ut fieret evangelium eternum*'; the claim that the
Eternal Evangel was especially committed to a barefoot order. In
the third *status* Gerard expected the active life of the secular
clergy to give place to the contemplative life, especially of the
ordo parvulorum. It was the arrogance—the 'incredible exaltation'—of Gerard's claim for the new order which most shocked
the commissioners. Passions were deeply stirred in Paris. William
of St Amour, the chief protagonist of the Secular Masters' party,
preached and wrote furiously against these pernicious
Mendicants.[13] Indeed, Gerard's dramatic announcement of the
third age evoked an equally dramatic denunciation of the friars as
the pseudo-prophets presaging the Last Things, and in support
of this attack William of St Amour actually cites a pseudo-
Joachimist prophecy.[14] Two contemporary poets reflect the tur-
moil created:[15] Ruteboeuf sees the new evangel as a sign of the
advent of Antichrist, while Jean de Meung, in the *Roman de la
Rose*, writes of:

> Uns livres de par le diable
> C'est l'Evangile pardurable.

The Pope condemned Gerard's *Liber Introductorius*—ironically enough together with William of St Amour's most rash counterblast—but left the Order to discipline him. The papal condemnation carefully excluded mention of Joachim and, indeed, Gerard had pushed the Abbot's doctrine to an extreme which he would have repudiated. In particular, the idea of a third evangel composed of his own works which abrogated the authority of the two Testaments would have been abhorrent to him. But one of the commissioners of Anagni, at least, must have been convinced that the real poison lay in Joachim's works, for in 1263 Florentius, now Bishop of Arles, secured at the provincial Council of Arles a full condemnation of the doctrine of the three *status* and the writings of Joachim on which it was founded. Thus one ingredient in Joachim's curiously contradictory reputation in later ages became his authorship of that pestiferous work, the Eternal Evangel.

His enemies managed to implicate John of Parma in the affair. He was forced to resign the Generalship and, after Bonaventura had succeeded him, John and Gerard, together with a certain Brother Leonard, were examined by him in 1256. If we may trust the account of the later Spiritual leader, Angelo Clareno, John declared the *status evangelice perfectionis* to be *altissimus* and exalted the Testament of St Francis as the embodiment of the *spiritualis intelligencia*.[16] In defending these high claims and their confidence in the ultimate *reformacio*, John and his companions seem to have based themselves on the doctrine of Joachim whom they stoutly cleared from the charge of heresy. John was allowed to retire quietly to a hermitage but Gerard was kept in detention by the Order for the remaining eighteen years of his life. He apparently never lost his itch for prophecy, for Salimbene, an old friend of his, recounts a vivid little conversation when they met years later.[17] Salimbene: 'Shall we dispute about Joachim?' Gerard: 'Don't let us argue, but talk together. And first let us find some secret place.' Then Salimbene leads him behind the dormitory and starts off: 'My question is about Antichrist—where and when he will be born?' Then they launch into a long, stolen conversation.

The fact that one not very distinguished friar could have created such a stir and aroused so much polemic shows that Joachimism was the focus of considerable attention by the mid-thirteenth century. Two non-events about this time affected the outlook of Joachites: in 1250 Frederick II died in his bed, instead of revealing himself as one of the limbs of Antichrist; the year 1260, the supposed year of crisis in the calculations of Joachim's disciples, passed without visible signs of transition to the third *status*, although it was marked in many places by outbursts of the Flagellant movement, expressing a general expectancy. From this point onwards two types of interest in Joachimism are displayed in the Franciscan Order: on the one hand there is the moderate outlook which seeks to read the signs of the times but does not look for sudden change; on the other hand, there emerges the Spiritual group which progressively distinguishes itself from the Order as a whole by its heightened expectation of calamity and by its passionate assumption of an eschatological role in bringing about the *reformacio*. Fra Salimbene represents the moderates. In a detailed study[18] Professor Delno West has concluded that although Salimbene professed disillusionment at the undramatic death of Frederick II, he remained a moderate Joachite, living in expectation of a gradual transition from the 'time of troubles' to the third age. His interpretation of events and social trends is governed by this perspective, so that his famous *Cronica* is not straightforward historical narrative but a Joachimist interpretation of his age. We find evidence of pseudo-Joachimist tracts circulating in the Order, as well as anthologies of *figurae*, especially the figure of the Dragon with seven heads. A general interest in the prophetic future was probably maintained.[19]

We have a significant piece of evidence revealing the way in which Joachimist imagery could influence the mystical experience of Franciscans.[20] In the *Fioretti* there is a vision of a robber-turned-friar who is led by an angel to a narrow bridge over a river full of horrors which can only be crossed at great peril. Petrified on the middle of the bridge, he prays and wings begin to sprout with which he attempts to fly after the angel. But they fall off. This is repeated a second time, but the third time he waits for the wings to grow fully and then successfully flies after the angel and up to a palace of translucent light on top of a high mountain. A Latin poem, discovered in a thirteenth-century manuscript, proves to be another version of the same story. Here a *vir religiosus* travels through great dangers and tortures until, on the sixth day, he comes to the final trial of lions and dragons and the narrow bridge over the horrible river. Here, he realizes, the righteous receive their wings and cross triumphantly to reach Paradise on top of a silver mountain:

> Et induti vite pennis exuunt spurcieiis,
> Hi securi et veloces ac si leves aquile
> Transeunt per artum pontem in ducatum patriae.

This poem is, in fact, the *Visio de gloria Paradisi* which is printed after the *Psalterium decem chordarum* (f. 280r-v in the 1527 edition of Joachim's works, and, since it is also found in one of the earliest manuscripts of his work, can be fairly attributed to him. The six days' labour, the perilous transit, the mounting on eagle's wings (which echoes the *Psalterium*), the paradise of spiritual light, are all Joachimist themes, while the success only at the *third* attempt in the *Fioretti* version adds another Joachimist touch.

This vivid figure of the perilous transit from the second to the third *status* leads directly to a consideration of St Bonaventura's attitude towards Joachimist eschatology. As the General who had to judge John of Parma and Gerard of Borgo San Donnino, Bonaventura has commonly been seen as a moderate whose task was to curb the fantasies of the Joachites, a view supported by his open repudiation of Joachim's condemned doctrine of the Trinity.[21] But in his latest work, the *Collationes in Hexaemeron*, he develops a philosophy of history which seems to draw on the original thought of Joachim himself, while avoiding dangerous exaggerations.[22] Thus he takes his stand firmly on the two Dispensations and two Testaments, pointedly emphasizing that '*Post novum testamentum non erit aliud.*' Yet he uses a number of sequences of threes, including one of three orders corresponding to the three Persons which echoes Joachim's words closely, and, though he divides history into four *tempora*, he sub-divides each into three *sub-tempora* which represent the particular operation of the separate Persons. Above all, so it has been argued by Joseph Ratzinger,[23] Bonaventura uses Joachim's scheme of 'double sevens', that is, of seven *tempora* in the Old, and seven in the New Dispensation, leading, of course, to the climax at the seventh, and especially the Sabbath Age of history at the Opening of the Seventh Seal. It would seem that Bonaventura, while reacting intellectually against the dangers of Joachimism, was gripped in the imagination by a belief in a culminating period of spiritual illumination when the Scriptures would be opened (*tempus reserationis Scripturarum*). In a number of passages he expects an ultimate flowering of the Church within history and follows Joachim in placing the seventh age between the destruction of Antichrist and the Last Judgement, thus distinguishing it from the eighth age of eternity.[24]

Bonaventura's sobering influence, however, may be seen in the place he assigns to the Franciscan Order itself. In a pattern which recalls Joachim's Psaltery with ten strings, he equates the three orders (*laicus, clericalis, monasticus*, each assigned to a Person of the Trinity, and each subdivided into three) with the nine hierarchies of angels.[25] In the final monastic order of the Spirit, the three suborders of *supplicatorii, speculativi* and *sursumactivi* are assigned respectively to Thrones, Cherubim and Seraphim. St Francis alone belongs to the Seraphic Order, a harbinger of the perfection yet to come, but the Franciscan Order is still at the 'speculative' stage of the Cherubim, belonging to the sixth age rather than the seventh. Bonaventura, then, believed his order to be still journeying towards full illumination through the intellectual stage. There must be a crucial *transitus*—the narrow bridge —by which the *viator* would transcend speculation and, through union with Christ, attain the perfection of the contemplative state. This was closely bound up with the perfection of evangelical poverty revealed by St Francis. This to Bonaventura was the final stage in a progressive revelation of history: in the first age the apostles and their disciples destroyed idolatry; in the second, men of discernment in the Scriptures destroyed heresy; in the last age, God is bringing forward men of voluntary mendicancy who will destroy avarice. The fact that Bonaventura accepted the Joachites' identification of St Francis as the Angel of the Sixth Seal and also saw him as the Angel of the Church of Philadelphia, a key figure in Joachim's exegesis, places St Francis' eschatological role beyond doubt: the first 'sealed' the 144,000 Redeemed, the second held the key to unlock the door of spiritual understanding.[26] So St Francis revealed both the nature of the final order and that of the final illumination. But the last stage was not yet: St Francis had made the *transitus*, but the Order was still 'in the way'. Yet, while refusing to make the highest claim for the Franciscans as they were, Bonaventura followed Joachim closely in believing that history must finally produce the perfect, the Seraphic, order:[27]

Et sicut sex diebus factus est mundus et sexta aetate venit Christus, ita post sex tempora Ecclesiae in fine generabitur Ecclesia contemplativa. . . . Unde oportet quod in Ecclesia appareat status qui huic angelo (i.e. Sixth Angel) respondeat habens ultimatum et perfectum Dei cultum et hanc triplicem lucem elevantem tripliciter.

By contrast, the commitment of the Spiritual Franciscans was to a practice of what they conceived as the absolute perfection here and now. They believed that their own struggle to preserve the Rule and Testament of St Francis in every syllable was part of a cosmic conflict, that the crisis of evil must rise in a crescendo before the Church could pass over Jordan and that their role was to safeguard the spiritual treasure of the future. Theirs was not the optimism of a evolutionary view of history, but a cataclysmic: step by step the situation must worsen until the seventh tribulation; then the tremendous miracle of the *reformacio* would happen. Their sufferings are enshrined in the *Historia Septem Tribulationum* of Angelo Clareno,[28] one of the leaders of the Italian Spirituals. This is not a straightforward and accurate record of events but rather a drama based on the pattern of the sevens which vividly conveys the cosmic meaning of their conflict. Their passionate belief in the future was the driving force of the Spiritual group; it lay behind their bitter opposition to the growth of the Order in terms of buildings, legacies and libraries, their passionate devotion to their patched and skimpy habits as symbols of absolute poverty, their audacious defence of their position before the Provincial Chapter in 1274. They were imprisoned, exiled and harried even in exile. There was one dramatic interlude in their persecution. In 1294 Pope Celestine V, the hermit pope, was elected. We shall consider later his relation to the already circulating prophecy of an Angelic Pope. The Italian Spirituals certainly hailed this election with intense joy and at once sought from Celestine absolution from their Minorite vows and permission to follow the strict Rule and Testament of St Francis as a group within Celestine's own Order of Poor Hermits. But the renunciation of Celestine followed immediately, and under Boniface VIII the little new order was abandoned to the fury of enemies from whom they had thought to escape. In 1295 Angelo Clareno, Peter of Macerate (Fra

Liberato) and others fled to Greece whence they returned after Boniface VIII's death. Perhaps their attention was now focused on a revolution in the papacy itself as the only means to bring in their visionary future. At any rate the Zealots grouped around Clareno and Liberato have been credited with the authorship of the famous *Vaticinia de Summis Pontificibus*[29] (first series) which we shall be discussing later. If they were indeed waiting for a revolution at the time of the papal election in 1304/5, their disappointment must have been bitter, for instead of an Angelic Pope there came Clement V, removing the Holy See to Avignon.

After the moment of hope had passed the Clarenists were allowed to retreat into the separatist, hermit life of those who wait for the crisis of history. In the March of Ancona Fra Angelo formed his disciples into the Order of Poor Hermits and until his death in 1337 exercised a restraining influence upon them. But the problem of authority faced them acutely. On the one hand, in his *Epistola Excusatoria*, Angelo vehemently repudiated the charge of being schismatic and declared his unwavering loyalty to the Roman See.[30] On the other hand, his disciples looked for the manifestation of Antichrist in a pseudo-pope and the final overthrow of the 'carnal Church'. In his letters to disciples Angelo sets the Rule which they were to guard above all other obediences: in it Christ speaks and the gates of hell shall not prevail against it. Yet he also enjoins obedience to prelates who hold the place of Christ and His Apostles. They must both maintain their sense of mission and suffer in patience, for, so Angelo believes, the seventh and greatest tribulation is upon them. Yet his confidence in the inevitability of the spiritual revolution remains unshaken: the Dragon must be beaten down, the last darkness be dispelled, and the faithful finally dwell in the full sunlight of love.[31]

As with all such revolutionary hopes, this position of patient waiting in tension proved impossible for the more impetuous spirits. After Clareno's death the Italian Spirituals split into groups of so-called Fraticelli who in the later fourteenth century stood in declared separation from the Roman Church and attacked the papacy fiercely. We can trace their views in letters or tracts which they distributed.[32] These show clearly whither the logic of the Joachimist hope could lead. If the whole hierarchy of the Church opposed the perfection of the future *status* entrusted to the few, then it could not be the true Church but the expected

Antichrist. Thus they developed the mentality of the exclusive sect, for 'always the many have persecuted the poor faithful of Christ'.[33] The fatal agent of the Church's seduction had been John XXII. If anyone persistently denied the poverty of Christ, he was a manifest heretic whom to obey was contrary to God and the Rule. Pope John and his successors, therefore, had departed from the true Church and become schismatics. Some asserted that John XXII was the mystic Antichrist and that the Roman Church was the synagogue of the devil; to all it was clear that the Pope had no power to touch the Rule and Testament of St Francis. The Fraticelli saw themselves as the saving remnant gathered into the frail bark of the true Church, the Noah's Ark of the last age.[34] In the sixth age of the Church Christ had sent St Francis, another Noah, to build a new ark, the Ark of the Evangelical Rule, in which the seed of the elect would be saved from the deluge of the unfaithful. The navigators who had charted their voyage included the Abbot Joachim who had foretold these things. In this ark they would be preserved from *'molti falsi Christiani et falsi profeti'*. After the Deluge would come the *renovatio*, when the Gospel would be preached by twelve poor evangelical men—the last in a long sequence of twelves starting from the patriarchs.

Clearly many found these ideas attractive. In Florence, Fraticelli almost gained official approval during the anti-papal War of the Eight Saints. The Signoria was ready to use any stick to beat the '*Chiesa carnale*'—the term used in its propaganda— and the shopkeeper/artisan class was receptive of Fraticellian ideas.[35] But especially their campaign against the rich chimed with the aspirations of the sweated workers. There was, for instance, a Frate Silvestro, a wool-carder, who joined a Fraticellian group and was credited with the gift of prophecy. Fraticellian influence was strong in the revolt of the Ciompi (1378) who called themselves *Il Populo di Dio*. Prophecies circulating at this time exalted the cause of the common people and looked for a humble leader who would bring peace and renewal. When the revolution failed and the government made its peace with the papacy, official cooperation with the Inquisition in suppressing heresy was resumed, but heresy and prophecy remained associated with social unrest. Professor Donald Weinstein has found a number of fifteenth-century prophecies in which the hopes of the Fraticelli and the Ciompi for a new age are carried on, as, for instance, in the Vision of Fra Andrea da Rieti.[36]

The most powerful intellect among those Franciscans who fell under the spell of Joachim was probably that of Peter John Olivi, a Provençal who was also in touch with Italian Spirituals.[37] A scholastic philosopher, biblical exegete, lector at Santa Croce in Florence and then at Montpellier, he wrote so much in a key of moderate and sound scholarship that the high notes of fanaticism do not seem to belong here. Yet somewhere dangerous overtones were present, even at an early stage, and were heard by his enemies, for his career was punctuated by disciplinary examinations in which he was forced to defend his views. Perhaps his real crime lay in a magnetic personality which enabled him to attract disciples around him. But what did he teach them? Was his concept of Franciscan poverty set in a framework of Joachimist prophecy? The extent of Olivi's Joachimism is still under debate and requires a judgement based on all his works, not just the apparently most revolutionary *Postilla in Apocalypsim*. Pending a more definitive assessment, it can be said, however, that in the *Postilla* Olivi, while using a pattern of double sevens to match the stages of the Church to those of the Old Testament, specifically relates the seven *status* of the Church to Joachim's second and third general *status* of history, elevating the sixth and seventh *status* of the Church into the *tertius status generalis* which he explicitly derives from Joachim. Again, he takes directly from Joachim the belief that, as the synagogue had been propagated by twelve patriarchs and the Church by twelve apostles, so at the last the Church must be propagated by twelve evangelical men whom he identifies with the twelve 'sons' of St Francis. In one passage of the *Postilla* his exposition of the three *status* in terms of the Trinity directly draws on Joachim's *Expositio*.[38]

There can be no doubt that Olivi expected a flowering of history between the defeat of Antichrist and the consummation of the age, and that St Francis held in his mind a unique position as the initiator of this final epoch. In order to combine a Christocentric view of history with the Trinitarian three-fold pattern, he uses a concept of three Advents of Christ: first in the flesh, second in the *nova ecclesia* of evangelical reform, third in final judgement.[39] Here St Francis occupies the position of

Christ in relation to the third *status*: just as carnal Judaism had been rejected when the *novus homo*, Jesus Christ, had instituted a new law and life, so now, with the rejection of the carnal Church, the law and life of Christ must be renewed by Francis. These were dangerous words. What did Olivi imply by the 'rejection of the carnal Church'? He certainly expected a mystic Antichrist who would be a false pope and believed that the new age would be ushered in by cataclysmic events. Did he, then, repudiate the existing hierarchy? On the contrary, in his own life he opposed separation and submitted to authority. It has recently been argued by Professor Brian Tierney[40] that belief in a progressive revelation in history placed both Bonaventura and Olivi in a position of needing an authority to authenticate the culminating revelation in St Francis. Although Bonaventura did not reach this point, Olivi, says Tierney, was led to develop a doctrine of papal infallibility in order to establish the immovable authority of Nicholas III's Bull *Exiit qui seminat* (1279) in which, according to Olivi, the Pope gave official sanction to the Franciscan claim that their Rule was the way of perfection revealed by Christ to the Apostles. The real 'authority' in Olivi's mind was the Rule of St Francis which was, to him, of final and cosmic significance: 'The evangelical state is absolutely immutable,' he wrote. The function of the Roman Church was to authenticate this new revelation of the Holy Spirit which would re-shape the whole life of the Church. But Olivi believed that the crisis of evil was at hand, when the Roman See itself would be corrupted and the pseudo-pope of the carnal Church would seek to overturn the true pronouncements of the papacy. Thus a doctrine of infallibility was needed to protect the once-for-all authentication of the Franciscan revelation in *Exiit*. There is a similar ambivalence towards authority in Joachim and Olivi: both based themselves on the authority of the Roman Church, both, it appears, submitted their writings at the end to the papacy, yet for both their passionate commitment to belief in a final revelation in history was an over-riding authority which transformed those who opposed it into forces of evil.

Olivi fused the Joachimist expectation of the Age of the Spirit with the Franciscan sense of a prophetic role in a new age of history. His contribution to Joachimism was an intellectual one, yet as a personality he seems always to have aroused heightened emotions—to his friends, a prophet of the final age, ranked with the Apostles and matched with St Paul; to his enemies, a manifestation of Antichrist. There is an interesting little example of his magnetism in the influence he exercised, by letter, over the young princes of Anjou, hostages at the Aragonese court.[41] The passions he aroused survived his death in 1298. In 1299 at the Chapter General of Lyons his writings were condemned and their possession forbidden. We cannot trace exactly how a fanatical Olivist group began to form, but the fury with which a group of his followers was persecuted and finally burned in 1318 for their refusal to surrender his books or give up their skinny habits shows how strong was the clash of emotions. Briefly, Bernard Delicieux, popular hero of Carcassone and Albi, appears as a leader of the Provençal Spirituals, until he is brought before John XXII in 1316, unfrocked and imprisoned.[42] After this brutal disciplining of the revolutionary friars, the teaching of the scholar Olivi passed, strangely enough, into vernacular texts in the hands of tertiaries and other lay groups. Perhaps this popularizing of prophecy was what the authorities feared most. These groups appear as the sect of the Beguins in the pages of Bernard Gui's Inquisitorial Manual and we read their pathetic depositions in the records of the Inquisition of Toulouse.[43]

Gui's analysis of their beliefs shows clearly the extreme consequences of arrogating to themselves the role of new spiritual men within the framework of a Joachimist future. The most perfect state in the Church is that of evangelical poverty; after Christ and His Mother, St Francis is the highest observer of the evangelical rule and its renovator in the sixth age of the Church; the Rule of St Francis *is* the Evangel of Christ. As no one can change the Gospel, so no one can change the Rule: neither Pope nor Council can prevail against it. They distinguish two churches—a carnal which, according to Gui, they identify with the Roman, and a spiritual which they claim to be theirs. At the end of the sixth age (*in quo statu dicunt nos esse*), the carnal Church will be rejected by Christ, whom it has crucified again in the persecuted *pauperes*, as once the synagogue was rejected. In the persecution of Antichrist all religious orders will perish except a third of the Minorites from which will be drawn the handful, perhaps a dozen, of spiritual men, *pauperes evangelici*, who will bring in the *ecclesia spiritualis* of the seventh and last *status* of the

Church. The depositions before the Inquisition of Toulouse *c.* 1322 bring out plainly the fact that their source of inspiration was the *Postilla* of Olivi which they read in the vernacular.[44] From it they derived a clear doctrine of the three general *status* of the world, embodying the Persons of the Trinity. Perhaps their unknown version pushed the logic further than Olivi had done, for they claimed, on the authority of the *Postilla*, to identify the Roman Church with the Babylonish Whore, soon to be destroyed.[45] The inspiration of their unswerving confidence was drawn from the inevitability of the third *status*. When all the forces of Antichrist had been beaten down, there would be a new outpouring of the Holy Spirit, the whole world would be converted by the saving remnant and the *ecclesia spiritualis* would flourish, *pauper, humilis et benigna*, until the end of the age. For this vision they were prepared to go to the stake.

It was probably while in Florence that Olivi attracted his greatest disciple, Ubertino da Casale, who remains for us as mysterious a figure as his master.[46] He appears as a Joachimist preacher in Italy, an able dialectician when arguing the case of the Spirituals at the papal court, a mystic who wrote a great spiritual work, and finally a fugitive from authority whose end is unknown. His great work was the *Arbor Vitae Crucifixae*.[47] He looked for a symbol of the inner growth of all history and found it in the image of the Tree of History, so dear to Joachim. Its roots, he thought, were in the early ages from Creation to the Incarnation, its branches were the works of Christ, its fruits the deeds of the elect. Book V summarizes his philosophy of history. His framework here was Olivi's adaptation of Joachim's scheme of history. Thus he used the pattern of the seven *status* of the Church, but also recognized the three general *status* and identified the sixth and seventh *status* of the Church with Joachim's third *status* of the world. The five preceding ages belonged successively to apostles, martyrs, doctors, anchorites, monks and clergy possessing temporalities; the sixth, initiated by the seraphic man Francis, '*est renovationis evangelicae vitae et expugnationis sectae antichristianae sub pauperibus voluntariis nihil possidentibus in hac vita*'; the seventh would see '*quedam quieta et mira participatio futurae gloriae ac si celestis Jerusalem videatur ascendisse in terram*'.[48]

Ubertino adopted from Olivi the concept of the three Advents of Christ. In St Francis the second Advent of Christ had actually occurred. Echoing Olivi he declared that the sixth *status* of the Church was of all ages most momentous '*ut videatur quoddam novum seculum seu nova ecclesia tunc formari*'.[49] For this reason St Francis had been hailed as the Sixth Angel of the Apocalypse. Ubertino himself had heard this identification first expounded by John of Parma.[50] St Francis had foretold persecution and Ubertino expected the conflict with Babylon, for must not St Francis be figuratively killed and buried before he could rise in glory? The attack on the Spirituals who guarded the Rule and Testament with their lives was nothing less than the final conflict with Antichrist, and in so far as the ecclesiastical hierarchy identified itself with this attack it had ceased to be the New Jerusalem and become part of Babylon *meretrix et impudica*. So, once again, the role of the Spirituals was to suffer and to wait. Ubertino's pages mirror the mood of a 'saving remnant'. They are the little flock of Christ, content to be '*quendam populum novum et humilem in hac novissima hora, qui est dissimilis in humilitate et paupertate ab omnibus aliis*'.[51] Their duty to the future requires that they should keep the Holy Rule and Testament—and wait. John of Parma, says Ubertino, had counselled one group to retire into Asia, since they could not live in evangelical observance in the midst of Babylon, there to await the fall of Antichrist.

Joachite groups penetrated into the western Mediterranean region by two routes. Some of the Clarenists fled south into the more inaccessible regions of the Neapolitan kingdom where they received some protection from the Angevins, especially Robert the Wise and his Queen.[52] In the mid-fourteenth century there must have been a considerable gathering of refugees in those parts, for Cardinal Albornoz instituted a process in 1362 against their patron Louis of Durazzo. On the other hand, the rival Aragonese dynasty also favoured similar groups. Here the main geographical route was from Provence into Catalonia and Aragon, while the personal influence of Arnold of Villanova, as well as Olivi, was also important.[53] Inquisitorial proceedings of the fourteenth century show a number of Franciscan Tertiaries, or *Fratres de Poenitencia*, attacked for beliefs which included a Joachimist expectation of the future.[54] A tract, originally written in Catalan, but known to us only in excerpts under the title *De*

Statibus Ecclesiae secundum Expositionem Apocalypsim, was an overtly Joachimist exposition of the three *status*, the seven ages and the role of the Franciscans in the apotheosis to come.[55] Under the rule of the Aragonese prince Philip, Majorca and Roussillon also harboured Joachimist groups, for Philip had fallen under the influence of Angelo da Clareno and actually tried to found a new order which would perfectly embody the Rule of St Francis.[56] The process against one of his counsellors, Adhémar de Mosset, again shows quite clearly that the interrogators were expecting to find evidence of a Joachimist philosophy of history in this group.[57] Finally, just as Olivi seemed able to cast a spell over the two young Angevin princes in Aragonese captivity, so Arnold of Villanova exercised a powerful influence over the Kings of Aragon, Pedro and James II, and more especially over Pedro's third son, Frederick of Trinacria, King of Sicily. So Sicily, like Naples, became a refuge for Spiritual Franciscans and others fleeing from ecclesiastical wrath.[58] Thus suppression of these revolutionaries could be delayed by powerful protectors, whether civic or royal, but gradually the authorities were able to whittle away such support and stamp out these scattered groups, although occasionally sparks light up again from smouldering ashes in the fifteenth century.

The Spirituals adapted to themselves the role of Joachim's new spiritual men. Their philosophy of history was more Christocentric than Joachim's. The manifestation of the Third Person of the Trinity was identified with a renewal of the life of the Second Person in St Francis who sought the re-enactment of the Passion in his own body. St Francis stood at the transition from the second to the third *status* as Christ stood between the first and second. Only the pattern of threes made it possible to claim for St Francis such a unique role and to permit the adaptation to him of biblical texts relating to Christ. Thus Angelo Clareno, without any sense of irreverence, could paraphrase from Hebrews and Philippians thus: 'Christ has in times past spoken to us in Fathers, Apostles, Prophets, Martyrs, Doctors and Saints, but in these newest days He has spoken to us in His seraphic son Francis whom He has constituted heir of all things following . . . who, being in this world in the form of Christ crucified, humbled himself . . . wherefore God has exalted him and given him a name . . .'[59] Thus the 'new age' was one of the re-enacted Word as much as of the illuminating Spirit, and the essence of the third *status* was now expressed as the *renovatio evangelicae vitae*, but the source of their ardent and inflexible purpose was still the Joachimist expectation of the new and last age.

The Spirituals played a disruptive role in the Franciscan Order, arousing passionate opposition by their obstinate determination to suffer and to wait. They petered out eventually with few marks of achievement. Yet there remains the question of the later Observant Movement and its roots. The obvious raison d'être for this was the desire to return to the early purity and idealism of St Francis and his companions without raising again the controversy over absolute poverty. But did this impulse draw any of its inspiration from a sense of the eschatological role of St Francis and his order? The fourteenth-century founder, Giovanni delle Valle, was a disciple of Angelo Clareno.[60] Ubertino's works, especially the *Arbor*, were read and used by Observants, notably St Bernardino of Siena.[61] Although denouncing crazy fanatics who stuffed themselves with prophecies, Bernardino does place St Francis within an eschatological setting and cites Joachim as the first witness to the identification of St Francis with the Sixth Angel of the Apocalypse. Indeed, there are various indications that Bernardino knew some of the works of Joachim, including a little tract on the Seven Seals which he quotes without naming his source. We shall return later to other Observant Franciscans who saw their order in the setting of the last age.

II

It was to be expected that the role of the *viri spirituales* would be claimed by wilder spirits and thus we meet the Apostolic Brethren, followers first of Gerard Segarelli and then Fra Dolcino.[62] Salimbene poured scorn on them as false prophets,[63] yet their inspiration probably came from the same source as his. There had been earlier movements in the twelfth century of people who sought to go back to the first century and imitate the Apostolic life, but it seems clear that this group saw its role not as a going back but as part of the eschatological future. Parma—also the home of Salimbene—may have contained Joachimist 'seeds' at that time. At any rate, this movement appeared in the crucial

Joachimist year of 1260 and its second leader, Dolcino, put forward a programme for the future in which he used Joachim's method of extrapolation from a whole pattern of history.

Dolcino believed that there were four *status* of history:[64] the first, that of Old Testament just men, had been lived in the good state of matrimony until it declined before the coming of Christ; the second, initiated by Christ and His Apostles, remedied preceding maladies and carried spiritual life on to a new plane until the time of Pope Silvester and Constantine, when it began to decline; the third saw the mass conversion of the Gentiles and, when love declined, the revival under St Francis and St Dominic. Now that, once again, love had grown cold among the clergy and religious, the call was to embrace the way of life pertaining to the fourth and last *status*, the true Apostolic life. This would be more radical in its poverty than that of the existing Mendicants and would alone endure to the Judgement Day: '*et propter hoc vita nostra major est et ultima omnibus medicina.*' It will be observed that Dolcino does not use Joachim's concept of a Trinitarian pattern in history. Nonetheless, he looks for an apotheosis about to dawn within history and he believes that the agencies divinely appointed to bring this in are human ones. Thus in his manifesto of 1300 Dolcino proclaimed that in these last days God had specially sent his own *congregatio* to preach the salvation of souls and lead the Church into the fourth period, when she would become *bona et pauper*. This period had been initiated by Gerard of Parma, most beloved of God, and would remain in perfection to bear its fruit until the end of the world.

The Apostolic Brethren carried repudiation of ecclesiastical authority to extremes. The Roman Church was no longer the Church of God but '*illa Babylon meretrix magna*'. Authority had now passed to the *Apostoli* upon whom had descended the power of St Peter. Thus they owed obedience to no man and could not be called by any authority to abandon their rule of liberty, for to do so would be to descend from the more to the less perfect. The outward transfer of authority, which they expected soon after 1300, would be accomplished by the violence of revolution. Pope Boniface VIII, the cardinals, prelates, clergy, and all religious would be exterminated by the sword of God, wielded by a new emperor. Dolcino believed that this emperor would be Frederick, King of Sicily, in whose favour he cited many scriptural passages.

After the holocaust a new and holy pope would be chosen by God and under his obedience would be placed the Apostolic order, with all the remnant who had been saved from the sword by divine grace and chose to become *Apostoli*. Then there would be a new outpouring of the Holy Spirit.

A second manifesto,[65] issued after the death of Boniface VIII, revises the time schedule a little, but still expects the general destruction of clergy and religious in 1305. In neither of these letters did Dolcino claim the role of Angelic Pope for himself, but this claim was made for him in the anonymous *Historia Fratris Dolcini Haeresiarchae* and Bernard Gui reported a revelation according to which Dolcino would become *ille Papa sanctus*. When Antichrist appeared Dolcino and his followers would be removed to Paradise, while Enoch and Elijah descended to dispose of him. After the death of Antichrist, they would descend again to convert all nations, while Frederick of Sicily ruled over the last world empire. Thus an Age of Spirit was expected after the crisis of Antichrist, one in which all the spiritual gifts of Joachim's third *status* would belong to the Apostolic Brethren alone, and their Church alone would flourish until the end of time.

In 1304 Dolcino gathered his partisans together into the mountains near Novara to await the fulfilment of events. They were undaunted by the passing of 1305, and when, in 1306, Clement V preached a crusade against them, they resisted to the death. The burning of Dolcino, together with the failure of prophetic fulfilment, should have put an end to the sect, but the astonishing vitality of this conviction concerning the spiritual role of the future is well demonstrated by the survival of *Apostoli* ideas. According to Clareno they wormed their way among the Franciscans.[66] They appear in Inquisitorial records in Bologna, Spain and Toulouse. In 1318 John XXII even warned the Bishop of Cracow against them and references can be found up to the fifteenth century.[67]

There are certain forms of mysticism in the later middle ages which seem to border on Joachimism, although direct links can seldom be traced. The characteristic which suggests some kind of connection with Joachimism seems to me to be a doctrine of history which points to a final apotheosis, begun or about to begin, in which a new manifestation of the Holy Spirit will mark out a new leader and followers. One of these would seem to have been Guglielma who appeared in Milan *c.* 1271 and around whom a cult gathered after her death in 1282. Our knowledge derives from the Inquisitorial process against the small group of initiated *Guglielmiti* in 1300.[68] It is not easy to determine how much of their doctrine sprang from Guglielma herself and how much was worked out by her chief disciple, Andreas Saramita. The *Process* is ambiguous, but at the end Saramita declared that he had received it from Guglielma herself. The main tenets, as stated by Saramita and his female companion, Manfreda, were unambiguous: as the Word had been incarnate in a Man, so the Holy Spirit had now become incarnate in a woman, Guglielma. She, too, would rise from the dead, ascend into heaven in the sight of her disciples, and send upon them the Holy Spirit as tongues of flame. All authority had therefore now departed from the existing ecclesiastical hierarchy and Boniface VIII was no true pope. The new spiritual roles were duly allotted, this time pre-eminently to women, for Manfreda would be the new pope and her cardinals would be women. She would baptize Jews, Saracens, and all other infidels, entering into peaceable possession of the Holy See. The idea of the Eternal Evangel reappears here, for the Gospels were to be superseded by new ones, in the writing of which Saramita would play the role of the first evangelists. He would produce gospels, epistles and prophecies, under the formula: *In illo tempore dixit Spiritus Sanctus.* The sect was too mad to be really dangerous and soon disappeared, though, curiously enough, it was drawn mainly from the well-to-do and Manfreda was probably the cousin of Matteo Visconti. The *Guglielmiti* pushed a daring Trinitarian logic to its limits: if the revolution in history was to be absolute there must be a new incarnation of the Godhead and this must be in the opposite sex. The Italian historian Tocco calls the dream of Guglielma the most beautiful and seductive of all contemporary hallucinations.[69] It reveals the most unassailable and the most absurd lengths to which the logic of a Trinitarian interpretation of history could be pushed.

Prous Boneta, a disciple of Olivi living in Montpellier, takes a similar, though not so extreme a line.[70] Her confession of 1325 shows a strange mixture of Catharism and Joachimism, but its chief emphasis is on the new era of history just beginning. To usher this in, the Holy Spirit must be incarnate, undergo passion and death, and rise again. The second Crucifixion was being accomplished in the condemnation of Olivi's works and in the persecution of Prous herself. She had been chosen to be the abode of the Trinity and the giver of the Holy Spirit to the world, baptizing with the Spirit all who believed the writings of Olivi and the words of Prous. As Eve had been the downfall of human nature, so Prous would be the instrument of all men's salvation. While St Francis was the angel with the sign of the Living God and Olivi the angel with the face of the sun, she herself was the angel with the keys of the abyss. Her confession ends with a strong affirmation of the dawning Age of the Spirit which had been initiated in Olivi: *et sic nunc est status ecclesiae novus in quo credere oportet in opere Sancti Spiritus.*

It is a strange little fact of history that the male claimants to the prophetic role of new spiritual men found female counterparts in this greater and more absurd claim. The human desire to find an enhanced role within the historical process lies at the root in both cases, but the women bring to the surface in a dramatic way the problem of sex in the Christian religion. We remember that the religious aspirations of women had received insufficient outlets, reluctantly accorded when given, in the twelfth and thirteenth centuries.[71] The great congregations of women in the Beguinages of northern Europe provided one answer to their quest for special vocation. The extreme prophetic claims of these heresiarchs was another.

III

The claim to a prophetic role was, on the whole, merely an external ornament to the Dominicans. On the other hand, as we have seen, it split the Franciscan Order with tragic consequences. It drove wilder spirits to revolution against authority. Could it be contained in milder form within a religious order, an inspiration to some but not a divisive force? The Order of the Augustinian Hermits (or Friars) contains traces of such an influence, though never in continuous enough form to be described as a movement. The prophecy of Joachim on which they fastened was the appropriate one of the hermit order which would emulate the life of angels. This was, it will be remembered, the more contemplative of the two orders of spiritual men to lead the world into the third age.

In 1334 an Augustinian hermit, Henry of Weimar, was writing a history of his order, *De origine et progressu Ordinis Fr. Eremitarum S. Augustini*.[72] He made high claims for his order. Although, he says, the communal religious life is a state in which perfection is being acquired, the anchorite life is a state of perfection achieved. Therefore it is not for every man but only for the perfect man who is moved by a special impulse from the Holy Spirit to embrace this '*artissimam et sanctissimam vitam*'. With this lead, it is not surprising to find Henry shortly afterwards claiming for his Order the prophetic role of Joachim's *ordo contemplantium*. He quotes from the *Expositio* the words which he believed had been revealed to Joachim: 'There shall arise an order which appears new but is not, garbed in black habits and girdled; they shall increase and their fame shall spread abroad. They will preach and defend the faith until the end of the world in the spirit of Elijah. They will be an order of hermits emulating the life of angels and burning with love and zeal towards God, to consume the thorns and thistles, that is, the lives of the wicked.' He reinforces this by referring to Joachim's exposition of the four angels in Revelation ch. 7, who represented *quatuor genera predicatorum*.[73] They will indeed emulate the life of angels, these hermits whose father was Paul the first to live the eremitical life. So Henry creates a prophetic role for his order which is quite distinct from that conceived by the Spiritual Franciscans, although both stem from the vision of Joachim.

There is, unfortunately, no evidence to show what Henry's contemporaries thought of these high claims, but it would appear from a curious episode rather more than a century later that some members of the Erfurt community became caught up in these prophetic interests. Fairly recently the record of a debate on Joachimism has come to light. Following a university disputation at Erfurt in 1465, Johann Bauer de Dorsten, a member of the Augustinian house, wrote a *quaestio* against Joachimist heresy.[74] It is significant that the doctrine which Dorsten attacked was the genuine Trinitarian view of history as developed by the Abbot himself. His account of the conception of the three *status* and the role of the new spiritual men is an unusually clear one, and we note that he is able to quote extensively from Joachim's own writings. But this was no mere academic exercise. Dorsten refers to the tenets of 'certain scandalous heretics' and it seems almost certain that these were heretics known as the Wirsberger brothers who appeared in Germany at this moment, announcing the immediate advent of the third *status*.[75] Dorsten's learned discussion was no doubt intended to give firm intellectual guidance at a moment when religious excitement might send people off the rails. The anxiety with which the proposition of the third *status* was debated shows how tempting it could be and therefore how menacing. From the way he handles it we can surmise that Dorsten himself was sufficiently attracted to this doctrine to be aware of its dangers. Were the works of Joachim which he used in the library of his house and was he concerned because members of his own community studied them too eagerly? At any rate his warnings did not quench the interest, for twenty years later another debate was held at the request of many monks and laymen concerning the problems of the last age, this time specifically linked with the teaching of the Wirsbergers.[76]

There is a case for continuity of interest at Erfurt, but it may be purely fortuitous that in the mid-fourteenth century the English Augustinian friar, John Erghome of York was also vigorously pursuing the study of prophecy. The catalogue of his private library, which was afterwards incorporated into that of the Augustinian house at York, reveals his interest in astrology, magic and prophecy.[77] One item in this catalogue lists a number of prophecies of which about half are ascribed to Joachim or written by Joachites. Another item lists both the *Liber Concordie* and the *Expositio* of Joachim. From these Erghome is said to have composed a book, *Compilationes Vaticiniorum*, which he dedicated to Humphrey de Bohun, Earl of Hereford. As we shall see, a copy of this work, now lost, must have been in the hands of the Protestant John Bale. What we do have of Erghome's work is a commentary on the prophecies ascribed to John of Bridlington, a well-known Augustinian Canon, which Erghome also dedicated to the Earl of Hereford. The work was in part a political satire on the times, but it also gave apocalyptic meaning to Edward III's struggle with France and expected an Age of Gold to begin shortly under the Black Prince.[78] Here Joachimist expectation has been translated into political terms and there is no sign of the role for new spiritual men. Whether Erghome took up the promise and the challenge of prophecy to his own order in the *Compilationes* we do not know.

Erghome may have been little more than a dabbler in prophecy, but a distinctive little Augustinian circle devoted to the
serious study of prophecy formed itself at a late date around the
Joachimist themes, and especially that of the angelic hermit
order. This reached the group as a clear prophecy of their own
order through Henry of Weimar's work and also through a recognition of it by the famous Dominican, S. Antonino, Archbishop
of Florence in the mid-fifteenth century.[79] The centre of the
group was Silvestro Meuccio, a friar of San Cristophoro della
Pace in Venice.[80] He was able, it seems, to lay hands on a
Joachimist compilation made by a Venetian Dominican, Fr
Rusticianus, in the mid-fifteenth century[81] and became fired with
the project of publishing what he took to be the works of Joachim
as containing the vital message for his age. He began in 1516 with
a pseudo-Joachimist work, a commentary, supposedly by
Joachim, on a prophecy attributed to Cyril the Carmelite.[82] From
this point Silvestro proceeded with great industry to publish all
the works of Joachim he could find, taking the false along with
the true quite uncritically. From the Venetian printing presses
there went forth in steady succession his editions of the *Super
Hieremiam* (1516 and 1526), the *Super Esaiam* (1517), the *Liber
Concordie* (1519), the *Expositio in Apocalypsim* (1527) and the
Psalterium decem chordarum (1527).

We know little about Silvestro outside these publications, but
he reveals himself in the prefaces he writes and here we also meet
three of his circle of friends. Anselmo Votturnio (Bochturnus) of
Vicenza possibly helped Silvestro—who dedicates one work to
him—in his labours. Filippo of Mantua wrote *lucubrationes* on the
Apocalypse. The third was a hermit mystic, Bernardino Parentino
of Padua, who was the interpreter of God's mysteries to the
group. So highly do they prize his prophetic utterances that once
Silvestro inserts his words into the Joachimist text he is editing.[83]
The little group of searchers is closely bound together: 'We two
are one and you a third most intimate with us,' writes Anselmo to
Silvestro.[84] A fourth inquirer into Joachimist mysteries was Paolo
Angelo, a 'Byzantine stranger'. Once, on a bridge in Venice,
Silvestro encountered a friend who showed him a newly-
published book, *In Sathanae ruinam tyrannidis*. With the book
under his arm Silvestro went home and did not cease reading
until he had finished it. In three days, it appears, he was dedicat-

ing his edition of the *Super Hieremiam* to its author, Paolo Angelo, whom he greatly desired to meet.[85] In fact he became Angelo's spiritual adviser and drew him into the Joachimist circle. In 1530 Angelo published *Profetie certissime . . . dell' Antichristo* which is practically an Italian translation of Silvestro's first Joachimist publication.

In his preface to the *Expositio* Silvestro stated the high claim of the Augustinian Hermits to be Joachim's new spiritual men quite clearly: '. . . he (Joachim) asserts that in the last age of the world this order of Hermits, . . . burning in zeal and love for God like a glowing fire, shall reform the ruined Church and restore all things.' Then he immediately quoted Joachim's great prophecy 'There shall arise an order which seems new but is not', and who would not thrill at the prospect of such a future? Silvestro carefully distinguished the prophecies which he appropriates for 'our order of hermits' from those which were generally held to apply to the Mendicants. So, by means of marginal notes such as *Ordo Eremitarum S. Aug.*, he claims all the references to the hermit order. An even bolder assertion was made in his edition of the *Expositio . . . in librum Cyrilli* where a picture of the future Angelic Pope is represented in Augustinian friar habit.[86]

Silvestro's prefaces reveal a man who viewed the future with deep foreboding. 'Any sane man', he wrote, 'will battle with all his powers against overwhelming waves, but in unknown calamities he sinks. How great, then, is the value of a prophet who marks out for us a way through the tempests.'[87] So the circle of Silvestro looked out upon the world with the eyes of Joachim *'noster divinus magnus modernusque propheta'*—expecting at once the bitterest tribulation of all time and the angelic state of reform and peace to follow. There would be a three-fold scourge upon the carnal Church: the German Emperor, the mystic Antichrist (the Heretic) and the open Antichrist (the Saracen). But beyond they expected the Church to be raised from her ruined state into that contemplative and celibate life which was to be the third *status*, enduring until the consummation of the ages.

The problem is how to assess the influence of this prophetic thinking among the Augustinian friars. There is not enough evidence to speak of a movement either earlier or in the sixteenth century. Yet one important personality was certainly interested in the Joachimist studies of Silvestro Meuccio as a guide to the *renovatio mundi* which he looked for. This was Egidio of Viterbo, the famous General of the Augustinian Friars in the time of Luther. Silvestro dedicated his edition of the *Expositio* to the General, describing in his prefatory letter how once in Venice he had had the privilege of an audience with him and how the great Cardinal had asked Silvestro to bring with him certain works of the Abbot Joachim: 'Which, when I had brought and he had read, pleased him not a little, so that he urged me to publish other works of Joachim and especially the *Expositio*.' Silvestro saw Egidio as a worthy General to lead the Order into its great Joachimist future, and so he offered him the *Expositio* 'above all, because in the days to come I do not doubt that our Order will be reformed under your leadership.' We shall see later how very clearly Egidio's mind was directed towards a prophetic future. It is impossible not to connect this visionary outlook with the prophecies of Joachim, but there is an irony in the situation, for while Egidio's gaze was on a great ecumenical dream ahead, developments within his own order in Erfurt and Wittenberg were propelling the future in quite another direction.

Yet again, one remembers that in the sixteenth century the Augustinian Hermits were moved by an extraordinary zeal to go forth and preach the Gospel in newly-discovered lands. Did some of these missionaries feel themselves to be Joachim's new spiritual men, sent to lead the world into the new age? A last echo of Joachimism among Augustinian Friars which comes from the year 1643 can perhaps be linked with this missionary zeal. Athanase of St Agnes paraphrases the prophecies of Joachim thus:[88]

> ... qui parle hautement de cette religion, lors qu'il la compare au Lionceau de Juda ... L'habi noir et la ceinture de cuir est la marque des Pères de cette religion, laquelle s'estrendra par tout et respandra par l'Univers les plus brillans rayons de la Predicator et les plus claires lumières de la parole de Dieu; c'est cette religion laquelle subsistera usque á la consommation du siècle et desployera tous ses efforts pour deffendre la Foy de Jesus contre la piussance de l'Anté-Christ. Ailleurs il dit ... c'est cette Religion laquelle n'a point éclipse parmy toutes les iniures du temps; c'est cette religion laquelle est assurée de sa grandeur et de sa durée; c'est cette religion laquelle jouyra du temps de la justice et de l'abondance de la paix; c'est cette

religion qui brisera la statue que fut montrée a Nabuchonazare.
Bref, c'est cette religion qui régnera sur toutes les nations et les
royaumes, qui s'opposent á l'Empire Chrestien.

The idea of the *viri spirituales* as leaders into the new age about
to dawn was by no means played out by the end of the Middle
Ages. Not only did it linger in the Augustinian Order, but we
shall find some of its most surprising adherents in the new order
of the Jesuits, and even some echoes among Protestants. It was,
without doubt, a most powerful idea. For, although the back-
ward-looking motif of return to primitive Apostolic purity also
played an important part in many movements of religious reform
during our period, the distinctive characteristic of the groups we
have been studying was that their faith sprang from a myth of the
future—not the past. Their reading of past history enabled them
to complete the pattern of things to come in the Last Age and to
find their own cosmic role within this pattern. Their models
might be drawn from the past, but their belief was that the life of
the future would far exceed that of the past. Thus, like early
Marxists, they believed they had a purchase over the future. It
was not so much a recapturing of the life of the first Apostles that
they expected as the creating of the life of new apostles. To the
orthodox the most unpalatable part of this Joachimist doctrine
was the belief that the future would transcend the past—a claim
that so easily passed into arrogance. In Inquisitorial proceedings a
major accusation against Joachites was the claim to greater perfection than Christ and the Apostles, yet the Joachite was almost
driven into this extreme position for it was in the nature of the
'myth' that the future must transcend the past. Perhaps it was an
instinctive avoidance of the extreme consequences of this logic
that led Spiritual Franciscans to combine faith in the future with
special devotion to the person of Christ and to find the focus of
this combination in the life of St Francis. But the role of Francis
was not simply that of imitating the earthly life of Christ as
closely as possible: it was to be conformed to Christ in order that
at the opening of the third age Francis might stand as Christ had
stood at the crossing from the first into the second. The fusion of
this christological emphasis with Joachim's on the outpouring of
the Spirit is best seen in their concept of the three Advents of
Christ, first in the flesh, secondly in the new spiritual life em-

bodied in Francis, thirdly in judgement at the end of time.

Whether the new age was conceived in terms of a Second Advent or an Age of the Spirit, the dynamic quality of the conception lay in the belief, received from Joachim, that a new illumination had been given to the *viri spirituales*. They were brought up into the high mountain and shown both the Promised Land and the crossing of Jordan which must first be accomplished. Then they saw their own calling: on the one hand to embody the true spiritual life of the future and, on the other, to lead the world towards it. Thus one aspect of this great spiritual adventure was the evangelization of the world, but in essence it led towards the silence of perfect contemplation which was to be the fulfilment of history.

3

LAST WORLD EMPEROR AND ANGELIC POPE

I

Politically, Joachim's expectation for the future struck a deterministic note. God had ordained the tribulations which punctuated the history of his Chosen People, both in the Old Dispensation and the New, in the Seven Seals and the Seven Openings. In the figure of the Dragon with Seven Heads Joachim identified the Saracens with the fourth head, once wounded unto death but now to be resurrected as the sixth head, which no crusading effort would be able to smite down until God willed it.[1] The Roman Empire had been ordained to hold back barbarian hordes, but when God's Sixth Angel poured his phial on the Euphrates (i.e. the Roman Empire), it would collapse, an event already foreshadowed in the disaster of Frederick Barbarossa and his army in 1187.[2] There was no future political order in Joachim's Sabbath Age: significantly, when he used the symbol of David's triumphal assumption of power in Jerusalem, it was with the papacy that he placed him in concord.[3] The only *figurà* of Joachim's which has a circular and therefore pessimistic movement is a political one showing the Chosen People moving out of captivity in Babylon and finally returning to it again.[4] There was to be no salvation through political agencies.

But there was an older legend of a last golden age under a world emperor which had been crystallized in Byzantium and brought to the west in Sibylline oracles and prophecies attributed to Methodius.[5] This legend proclaimed the coming of a mighty king to rescue Christendom just when tribulations were at their height. He would destroy or convert all the heathen and inaugurate an age of peace and plenty when men would eat, drink and be merry without fear or care. Finally, however, this period of blessedness would be rudely shattered, the gates of the north would burst open and all the tribes shut in by Alexander sweep forth to burn and kill. The Emperor would go to Jerusalem to await the onslaught of Antichrist and at the appearance of the Son of Perdition, he would lay down his crown on Golgotha and give up the ghost. Then Antichrist would reign until the true Christ appeared in clouds of glory to destroy his last enemy and sit in judgement. Thus the vision of an earthly Age of Gold merges into the pessimistic conviction that against the cosmic power of evil no human institution can stand: the greatest battle is Christ's alone.

In the west these expectations became linked with the theme of a great monarch who waits to be resurrected, such as Arthur, Charlemagne and, later, Frederick Barbarossa. In a political sense these legends did represent a certain apotheosis of history, but it is not clear that they were linked with a great spiritual *renovatio* and they certainly did not carry a Trinitarian implication of a final Age of the Spirit. In the pre-Joachimist legend, as we have seen, the age of peace and plenty *precedes* the onslaught of Antichrist, and the Last Emperor cannot withstand him. In Joachim's programme, on the other hand, the greatest Antichrist is defeated before the apotheosis of history and the final recrudescence of evil at the end of time is a mere flick of the dragon's tail. It needed the combination of this political dream with the Joachimist spiritual illumination of the third *status* to create a powerful form of political prophecy which was eagerly taken up as propaganda of many types in the later Middle Ages.

Frederick II appears to have been the first monarch to be placed in the dramatic context of a Joachimist future. He was a natural candidate for extreme roles, both bad and good. As the personification of evil he appears in the *Super Hieremiam*, the first pseudo-Joachimist work of the Italian school, as the *leo saevus de aquilone*, the Leviathan, the terrible *aquila*, the sixth or seventh head of the Dragon. The German empire is always 'nostris durum, dirum et mirum'. There would be a monstrous coalition between the Roman *imperium* and the Saracen, but finally both would be destroyed. Then, in the third *status*, 'which we believe to be already at the gates', the only authority would be the *ecclesia contemplantium*.[6] When Frederick II died undramatically, Salimbene, as we have seen, professed to have given up this doctrine *totaliter*,[7] but in fact neither Salimbene nor others could give up their Joachimism so easily. They could not believe that the Hohenstaufen had done his worst: he must be resurrected or reborn in one of the serpent's brood. Thus the next crop of pseudo-Joachimist works emanating from the same group still portrays the Hohenstaufen house as the cosmic centre of evil, the *malleus ecclesie*. The evil brood of Frederick II is symbolized in the adder, the viper and the flying serpent of biblical prophecy, while the German *imperium* is still the scourge of the Church.[8]

But in days when prophecy was so powerful a weapon, there quickly developed a prophetic counterblast. How far did Frederick II himself encourage a kind of imperial Joachimism for purposes of propaganda? There is no doubt about the heightened language and biblical parallels used by Frederick and his servants to describe his role in history.[9] Frederick hailed his own birthplace, Jesi, as a second Bethlehem and dared to adapt to it the words of the prophet Micah: '*Ex te enim dux exiit, Romani princeps imperii qui populum tuum reget.*' In a letter to the city of Worms (1241) he claimed to have been raised up by God in the spirit of Elijah—and, since the mystical return of Elijah was a key symbol of the *renovatio* for Joachites, the eschatological overtones here would not be lost. Frederick's servants and admirers carried further the application of messianic texts to the Emperor. Pier della Vigna identified him as the *Aquila grandis* of Ezekiel 17:3, again a text of significance to Joachim, and also applied a prophecy of Jeremiah to him. Biblical prophecy was extended to Pier himself by the notary Nicholas de Rocca who audaciously made him the cornerstone upon which the new Church would be founded. The first Peter denied his master three times, but the new Peter would not do it once. Other friends, playing on the same theme, made the Emperor address to him the words of Christ: '*Petre, amas me, rege oves meas,*' and compared his relationship to Frederick with that of Peter to Christ at the Last Supper. How far this was all propaganda and how far genuine, it is impossible to say, but this bold adaptation of biblical prophecy and symbol betrays a Joachimist current of influence. It implies a sequence of threes, making possible the claim that as events and persons in the Old Testament foreshadowed those of the New, so both would be paralleled by their counterpart in the new age. No doubt the Joachimist basis of this symbolism was generally unrealized, but the emotional tone of these writings, propagandist though they may be, is eschatological. To his supporters Frederick was the ultimate *renovator mundi*.

Whether or not stimulated by imperial propaganda, there is clear evidence of a group in Swabia committed to the expectaion of a *renovatio* which would be brought in by the Hohenstaufen. It is first recorded in 1248 by Albert of Stade. Between 1248 and 1250 one of its leaders, Frater Arnold, a Dominican, published his manifesto, *De Correctione Ecclesiae*, addressed to Frederick II.[10] He believed that the sixth age now approaching had been given to the Church for correction and that afterwards would come the seventh of peace, justice and renovation. The agencies to effect this spiritual revolution were the Dominican brethren, the Emperor and his son Conrad. The writer's hope is focused on the belief that after present tribulation and the death of Antichrist there would be an age of peace in the Church. Here for the first time we meet Joachim's third *status* recast in political terms, with the second great luminary of the world substituted for the papacy in the work of renewal. So the two streams—of Joachimism and of the ancient World Emperor tradition—meet in this political programme to bring in the seventh age. The influence of Joachim's emphasis on spiritual revolution is seen in the attribute now added to the image of the Last Emperor, that of the just chastiser and renewer of a depraved Church. The anti-imperialists called the emperor the *Rex impudicus facie* of Daniel 8.23, but by a bold counter-stroke the imperialists hailed him as the *Rex pudicus facie*.

When Manfred, the last of the 'serpent's brood', died at the Battle of Benevento in 1268, these indestructible prophetic images simply took on a new name, that of a future Third Frederick. He first appears in a Ghibelline prophecy which focuses hope on a new figure almost certainly intended to be Frederick, Landgrave of Thuringia, a grandson of Frederick II.[11] The power of his arm would extend to the end of the world: *Ipse enim imperans imperabit, et sub eo summus pontifex capietur*. A popular Ghibelline verse, beginning *Gallorum levitas*, states the imperial triumph over the papacy explicitly: *Papa cito moritur, Caesar regnabit ubique*.[12] Prophecies were now circulating briskly and a counterblast was soon forthcoming in a verse which expected the destruction of Frederick's brood and the apotheosis of history under the papacy, when all nations would be gathered into one fold.[13] Thus, out of this prophetic contest, a political Joachimism was born in two opposed versions in which a Saviour-Emperor and Antichrist-tyrant are juxtaposed on the stage of history.

Writing *c.* 1281, Alexander von Roes, in his *De Translatione Imperii*, seeks to boost his hope for the future of the *Imperium* by prophecy.[14] But on the German side he seems to know only an oracle concerning the bad Third Frederick which runs: *De huius Frederici germine radix peccatrix erumpet Fredericus nomine, qui clerum in Germania et etiam ipsam Romanam ecclesiam valde humiliabit et tribulabit vehementer.* This forces him to turn in quite a different direction for the promise of a glorious ruler. It is the old legend of a Last World Emperor which he revives in its Charlemagne form. There is a popular prophecy, he says, which expects an emperor to be raised up from the Carolingian stock who will be *princeps et monarcha* of all Europe. He will reform the Church and after him there will be no other emperor. To Alexander, of course, Charlemagne had been a Teuton and the Empire had been translated to the German monarchy. Thus in Alexander von Roes's work we encounter for the first time the Third Frederick as tyrant and the Second Charlemagne as saviour placed in the dramatic juxtaposition in which we shall meet them many times. The agents both of *tribulatio* and *renovatio* are imperial and, indeed, the line between evil oppressor and just chastiser is not always very clear-cut. We may observe also the use of the symbol of a new branch springing from an old root for both good and bad rulers. The one probably carries an echo of the 'rod out of the stem of Jesse' and the other of the evil tree of Antiochus Epiphanes.

One candidate for the role of a good Third Frederick in this period appears to have taken prophecy seriously. This was Frederick of Trinacria, King of Sicily, also descended from the Hohenstaufen.[15] A close friend of his was Arnold of Villanova, a Joachite associated with Spiritual Franciscans. To Frederick Arnold poured out his passionate dream that the King might be the divine instrument of the *renovatio mundi*, to cleanse Church and State, convert the Saracens and bring all men into the true evangelical life. God would raise up an Angelic Pope who, together with the King, would bring the whole world into one fold. Frederick was not unmoved, for he took his religious vocation most seriously. Perhaps at the court of Sicily in the early fourteenth century we witness a unique desire to realize this eschatological dream on the plane of politics. Others, too, observed that here was a Third Frederick descended from the Hohenstaufen. He caught the imagination of the Fraticelli, many of whom he sheltered. Fra Dolcino expected him to fulfil the programme of the Apostolic Brethren. A Catalan chronicle of this period hailed him as the Third Frederick and expected him to become '*senyor del imperi e de la major part del mon*'.[16] Frederick resisted papal pressures to give up these doubtful connections for some time but nothing positive came of these dreams.

The greatest exponent of an earthly beatitude under the rule of a single emperor was, of course, Dante. In his letter to the Princes and People of Italy in 1310 he hailed the coming of the Emperor Henry VII in almost messianic phrases and he saw the true freedom of Florence and the other cities of Italy in terms of their obedience to God's chosen vessel.[17] Whatever the date of the *Monarchy*, Dante set down in it his belief that the true potential of mankind could only be realized through the harmony of one world government, and in the *Divina Commedia* he was still—if one accepts the usual interpretations—looking forward to a great ruler or leader who would end civil strife and set the world aright.[18] How much was Dante influenced by Joachimist prophecies? He saluted Joachim himself as a great prophet, placing him in the *Paradiso* as one endowed with the spirit of prophecy.[19] He knew Ubertino da Casale's *Arbor Vitae Crucifixae* and he perhaps listened to Olivi when he was lector at Santa Croce in Florence. It does not seem possible, however, to pinpoint any direct connection between Dante's political messianism and the World Emperor prophecies we have just been considering, for Dante took his own route to his political philosophy. On the other hand, we have almost incontrovertible evidence that Dante knew Joachim's *Liber Figurarum* and used at least two of these figures in the *Divina Commedia*.

In the sixth heaven of Jupiter Dante describes the moving stars, flames of the Holy Spirit, which form in heavenly writing the words: '*Diligite justitiam qui judicatis terram*.'[20] While the rest fades, the stars gather on the final *M* which, entwining with lilies, they transform into an eagle. This image has confounded many interpreters but the clue surely lies in Joachim's Tree-Eagles.[21] Here the formal pattern of upturned branches is easily seen as a gothic *M* when turned the other way up. This again transforms itself into an eagle by the addition of the head and tail, while the rich ornamentation of heraldic lilies and fruits explains the enigmatic phrase of Dante: '*d'ingigliarsi all' emme*'. In its five/seven symbolism, incorporated into the form of the eagle and embellished with the lilies of the Holy Spirit, Joachim's figure does, as we have seen,[22] most powerfully express the hidden promise of the coming Age of the Spirit. In the *Paradiso* the eagle is the bird of Jupiter, embodying ideal justice, but for Joachim it is the bird of St John, embodying the third *status*. May not Dante here be expressing his expectation of the renewal of justice and right government in the world, when the Tree twice-despoiled flourishes again in the third and last age? His hope for the world was couched in political terms but in the *Paradiso* this must be seen in the context of spiritual blessedness. It seems possible, then, that Dante not only used the figure of the Tree-Eagle but understood its hidden promise of the Age of the Spirit and used it because the eagle of Jupiter and the eagle of St John together embodied his conception of the third age.

Secondly, Dante used Joachim's powerful image of the Godhead as three intertwined circles in the final vision which is the climax of the *Paradiso*. Some commentators have declared that Dante could not have intended a literal geometrical figure here, since this would be grotesque. But after studying the mystical uses of geometry in Joachim's *figurae* it no longer seems incongruous in Dante's highest poetry:

> Nella profonda e chiara sussistenza
> dell' alto lume parvermi tre giri
> di tre colori e d'una contenenza;
> e l'un dall'altro qual iri da iri
> parea riflesso, e il terzo parea foco
> che quinci e quindi igualmente si spiri.
>
> (canto xxxiii. 115–20)

Dante's lines seem precisely to describe the three interlacing circles in the *Liber Figurarum*:[23] three equal circles (*d'una contenenza*), side by side and interlinked (*l'un dall'altro*), of three colours, the third the colour of fire. Instead of being deliberately obscure, Dante's vision seems to be one of marvellous clarity and exactitude. We should note that in both the chief manuscripts of the *Liber Figurarum* the third circle is red and also that the particular way in which Joachim interlaced the circles to express the double procession of the Spirit is exactly indicated by Dante: '*il terzo parea foco, che quinci e quindi igualmente si spiri.*' The phrase '*qual iri da iri*' has always caused problems. Mgr Tondelli pointed out[24] that in one medieval tradition the fundamental colours of the rainbow were only three and that these were named by Joachim in the *Expositio* as precisely the colours used in the Oxford and Reggio manuscripts of the *Liber Figurarum*:[25] green, blue and red. The true interpretation therefore seems to be that Dante saw the green, blue and red of the three circles as iridescent, each reflected in the others, together making one rainbow and yet appearing as three. This mystery expresses the activity of the three Persons and their intimate relations, radiating supernatural light and colour which is at once three-fold and one. This recalls strikingly the various symbols and metaphors used by Joachim in his struggle to describe his concept of the Three-are-One. In this final moment of the *Commedia* Dante had no longer thought for an earthly beatitude. It was the essence of the Triune Godhead that filled his vision. Detached from other relationships, he sees the simple but aweful *circumincessio* of the Trinity in the flashing, quasi-electric contact of each circle with the other two. It would seem that Dante had been struck by the clarity of Joachim's concept and the beauty of its expression in the figure. These elements he could transform by his poetry into a vision of the Godhead which exalts geometrical shape into the luminosity of the rainbow. Thus, while Dante's political vision seems to have received a stimulus from Joachim's Tree-Eagle, he also found some of his final inspiration in that strange mixture of theological concept and artistic imagery which distinguishes Joachim's view of the Trinity.

Dante's use of Joachim's circles has taken us away from the theme of the Last Emperor. From this digression we turn now to the French role in political prophecy. France had played an ignominious part in thirteenth-century writings, figuring either as the broken reed of Isaiah 36.6, or as a power to be broken by a triumphant German Emperor. With the Second Charlemagne prophecy ready to hand, however, a French counterblast was obvious. Yet it was not until the early fourteenth century that the marriage between the old legend and the Joachimist *renovatio mundi* appears clearly. Had this anything to do with that enigmatic monarch Philip IV, who—it has recently been suggested— was not without his grandiose dreams of world crusade, conquest and renewal?[26] At any rate it was his servant, Pierre Dubois, who, in claiming a cosmic role for the French monarchy in his *De recuperatione Terrae Sanctae*, deliberately linked this claim with the descent from Charlemagne.[27] From this source alone, he believed, could flow the universal peace desired by all. So the imperial title must be transferred to the French royal house and, the Holy Land recovered, the French Emperor must rule a federation of nations from Jerusalem.

This political propaganda, closely associated with the French court, is understandable, but what led the authors of a little tract of religious prophecy, the *Liber de Flore*, to partner the Angelic Pope with a *rex generosus* from the line of Pepin?[28] We shall look at the problem of the authorship of this and its associated tracts a little later. If they emanated, as has been assumed, from Angelo Clareno's group of Italian Joachites, this turning to the French monarchy seems strange, but we note that Ramon Lull, in his missionary zeal, also looked to the French monarchy to support his programme of world evangelization. There is something not yet explained here.

At any rate, the seed dropped in the *Liber de Flore* springs into a full-blown tree in the French Joachimism of Jean de Roquetaillade (Rupescissa).[29] Born near Aurillac, this mid-fourteenth-century Franciscan fell under the spell of Olivi's writings when studying at Toulouse and became a convinced Joachite, with a mind peculiarly receptive of visions and prophecies. From 1344 onwards he suffered a long series of imprisonments in Franciscan convents and, finally, in the papal prison at Avignon. From prison he poured out a series of prophetic writings, of which the most important are a Commentary on the pseudo-Joachimist *Oraculum Cyrilli*, the *Liber Secretorum Eventuum*, the *Liber Ostensor* and *Vade Mecum in Tribulatione*. In spite of orthodox suspicions, they were read and discussed by eminent churchmen and some were widely disseminated. Their influence probably lay in their fusion of national aspirations and

Joachimist dreams. Roquetaillade's prophetic politics were convincingly simple in their range of black and white, and—whilst the authorities dealt harshly with the poor fanatic—no one was quite prepared to disbelieve him.

For Roquetaillade the source of all political evil still lay in the accursed seed of the *serpens antiquus*, Frederick II, from whom had sprung a multiple Antichrist in Frederick and Louis of Sicily, and Louis of Bavaria. Linked with them were the bad sons of St Francis. The forces of good stood in gratifyingly clear contrast. Roquetaillade expected a holy Pope, *corrector et reparator*, who would take refuge with the King of France when the evil powers were in the ascendant. The blessed race of the French princes was that of the new Maccabees, sent to defend the Church. In the *Liber Secretorum* the world is lined up in two camps: Antichrist and his allies, that is, Italian Ghibellines, the Spanish kings and the German tyrants, against the true Pope, the King of France and Charles IV of Bohemia. Evils will mount to a climax, with famine and plague added (a sinister note in 1349), but in a final battle the true Pope will triumph, aided politically by the King of France and religiously by the true children of St Francis. In his earlier works Roquetaillade had merely assigned the role of aid to the French monarchy, but his latest versions of the future, written *c.* 1356, when French fortunes in the Hundred Years' War were at their nadir, exalted the 'King from the race of Pepin' into the temporal instrument through whom God will bring in the final age of beatitude. Such is prophetic hope! Roquetaillade expects him to be elected as Roman Emperor and to rule the entire world from Jerusalem. Together with the Angelic Pope, in whom, says Roquetaillade, the third *status* will begin, the French Emperor will 'repair the whole globe', destroying Mohammedanism, subduing Turks and Tartars, converting Jews and infidels, and bringing all into one flock under one shepherd. Through all the tribulations the pure seed of the Minorites will have been preserved to replenish the world and in this last time, when a new plenitude of the Holy Spirit will be poured out, they will embody 'this new state of being' so accurately prophesied by Joachim.

Roquetaillade's works sparked off a mysterious person who called himself Telesphorus of Cosenza (Calabria).[30] Whether or not he was really a Calabrian hermit, he was certainly a

Francophile Joachite. In his prefatory letter he tells us that in a vision on Easter Sunday, 1386, he was directed to search the oracles of Cyril, Joachim and others. In fact, he probably began to write *c*. 1356 and put his *libellus* into final shape between 1378 and 1390. The dramatic alignment of the world into 'good' and 'bad' camps, as foretold by Roquetaillade, received startling confirmation in the Great Schism and Telesphorus, already thinking along these lines, must have felt his prophetic authorities to have been strikingly vindicated in 1378 and the following years. In his *libellus* which is partly a commentary on the *Oraculum Cyrilli*, he proves that this last and most monstrous schism has long been foretold by the Holy Spirit. Its cause is God's anger at the sins of the clergy. The chief agents of destruction will be a 'Rex alemanus' and a pseudo-pope of the same nation. In his original version (but not in the sixteenth-century printed edition), Telesphorus names the German tyrant as a future Frederick III who will be crowned as the diabolical emperor by the German anti-pope. Then the stage is set for the great conflict between these forces of Antichrist and those of the *nova religio sanctissima*, championed by the Angelic Popes and the French King, that generous monarch whose name will be Charles and who will spring from the seed of Pepin. After some vicissitudes, all the forces of evil will be destroyed and the Angelic Pope will crown the French King as the true Emperor. Then in a holy partnership Emperor and Pope will reform the Church and recover the Holy Land in the seventh and last crusade. This will be the millennium when Satan is bound for a thousand years. At the end of this there will, indeed, be a short recrudescence of evil, but before the end of the world there will supervene a second age of beatitude, conceived in the religious terms of the series of Angelic Popes.

From the widely scattered manuscripts it is clear that Telesphorus's *libellus* enjoyed a great vogue. This may have been partly due to the dramatic and lively little pictures which often embellish it. In one of the earliest manuscripts, finished in 1387, the illustrations pick out especially the four Angelic Popes and the Last Emperor who is crowned as the 'Second Charlemagne'. Immediately following this is a separate prophecy of the Second Charlemagne which soon becomes the most popular of all oracles.[31] He is hailed as Charles, the son of Charles, from the

nation of the most illustrious Lily and described as having a
'*frontem longam, supercilia alta, oculos longos, nasum aquilinum*'. He
will be crowned in his thirteenth year and at fourteen will start on
a triumphant career that will begin with the destruction of all
tyrants in his own kingdom and carry him triumphantly through
the subjugation of western Europe, the destruction of Rome and
Florence, the conquest of Greece and the eastern nations, until at
last he reaches Jerusalem. The divine arm will be always with
him and no one will be able to resist him, so that he will attain the
dominion of virtually the whole earth. Finally in the thirty-first
year of his reign he will lay down his crown on Mount Olivet and,
rendering thanks to God, give up the ghost. He will be crowned
as Emperor by the Angelic Pastor, being the first emperor after
the Third Frederick.

I have given a full summary of this text since we shall meet it
again and again from the fifteenth to the seventeenth centuries.[32]
It is not at all certain that Telesphorus wrote this in the first
place. A version has been found which can be dated to 1380 and
which was composed in honour of the young Charles VI of
France.[33] It lacks the final sentence about the Angelic Pope and
the Third Frederick which, in any case, is very awkwardly tacked
on the end. Perhaps, then, this was originally a version of the old
Second Charlemagne prophecy which was seized on by
Telesphorus and put into a Joachimist context. By placing the
Second Charlemagne *after* the Third Frederick and in association
with the Angelic Pope, the embodiment of the third *status*, the
author of the addition contrives to put this old symbol of the Last
World Emperor within the eschatological framework of the
Joachimist third *status*. The assumption that this author was
Telesphorus rests on the persistent association of this text with
his *libellus*. Long after the unfortunate Charles VI had sunk into
insanity, this symbol presented a bright image of political glory
coveted by the most varied claimants.

On the whole the French prophets did better than those on the
Teutonic side in the fourteenth century. But Rome produced a
prince of political prophets in Cola dei Rienzo.[34] His eloquent
letters show that the focus of his expectation was not so much the
tribulation of Antichrist as the new outpouring of the Holy Spirit
which was to come. In this he was deeply a Joachite. Again and
again in glowing words he expressed his vision of the great time

when a more ample gift of the Spirit would be manifested to all flesh, to illumine and make new the face of the whole world. The source of his Joachimism can be traced to a Fraticelli group at Majella with whom he sojourned in hiding for a season. But Rienzo's Age of the Spirit was also to be a political golden age in which the ancient City of Rome would rise to new life and, adorned as a bride, receive again her spouse, the Roman pontiff. Rienzo conceived his mission as a call to restore Rome to her pristine glory, renewing in her justice, liberty and security, so that, by the grace of the Holy Spirit, she would enjoy a sweetness of peace greater than ever known before. It was always the *pastor angelicus* who, in Rienzo's mind, was the central figure in this great revival, but when the Avignonese popes remained unmoved, he turned to the Emperor Charles IV to carry out the great work of emancipating Rome and bringing in the *reformacio*. His two letters to Charles sketch out his programme. If Charles will only believe the prophets and start his campaign in Italy, he will receive prosperity and empire. Italy will be conquered in seven months and Rome, the new Jerusalem, will, under his sceptre, become the head of the world. Charles, however, was much too shrewd to listen to this revised Ghibelline programme of prophecy—or to the ambassadors from Majella who waited on him to announce the advent of the Age of the Holy Ghost.

It was inevitable that the period of the Great Schism should produce a Teutonic *riposte* to the popular French programme disseminated by Telesphorus. So in the early fifteenth century we find Germanic prophecies circulating in the name of Gamaleon, reputedly a relation of Pope Boniface IX.[35] He sees in a vision an armed man clothed in red and crowned with a ruby. This is the French tyrant who will seize the *imperium* and bring desolation on Church and people. Of this tyrant it is written: *Tu es horribilis et quis tibi resistet?* But in the Rhineland there will arise a prince whom the Germans will elect as Caesar. He will call a Council at Aachen where the Schism will be ended by the crowning of the Patriarch of Mainz as Pope. Then the Caesar will destroy the French pretender and prevail over all peoples, exterminating the Jews and reducing the clergy to Apostolic poverty. Rome will be remembered no more as the seat of the Apostles, for the Patriarchate of Mainz will become the centre of the Church: '*Et sub isto Caesare Germanicae regiones ac nationes exaltabuntur.*'

Here an upsurge of something akin to nationalism is sweeping into political prophecy, claiming for itself, not only the righteous political agent who will fight for the true Pope, but the whole spiritual *renovatio* as well. Emotionally, the aspiration expressed here seems to be anticipating the German Reformation.

II

Yet alongside the World Emperor stands the Angelic Pope. One of the most moving dreams of the later Middle Ages is that of the Angelic Pope whose expected advent would usher in the Age of the Spirit. This was one mode in which the visionaries dealt with the problem of reconciling continuity of authority with spiritual revolution. For many the see of St Peter remained the immovable rock which would endure until the end of the age, whatever storms beat against it. Yet their eyes of longing were fixed on the tremendous dream which hovered on their horizon, sometimes nearer, sometimes farther off. Their question was the question of all revolutionaries: how do we get from here to there? Their answer was to postulate a revolution in the very central institution itself. But, given the nature of its authority, what hand could revolutionize it except God's? In some form or other God must intervene to create a new papal image—hence the emphasis on *Angel* or *Angelic* Pope.

Joachim himself created the basis for this dream, but we must first be clear that institutionally the church of the third *status* remained for him the Roman Church, with the successor of St Peter as its head. However much he might speak of the active life symbolized by Peter being superseded by the contemplative life designated by John, the context of these statements was always the *quality of life* in the Church, which must be transformed, never the *institution* which must be replaced. Institutionally, the Church is the *novam Hierusalem que est Petri navicula*, which must endure to the end.[36] 'Peter is great,' exclaims Joachim once, 'Prince of the Apostles and of the prelates of the whole Church, but oh! how blessed in John! . . . The former is greater in glory: the latter more felicitous in love.'[37] This seems to sum up both Joachim's loyalty and the focus of his affection.

The spiritual revolution was seen by Joachim in terms of a geographical movement of the same authority from one place to another. David reigned first in Hebron and then was exalted to Jerulsame; even so the papacy, for the popes must first rule over the *ecclesia laborantium*, sweating through the active life, and then over the *ecclesia quiescentium*, exulting in the contemplative life.[38] But the historical concord with David does not give a clue as to how the 'movement' will take place: it simply must be, because of the pattern of history laid down by God. Thus we do not get from Joachim any statement on how the new spiritual leadership will arise. We also find the Roman pontiff of the third *status* typified in some of the great figures at the end of the Old Testament: Zorobabel, for instance, the *novus dux* to lead the chosen people from Babylon back to Jerusalem, and Mordecai who is exalted after great tribulation.[39] The Roman pontiff in the last days will be both the great champion in the time of the sharpest tribulation and the focus to which in the Sabbath Age all peoples will flow. The new qualities in Joachim's third *status* include not only spiritual understanding and holy liberty, but also ecumenical unity, and it is this last aspect which is most clearly symbolized in the spiritual authority of the transformed papacy. Its dominion will extend from sea to sea and to the ends of the earth. Immutability and transition are summed up thus: 'The Church of St Peter which is the throne of Christ cannot lose its authority, but, transformed into greater glory, will remain firm to eternity.'[40]

But what would be the nature of the transition? This urgent question, only dealt with figuratively by Joachim, received a variety of answers in the thirteenth century. The first group of pseudo-Joachimist prophecies express a somewhat harsh view of the papacy. The wealth, worldliness and pride of the Roman Church must be chastised and from this develops a more extreme attitude towards the transition from the second to the third *status*. A violent gesture, either by the papacy itself, or by others towards it, begins to appear in the prophetic programme. Peter must cast off his coat and plunge naked into the tempestuous seas, while the ark of the Church is almost submerged, yet rides the waves. The Church must fall among thieves. The transition across Jordan must be one of persecution.[41] For some time the image of Peter wallowing naked in the sea obsesses the prophetic imagination and we can hardly put our finger on the origin of this famous myth of the Angelic Pope which takes its place.

Our first clear reference comes, not from a Joachimist work, but from the writings of Roger Bacon.[42] Addressing the Pope in his *Opus Tertium* (1267/8), he says that for forty years there has been a prophecy of a pope who would come to purge canon law and the Church from all cavilling and fraud, dispensing universal justice without litigation. His goodness, truth and justice would be such that the Greeks would return to the Roman obedience, the major part of the Tartars would be converted, the Saracens destroyed, and there would be one sheepfold and one pastor. Bacon goes on to say that one who had seen this vision by revelation declared it would happen in his own time. In another reference to this prophecy he speaks of *unus beatissimus papa* who would purge all corruptions from learning and from the Church, convert the remnant of Israel, renew the world and bring the 'plenitude of peoples' into the fold.[43] Bacon's source remains an enigma but his words suggest a circulating prophecy and this is borne out by a passing reference which Salimbene—that sounding board of prophecies—makes in connection with the death of Pope Gregory X (1276).[44] He says there are some verses circulating which speak of a *papa sacer* of *angelice vite* who will carry out a programme of reform:

Hunc Deus ornabit et mire clarificabit,
Sanctificabit, magnificabit, glorificabit.
Mundum pacabit et Ierusalem renovabit
Fructus terra dabit, Deus orbem letificabit.

We also find a strange reference to an *ursus admirabilis* as a figure for the reforming Pope in the *Oraculum Cyrilli*, a pseudo-Joachimist tract written *c.* 1280–90.[45] Somewhere amongst these visionary Joachites—whether in the circle of Joachim's Calabrian disciples or that of the Spiritual Franciscans—the image of the ideal Pope was created.

That it caught the imagination and circulated rapidly would seem to be the conclusion to be drawn from an extraordinary episode which appears to be the sudden embodiment of this dream in action, even before it was fully articulated. It is almost impossible now to assess the various currents of emotional aspiration and political scheming which flowed together to bring about the election of the hermit Pope, Celestine V, in 1294. Once chosen, he was certainly hailed in messianic terms as he journeyed from the wilderness, meekly riding on an ass, to take up the pontifical office.[46] The lack of evidence makes it impossible to assert that a Joachimist vision inspired the election, but it is clear that, once this astonishing event had taken place, it 'precipitated' the image of the Angelic Pope in clear and powerful form. Celestine became the proto-type of the angel-pontiff to be. Moreover the tragedy of his fate underlined the stark juxtaposition of good and evil which characterized the Joachimist programme. It was tempting to see the drama of Celestine V and Boniface VIII in terms of the Antichrist who was to capture the high places and thrust in a pseudo-pope. Angelo Clareno's group of Spiritual Franciscans suffered much from Boniface VIII and therefore, it has been suggested, it is from their circle that the famous *Vaticinia de summis pontificibus* emanated, with their sudden transition from harsh judgement of a worldly papacy to proclamation of a series of angelic popes.

Neither the date nor the authorship of the *Vaticinia* is quite certain. Professor Grundmann's theory that they were produced in the summer of 1304 by the Spiritual group led by Clareno and Liberato, when they were gathered at Perugia to await the election of a new Pope, rests mainly on two types of argument.[47] In the first place, the Byzantine source which was undoubtedly the basis of the *Vaticinia* can most easily be accounted for by the fact that Clareno and his followers had recently returned from exile in Greece. Secondly, Grundmann suggests, one can detect the point at which *post eventum* prophecy becomes real prophecy and thus fix the date. The enigmatic character of the prophecies makes the second point, to my mind, less clear than Grundmann thought and so the date remains in doubt. But of the Byzantine source there can be no doubt, and therefore the likelihood of a Clarenist authorship seems to follow.

The prophecies consist of fifteen figures, each with oracular caption and text, which represent a series of popes.[48] From the earliest outside reference to them (before 1314) we learn that the series started with the Orsini Pope, Nicholas III (1277–1280), pictured with little bears besieging him. Figures and texts are adapted from the so-called Oracles of Leo the Wise, the Byzantine emperor who ruled from 886 to 912. In fact it has been shown that the Oracles were probably a product of the Comnenian period, collected together, perhaps, *c.* 1180. The very

nature of the enigmatic figures—two crows attacking the eyes of a
serpent, an eagle, a unicorn, a bull or cow accompanied by two
heads of young men, a bear suckling its young, a severed head in
a dish, a fox with three standards, and so on—made them amen-
able to adaptation. But the real value of the Oracles to the
Joachites lay in their hidden message of revolution. After prophesying by means of these figures the fluctuating fortunes of a
series of emperors, an empty throne appears, representing a
moment of crisis. Then comes the crucial turning-point in the
figure of a holy half-naked hermit seated on a rock or tomb who is
approached with reverence by a robed man. In the text to this the
voice of God commands the electors to seek a new emperor in the
west of the seven hills. Thus the spiritual revolution is initiated
by divine revelation. In the next picture the holy emperor is
actually being sought among the dead, but in the final ones he is
installed with crown and sceptre, supported by angels and in
alliance with the patriarch. The concluding sequence of captions
—*Innocentia, Praehonoratio, Electio*, compared with such earlier
ones as *Sanguis, Confusio, Membrorum Divisio*—emphasizes the
complete contrast in regime. Thus it seems that the original series
itself embodied a revolutionary change from corruption and ruin
to spiritual revival through the revelation of a Saviour-Emperor.

This gave the Joachite adapters exactly what they wanted: a
series through which to express continuity of office, a sharp break
necessitating divine intervention, a spiritual revolution culminating in an angelic regime. By fathering the series on Joachim, they
could contrive, under the guise of prophecy, a bitter and telling
attack on recent popes, before moving into real prophecy. The
contrast of evil and good could be presented in dramatic juxtaposition and expectation of the great moment could be crystallized into the substitution of a holy for an unholy series of pas-
tors. For their purpose the figures—which they rearranged—
adapted wonderfully well, mitred popes being easily inserted into
the animal pictures or substituted for crowned emperors. The
bear and young obviously suggested the Orsini and became the
first picture, indicating the nepotism of Nicholas III. Captions
such as *Ypocrisis habundabit principium malorum* show the tone
of the early prophecies. Early in the Leo series—either four, five
or six—appeared a man with a sickle in one hand and a rose in
the other, who is being crowned by an angel. This was clearly

meant to be an angelic type appearing out of season and of course it was at once turned into a monk to represent Celestine V, interrupting dramatically the 'unholy' sequence. To this the caption was given *Elacio paupertatis. Obediencia. Castitatis Temperacio. Ypocritarum Destructor.* Though the following picture is enigmatic, its caption surely indicates Boniface VIII: *Incisio hypocrisis in abominatione erit.* The hermit on the rocks was of course the appropriate symbol for the first Angelic Pope and this is emphasized in the caption *Bona honoracio. Et revelabitur unctus qui habet prenomen monachi, petram habitans.* In all the early manuscripts I have examined this is the eleventh prophecy, followed by four more or less angelic pictures with suitable captions: *Bona gratia. Symonia cessabit. Bona interio. Caritas abundabit/Prehonoratio. Concordia erit./Bona Occasio. Reverentia/ Devotio augmentabitur.* These are the key pictures. For the rest, the earliest versions of the Pope-prophecies vary in order and sometimes in actual figures, but all derive the elements of their figures from the Leo Oracles. There are some strange variations, however, which at times seem to hint at imagery arising out of the subconscious.

The relationship of the *Vaticinia* to the *Liber de Flore* and the commentary on it by 'Rabanus' is not quite clear. The *Liber* does not draw on the Oracles, it has no figures, and its style is different. Nevertheless, it has the same theme—a papal series culminating in a sequence of angelic popes—and the angelic group begins with the same hermit, *pauper et nudus*, who must be sought out and crowned by the angel. From this point onwards the political programme we have already referred to will be carried out. The Hermit Pope will form an alliance with the *rex generosus* of Pepin's line and together they will conquer east and west, recover Jerusalem and bring the Greek Church back to its true obedience in conjunction with the French monarchy. The Pope will create the French king Emperor, while renouncing all temporal wealth for the Roman See and the clergy. The second Angelic Pope will be a Frenchman and will reform Germany. The third Pope will be an Italian Franciscan and the last a Gascon who will make pilgrimages throughout the world, until in Palestine the two barbarian peoples of Gog and Magog will meet him with palms and songs. He will rule the world until its end. Here was a splendid programme embodying the passionate hopes of a particular

moment in history. But it did not wear well, for it was too rash in
its specific detail. So the *Liber de Flore* is today only known in
three manuscripts.

The *Vaticinia de summis pontificibus* also locates the moment of
spiritual revolution in a historical series, but its programme for
the future is couched in far more enigmatic terms so that, when
the crucial moment had slipped away uneventfully, it provided
unending attraction in reinterpretation. In all about seventy
known manuscripts and printed editions survive from the fourteenth to the seventeenth centuries. Some of these merely expressed an interest in figuring out how well the prophecies fitted
succeeding popes. Thus in a number of them names of popes are
scribbled in beside each figure. Before the original number of
fifteen had been exhausted, a second series of *Vaticinia* had appeared, also based on the Leo Oracles, with similar figures, captions and texts. The second set does not have the same thrust
towards a climax in the Angelic Popes—indeed, the last one
clearly represents the advent of Antichrist. Before the end of the
fourteenth century, however, the two sets had been put together
as one set of thirty, with the earlier fifteen as the second half.
This suggests that the vision of the Angelic Popes still exercised a
strong pull, for this arrangement meant that the pessimistic prog-
nostication of Antichrist was harmlessly lost in the middle of the
series which still mounted up to its beatific climax from numbers
twenty-five to thirty. The extension to thirty also meant that the
series was extrapolated well into the succeeding century. Thus
there was plenty of scope for eager interpreters. Continuing interest in the *Vaticinia* is well illustrated in the variety and widespread distribution of manuscripts, ranging from crude pen-and-
ink sketches to superbly illuminated productions, such as MS.
Harley 1340 in the British Museum which is claimed by Berenson
to be the work of the Master of the San Miniato altar-piece.

The concept of the Angelic Pope evolved only as ardent visionaries, such as the Spiritual Franciscans, were pressed into an
impossible dilemma by the attempt to hold together two incom-
patible principles: obedience to the papacy and loyalty to their
vision. The inexorable logic which drove Franciscans such as
Olivi, Clareno and Ubertino da Casale along could be stated thus:
the true Pope could not err, the Rule of St Francis could not be
modified, therefore a pontiff who did so and manifestly erred

must be the pseudo-pope of prophecy, presiding over the carnal Church of Babylon. Whilst maintaining a knife-edge position in his obedience to Rome, Olivi expected the forces of good and evil to range themselves ever more sharply against each other. In the statements of the Spirituals, and still more in those of the Fraticelli, the expectation of the pseudo-pope, persecutor of the true church, appears prominently, sharpened especially by John XXII's hostility to them. Thus Olivi's followers in the south of France openly assert that John XXII is the pseudo-pope or *Antichristus misticus*, and similarly the Fraticelli in Italy.[49] The second series of *Vaticinia* was probably the work of Tuscan Fraticelli and expresses their viewpoint in the harsh indictments of wealth, political intrigue and nepotism in the papacy.[50] The roles allotted to Celestine and Boniface stand out dramatically. Celestine is represented by a holy mitred pope being blessed, with a text that begins: '*Benedictus qui venit in nomine Domini*', but there is a fox tugging at his robe from behind. The next, with the caption '*Fraudulenter intrasti . . .*', shows Boniface at his worst, piercing the dove of peace and embroiled with the cock and eagle, while behind him the rejected holy monk sits disconsolate. Indignation against the Avignonese popes is fierce. If our dating is correct, the last three, that is, after Innocent VI, are real prophecies. The last is clearly Antichrist, the only one in which the Pope is represented by a beast, with the caption: '*Terribilis es, quis resistet tibi?*' This is an uncompromising assertion that Antichrist will appear in the supreme pontiff's seat. The idea of the Angelic Pope had to develop over against this menacing manifestation of evil.

Babylonish Captivity, schism, pseudo-pope or *Antichristus misticus*, Angelic Popes—these are already elements in an established prophetic tradition by the mid-fourteenth century. The black and white lines of the great final drama were worked out in detail by John of Roquetaillade and Telesphorus of Cosenza, with, it seemed, extraordinary confirmation in the Great Schism. For Roquetaillade a worldly hierarchy in the Church was the antithesis of the true evangelical Church and therefore a manifestation of Antichrist.[51] Thus one or more pseudo-popes were inevitable. The true Pope would be stripped, persecuted and forced to flee into the desert, perhaps to hide himself in France. Schism was inevitable, yet the Angelic Pope remained as a thread of gold through all Roquetaillade's gloomy prognostications. The *Papa Angelicus* appears in his writings under a number of names and figures: he will be the *Corrector*, the Reparator, the *Reformator*; prefigured in the schism of Israel and Judah, he is Rehoboam against Jeroboam; he is the *ursus admirabilis* foretold by 'Cyril the Carmelite'. He will resemble both St Francis and Celestine V and, like the latter, be elected at Perugia. He will be the hermit called forth from the rock of the *Vaticinia*. Roquetaillade expects him to be chosen from the Minorites and himself to choose evangelical men of poverty for his cardinals. As we have seen, he will carry out his great programme in collaboration with the King of France. Peace will be made in Italy, all schism ended, and the clergy drastically reformed. Together the two world leaders will visit Greece and Asia, bringing even Turks and Tartars under their rule. The Angelic Pope will then leave the political role to the French Emperor who will execute the mandates of the *Reformator* throughout the world, while he wields the spiritual power. After the conversion of the Jews he will transfer the Holy See to Jerusalem, holding seven general church councils on the conversion of the world. The New Jerusalem will be built but no secular ruler allowed there for fear of contaminating the clergy. Then there will be such an outpouring of the Holy Spirit that Paradise will seem to have descended again. All will aspire to the contemplative life, following the Rule of St Francis. Forty-five years after the death of Antichrist there will be one empire embracing the whole earth, one sheepfold and one shepherd.

We catch echoes of the *Papa Angelicus* in various prose and verse prophecies scattered around Italy from the mid-fourteenth century onwards. Thus a Fra Gentile *c.* 1345 clearly knows the Oracles of Leo as well as the *Liber de Flore* when he quotes a prophecy in which the voice of God directs the electors to the naked hermit, the first *Reformator*, to be followed by two more.[52] Among prophetic verses, the well-known *Apri le labbra mie* ends:

> Poi fie la Chiesa ornata di pastori
> Umili e santi come fur gli autori.

Another, beginning *Vuol la mia fantasia*, dreams of *Li sancti preti di novello stato*, while a later one specifically prophesies the coming of the Angelic Pope:

E sarà un Papa vero e naturale
Santissimo, giusto e governarà piano.[53]

As we have seen, Cola di Rienzo sought to recall Clement VI
from Avignon to fulfil the angelic role in Rome and bring in the
dream of the '*unum ovile et unus pastor*'. A little later St Bridget of
Sweden was making the same call.[54] Once more the greatest evil
and the greatest good are juxtaposed in her prophecies. She hears
Christ proclaim the coming age: 'Now will my friends bring me a
new bride', and calls on the Avignonese popes to return and fulfil
the vision. Again, the messages of St Catharine of Siena are
pitched in the same key. To such visionaries the return to Rome
was seen, not as a desirable political or moral move, but as an
essential part of the programme to bring in the new age. The
Jordan of tribulation must first be crossed before the seventh age
can dawn and this implies a significant element of discontinuity.
So the return to Rome is itself seen as a revolutionary act: the
physical discontinuity between Avignon and Rome, prefigured in
David's move from Hebron to Jerusalem, is symbolic of the
deeper discontinuity between the sixth and seventh ages of history.

By one of the ironies of history the longed-for return to Rome
in 1376 brought, not 'one sheepfold and one shepherd', but the
Great Schism. This was, of course, part of the prophetic programme and so the Great Schism, in sharply emphasizing that
the Jordan of the sixth age had not yet been crossed, put the seal
on the prophets from Joachim and St Francis to Roquetaillade.
Even Pierre d'Ailly wondered whether this was 'that great schism
to precede the advent of Antichrist of which much had been
written by St Hildegarde and the venerable abbot Joachim'?[55] He
was writing in 1414, on the eve of the Council of Constance. Even
while operating on a practical level to end the Schism, d'Ailly was
alive to the possibility that the Church might be in the grip of
cosmic forces to which the only certain guides were the prophets.

Telesphorus of Cosenza was, apparently, already thinking in
these prophetic terms when the Schism came upon western
Europe. His interpretation of these portentous happenings followed naturally.[56] Here was the terrible schism so often prophesied by Joachim, here was the pseudo-pope, the *Antichristus
misticus*. Now was come the ruin of the carnal Church, the pun-

ishment of the false clergy and mendicants. If Joachim's *nova religio sanctissima* was to come in, there must be violent revolution first, with the ruin of the Roman Church as it stood. Under the pseudo-pope, *natione alemanus*, the final persecution would be heavier and more inhuman than any before it.[57] But the advent of the New Dispensation was undoubted. In characterizing this sacred new religion, Telesphorus claims to be quoting from Joachim's *Liber Concordie*, although this is only partly so.[58] He says that it will be free and spiritual and at peace, beloved of God above any other 'religion and order' because its perfection will transcend all other. For the series of Angelic Popes Telesphorus draws on the four portraits of the *Liber de Flore*. Working in holy partnership, angelic pontiffs and new spiritual men will purify the Church and bring it *in statum paupertatis*. A general council will ordain poverty for all clergy and twelve will be elected from the *nova religio* to preach the gospel throughout the world. In the final sabbath of Telesphorus's intricate programme, the spiritual power alone will rule the world in a regime which he again describes in an unidentifiable quotation from Joachim's *Liber Concordie*.

4

JOACHIMIST EXPECTATION IN
THE RENAISSANCE PERIOD

I

In the age of the Florentine Platonists and Savonarola the elements of exaltation and apprehension were strangely mixed in their outlook on the future, just as in their view of knowledge rational and mystical approaches mingled. The Platonists were swept to a high excitement by the sense that the *plenitudo temporum* had arrived, yet at the same time were assailed by anxious expectations of Antichrist. It was to the astrologer Paul of Middelburg that Marsilio Ficino in 1492 wrote his famous letter proclaiming the Age of Gold to have arrived and listing all its manifestations, in humane letters, in the arts, architecture and music, in astronomy, in the invention of printing.[1] Yet at the same time general anxiety concerning the future was building up to a peak. Luca Landucci reported a miracle in his Florentine Diary because everyone was awaiting great signs from God.[2] There were wandering prophets crying 'Woe!' in Siena in 1472, and in 1492 Fra Guiliano was inveighing against *l'avara Babilonia* in Milan.[3] Various prophets appeared with strange foreboding messages in the streets of Rome. In 1490 Stefano Infessura described the advent of one dressed in the rags of a mendicant who threatened the Romans with immediate calamity which would spread to the rest of Italy.[4] In this case there are echoes of Joachimism, both in the method of concords between the two Testaments which he was reported to use, and in his expectation of an Angelic Pope after the tribulation. In these same years the strange and solemn prophecy attributed to St Cataldus was striking like a knell on men's ears,[5] and Paul of Middelburg's astrological prognostications were sweeping through Italy.[6] Again we meet here the conjunction of catastrophe and Antichrist with the advent of a holy reformer. The significant point to grasp is that we are not dealing here with two opposed viewpoints—optimistic humanists hailing the Age of Gold on the one hand, and medieval-style prophets proclaiming Woe! on the other. Foreboding and great hope live side by side in the same people. This dramatization of history as a juxtaposition of greatest tribulation and greatest beatitude was already present in the Joachimist view of history which we have been tracing. Thus the Joachimist marriage of woe and exaltation exactly fitted the mood of late fifteenth-century Italy, where the concept of a humanist Age of Gold had to be brought into relation to the ingrained expectation of Antichrist.

Again, the concern with prophecy was not at odds with the pursuit of humanist scholarship. To these Platonists knowledge could be sought along many routes and the very breakthrough to new light by rational methods raised the hope that many other clues to the meaning of the universe could also be read, so that its full structure might be revealed in all its logical spirituality.[7] Man was born to this work: to know the divine things and to dominate all things under the heavens. This was the theme so grandly embodied in Giovanni Pico della Mirandola's famous oration *On the Dignity of Man*. By all avenues of knowledge, occult as well as open, it was his destiny to ascend to celestial secrets. Alchemy, magic, the cabbala, astrology, prophecy, could all be viewed as aspects of the veiled language in which the Eternal divulged the fundamental secrets of existence. In 1463 Ficino published the first Latin version of the *Corpus Hermeticum*, a collection of treatises on the occult sciences, which had an enormous vogue right on into the seventeenth century.[8] Giovanni Pico della Mirandola studied the cabbala and knew the works of Joachim.[9] The religious dimension of this search for knowledge is clear. Plethon is reported to have prophesied the proximity of a true world-wide religion, united in spirit, mind and message.[10] Commenting on this, Chastel characterizes the mission of the Platonists thus: '*le platonisme était l'instrument d'une rénovation totale de la pensée théologique et des moeurs qui ouvrait une étape magnifique de l'histoire humaine.*'[11]

Paul Kristeller has brought to light two minor Renaissance characters who illustrate well the blend of humanism and mysticism.[12] Lodovico Lazzarelli pursued 'profane' studies in his youth, especially poetry, until he was converted by a strange person who called himself Giovanni Mercurio. In 1484 during the pontificate of Sixtus IV this enigmatic figure rode through the streets of Rome proclaiming a prophetic message and in the following years he made similar appearances in Italian cities and once even in Lyons. The name he adopted had hermetic significance and he adorned himself with hermetic, Hebrew and Christian symbols. His teaching seems to have been a mixture of Christian prophecy and ideas drawn from hermetical and astrological sources. Kristeller notes as significant the fact that he impressed not only the masses, but rulers like Pope Julius II and Louis XII and writers such as Sosenna and Lazzarelli, who viewed him as an 'initiate' able to perform the miracle of a divine generation in disciples. After his own 'regeneration' Lazzarelli devoted himself to the study of Hebrew and the cabbala and the publication of hermetical works. In his *Crater Hermetis* he sought to synthesize Christian and hermetic teaching, identifying Pimander with Christ and the classical Age of Gold with the Christian final world Sabbath Age, in which man would become godlike in wisdom and power. There are no specifically Joachimist traits here, yet Lazzarelli's emphasis on the emergence of the new man strikes the same note as Joachim's prophecy of the new man in the third age.

At the end of August 1494 Charles VIII of France was crossing the Alps with his army; in September Savonarola was proclaiming to the Florentines the fulfilment of prophecy in this advent. There has seldom been in western European history a series of events so widely viewed within the framework of prophetic drama as the Italian expedition of Charles VIII. On the French side it only needed the return of the magic name of Charles to the monarchy to arouse again the expectation of a Second Charlemagne. The poet André de la Vigne dreamed that Christianity, in the form of a woman, implored Charles to rescue her from the infidel. Michael Tarchianota Marullus from Constantinople exhorted Charles, in his *Epigrammata et hymni*, to take up his appointed role. A strong prophetic influence was exercised over Charles by Francesco di Paola, an exiled Calabrian, while Jean Michel, his doctor, had a prophetic vision which he presented to Charles as a treatise, *De la nouvelle réformation du siècle et de la récupération de Jérusalem à lui destinée.*[13]

Finally, Guilloche, a poet of Bordeaux, unearthed the very Second Charlemagne prophecy once written for Charles VI, and expanded it in vernacular verse:[14]

> Charles huitiesme de ce nom, Filz de très noble nacion
> Et très illustres fleur de lis,
> En soy aura haultes sourcis,
> Semblablement aura long front,
> Les yeulx longuetz comme seront
> Le nez agu . . .

Thus the young king, the son of the lily, assumes the prophetic features, the *'frons longa, supercilia alta, oculi longi, nasus aquilinus'* of the Second Charlemagne. The early part of the prophecy was extraordinarily apt, for Charles, as it forecast, had actually been crowned in his fourteenth year, and the first part of its programme—the destruction of all tyrants in his realm—could be regarded as already fulfilled. So the poet turns to the future with some confidence:

> Il fera de si grant batailles
> Qu'il subiuguera les Ytailles, . . .
> Et puis après conquestera
> Vaillamment la cité de Romme
> Et obtiendra double couronne,
> Nommé sera roy des Rommains . . .
> Par feu et par sang destruyra
> Un'autre cité qui sera
> Nommée la cité de pechié.

Here a note identifies this city as Florence. From this point the poem proceeds with the whole programme of the Second Charlemagne text. He will conquer Greece and be acclaimed King of the Greeks; he will conquer the Turks and all barbarians; all Christian kings will submit to him.

> Il possédera, en sa vie,
> La très-haultaine seigneurie
> De ceste terre universelle.

How far Charles VIII was influenced by this prophetic programme it is impossible to say with any certainty. Lauréault de Foucemagne, writing in the eighteenth century, concluded that a vital element throughout this expedition was the crusading motif and recalled the prayers and processions Charles offered for victory against the infidel.[15] Charles's programme suggests the duel prophetic role as chastiser/reformer and crusader most clearly, while the inclusion of Florence in his programme immediately recalls the Second Charlemagne prophecy. We get an echo of his belief in the prophecies from the *Diaria de Bello Carolino* of Alessandro Benedicto who, remarking that Charles confidently applied the prophecies to himself, gives a summary of the Charlemagne text. Guicciardini reports that, to flatter Charles, people would refer to 'that glorious Charles whose name you bear'. Whatever Charles himself believed, the Florentines saw him all too clearly, as he approached, in the role of the divinely-appointed instrument of chastisement.

On the Italian side, as we have seen, there was a build-up of prophetic anxiety from about 1490 towards the year 1494. Besides the phenomenon of the wandering prophets, the Sienese chronicler, Tizio, reports presages, phantoms and astrological conjunctions of dreadful import, while Alessandro Benedicto writes in the same vein.[16] It was in 1494 that a friar, Luke of St Gemignano, collected together prophecies of Joachim, Merlin, the Sibyls and others, adding the remark that he had copied these when Charles, King of the Franks, was marching towards Rome.[17] By a curious coincidence there was a parallel Jewish expectation of tribulation and messianic hope current at this time.[18] This mysterious anxiety abroad in Italy provided the perfect sounding-board for Savonarola's message.[19] Initially, as Donald Weinstein has shown,[20] this was one of impending calamity and punishment. The approaching Charles was the new Cyrus, the King-Chastiser. This was the Day of Deluge and Florence must build the Ark of Repentance if she was to ride out the Flood. But between September and the end of 1494, as Weinstein shows, Savonarola's prophetic emphasis was shifting from tribulation towards *renovatio*, and this was remarkably confirmed by the peaceable departure of the French from Florence on 28 November. Florence was now seen as the elect people of God, saved from destruction to fulfil a glorious new role. Once again, the ground of prophetic expectation was already prepared.

There were probably two main sources of Florentine belief in her own glorious destiny at this time. One was the ancient myth that Florence was the favoured daughter of Rome, the head and heart of Italy, from whom by virtue both of geographical position and gifts life flowed into all the members, the *sementa santa* ('sacred seed') of Dante, which would spring up as the new Rome.[21] The other was the Joachimist seed of the *novus populus* to bring in the *renovatio* after the great tribulation. This had been well-watered by Fraticelli groups and others in the fourteenth century and Weinstein has gathered interesting examples, many from unpublished material at Florence, to show how this theme had been kept alive throughout the fifteenth century.[22] Thus in the vision of Fra Andrea da Rieti already referred to, the Florentine lily is seen putting out ever more beautiful branches, flowers and leaves, until the Pope flees to its shelter and it covers all Italy. The 'Vision of the Holy Hermit of the Year 1400' sees Florence beset by tribulation but ultimately victorious and destined for a leading role in the 'new Church'. In this great future Florence was already associated with the Second Charlemagne. A *Prophetia Caroli Imperatoris* upbraids Florence for deserting the divine cause which the Second Charlemagne will carry forward. As the French army approached, a vision of a 'devout monk' revived this prophecy, looking forward to the final era of peace and reform. The Florentine canon, Prospero Pitti, prophesied the advent of Angelic Pope and *renovatio*, while at the approach of Charles Angelo Fondi, a Benedictine monk of Vallombrosa, exhorted Florence to believe the prophecies and support Charles.[23] Even Marsilio Ficino himself, in his oration welcoming Charles to Florence on 17 November, proclaimed the Second Charlemagne tradition.[24]

By the end of 1494 Savonarola was proclaiming unequivocally the full role of Florence as the new Jerusalem, God's elected instrument for world renewal, the centre of a new and glorious age. 'You, O Florence, will be the reformation of all Italy and from here the renewal will begin to spread everywhere, because this is the navel of Italy.'[25] In the biblical figures he used there were strong echoes of Joachim's exegesis. Thus the story of the Shunamite Woman (II Kings 4) became a symbol of the Florentine Church and its renewing role; similarly, the people of Florence were the new Israel to be led through tribulation to felicity by their new Moses.[26] Again reminiscent of Joachim, he promised that after six days, when men have escaped from the toils of material things, the sun would illuminate the world and men would be brought to the mountain of contemplation, where they would truly understand the Old and New Testaments. Here we have, argues Weinstein,[27] a fundamental transformation of Savonarola's eschatology: 'The preacher of repentance has become the prophet of the millennium; while the avenging new Cyrus is now the renewing new Charlemagne.' The parallel instrument to bring in the seventh age or World Sabbath was, of course, the Angelic Pope. This concept had already been well-implanted in the Florentine imagination and in some passages at least Savonarola implies that the seat of the expected *Papa santo* will be in Florence, the new Rome. Thence the springs of renewal will stream forth throughout the world, Turks and other infidels will be converted and men will rest at peace in the one sheepfold under the one shepherd.

Was Savonarola a Joachite? This question has been much debated. In his first prophetic sermons in Florence in 1490 he cited the Abbot Joachim and St Vincent Ferrer as authorities.[28] On the other hand, it is well-known that later he specifically repudiated any debt to Bridget and Joachim: when in an imaginary conversation the Tempter accuses him of possessing these prophecies, Savonarola replies that he has read none of Bridget and little of Joachim.[29] This might indicate either prudence or guilty interest. But the real question is not whether Savonarola consciously adopted or rejected Joachimism, but whence he derived the content of his message. In his juxtaposition of tribulation and renewal, in his vision of the Sabbath Age of peace and world unity, in his emphasis on human agencies to carry out this divine programme, and especially on the Angelic Pope and Second Charlemagne, Savonarola was clearly drawing on the Joachimist vision as developed in the fourteenth century, and, as we have seen, the source material for this was plentiful round about him. On the other hand, in two respects his thinking is not so close to Joachim's: his millennial promises to Florence are couched too much in terms of political and material gains, while he seems to have too little framework in terms of a philosophy of history for a Joachite. In so far as he had a scheme of ages, it was that of the seven ages of the Church but sometimes he seems to see history in a cyclical pattern of periodic decline and renewal, while at other times the impending *renovatio* is to be a once-for-all, final age of regeneration, towards which the whole of history has been progressing. Savonarola was spontaneous and eclectic in gathering inspiration for his developing message; this resulted in certain inconsistencies, but there can be little doubt that he belonged within the prophetic tradition we have been tracing.

The way in which this tradition updated itself is strikingly seen in the rapprochement between the Platonic humanists and the biblical-style prophets. Ficino himself, after the initial upsurge of faith in the prophecies at the coming of Charles VIII, seems to have been disillusioned and to have repudiated Savonarola's message.[30] Yet his belief that the time was dawning when the new illumination forecast by Plato would bring a revival at once intellectual and spiritual chimed with the prophecies of new spiritual men. With its emphasis on mystical as well as rational knowledge, the Platonists' vision of a new understanding which through love would transcend human barriers and bring men nearer to divinity could find its place beside that of the *vita contemplativa* in the third age. 'And the Church will be so full of love that angels will converse with men, because the Church triumphant will love the Church militant,' said Savonarola in his sermon of 13 March, 1496.[31] This was the message which drew some of Ficino's group into the circle of the *Piagnoni*, Savonarola's disciples.[32] Both the famous Giovanni Pico della Mirandola and his nephew Gianfrancesco were caught up in the movement, while the elder Pico apparently knew Joachim as a master of number symbolism. The most eloquent spokesman of the Platonist *Piagnoni* was Giovanni Nesi who, in his *Oraculum de novo saeculo*, gathered together a strange mixture of Neoplatonism, occult mysteries and Christian prophecy. It is addressed to the younger Pico and calls him to participate in this latest banquet of the *novum saeculum* or golden age.[33] Here Savonarola appears surrounded by hermetical and astrological symbols. Nesi was seeking to blend the Neoplatonism of Ficino's Academy with the prophetic tradition of Joachimism, as derived from the Bible. In his union of philosophy and Christianity he envisages the eagle of philosophy nesting with Christ, the phoenix. The nest is Florence and from this union will spring the 'new race' of fledglings which will spread throughout the world. The Christian millennium is now equated with the ultimate enlightenment when Man will fall heir to the secrets of all religions and mysteries, yet it remains a

Christian future, and Nesi's vision of the new city is as much the new Jerusalem as the Platonic Republic. Chastel describes the culminating vision as '*l'exaltation typique du millénarisme piagnone, où revit en somme le vieux joachimisme confiant dans le règne prochain de l'Esprit.*'[34]

We have already mentioned the similar synthesis made by Lazzarelli, but beside him we may place a Franciscan theologian, Georgio Benigno, who joins in the prophetic debate. He, too, accepts the vision of the *renovatio* and the role of Florence in bringing it in, but remarks that he had been sceptical until brought to belief by the fervour of Zanobi Accaiuoli, the humanist.[35] Another Ficinian who joined Savonarola's *Piagnoni* was Benivieni, a friend of Giovanni Pico.[36] These two were already turning from Platonism towards religious repentance before Savonarola's message fell on their ears. Both became associated with Savonarola and when Pico died in 1494, Benivieni was drawn even more strongly to religion. Like Nesi and others he expected both tribulation and a *renovatio* which would focus on Florence. He put his vision into a poem on the building of the new Jerusalem written for the Palm Sunday procession:

> Arise, O New Jerusalem and see
> Your Queen and her beloved son.
> In you, City of God, who now sit and weep
> Such joy and splendour will yet be born
> As to decorate both you and the world
> In those days of bliss.
> You will see all the world come to you
> Devoted and and faithful folk,
> Drawn by the odor of your holy lily
>
> (Translated Weinstein, *op. cit.*, p. 216).

In the commentary on this Benivieni declares that all peoples and religions will conform to Florence's true religion and there will be one sheepfold and one pastor. Florence will extend her hegemony in a benevolent *imperium*. The odour of her sanctity will spread throughout the world and people, seeing her felicity, will want to share her government and laws. All who return voluntarily within the paws of the Florentine lion will be blessed with temporal and spiritual rewards. Benivieni lived through all the tragic changes in Florence which followed Savonarola's death without apparently wavering in his belief, for had not Savonarola foretold the necessity of catastrophe before millennium?

Savonarola's message of three-fold tribulation before the age of beatitude could dawn obviously lent itself to reinterpretation as time passed. What had been thought to be a short, sharp series of woes extended itself, but faith survived. When the Medicean Pope Leo X was elected in 1513 Benivieni wrote a *Frottola* for him on the renovation of the Church.[37] The sheep, he said, were tormented by wolves, but God had sent a conquering lion to put them to flight and bring all into one sheepfold. The seed had been sown in Florence whence the new fruit would come forth. Another of the *Piagnoni*, Bartolomeo Redditi, also clung to the vision, declaring in his compendium of Savonarola's prophecies that he still believed, because 'his preaching made of Florence a paradise on earth, while since the cessation of his teaching it had become an inferno'.[38] The figure of the Angelic Pope begins to appear more strongly on the road to the future. A vision, attributed to 'Albertus Carthusiensis' or Albert of Trent and current in Florence *c.* 1502, focuses on this dream, with echoes from the Pope-prophecies.[39] A succession of preaching friars, such as Antonio da Cremona and Francesco da Montepulciano, kept the Savonarolan themes alive.[40] The fascinating question is what the Medici thought of all this. The Medicean ecclesiastics, Pope Leo and Cardinal Guilio, were sufficiently drawn to discuss prophecies with Benivieni and to allow a Carmelite preacher to identify Pope Leo with the Angelic Pope in 1514.[41] Did he really entertain this idea for a while? At any rate, there is a cluster of verses at this time in praise of Leo and Florence and in expectation of the *renovatio* they would bring in. Events carried these hopes away, but in 1530 Benivieni could still write in expectation to another Medicean Pope, Clement VII, pressing on his attention the essential and unchanging core of Savonarola's prophecies in four points: (1) the chastisement of Italy, especially Rome, (2) the renovation of the Church, (3) the conversion of the Turks and Moors, (4) the felicity of Florence.[42] He showed how many of Savonarola's predictions were proving true and appealed passionately to the Pope to further their fulfilment by assisting the liberation of Florence.

The most ecstatic expression of this visionary future in which 'angels will converse with men' is to be seen in Sandro Botticelli's famous eschatological Nativity which has been called one of the greatest documents of Joachimist thought.[43] That the Incarnation is here seen as the symbol of a future divine event is made clear from the inscription on the picture:

> I Sandro painted this picture at the end of the year 1500 in the troubles of Italy in the half time after the time according to the xith chapter of St John in the second woe of the Apocalypse in the loosing of the devil for three and a half years. Then he will be chained in the xiith chapter and we shall see him trodden down as in this picture.

Joachim saw this mysterious three-and-a-half-year span of time as denoting the period during which Antichrist would rage, but always for him there was the implication of the third *status* beyond it. The symbolism of Botticelli's picture, with angels embracing men in the foreground and dancing in the skies, while the beaten little devil crawls away, carries this Joachimist vision to a high point of ecstasy. Weinstein interprets another picture of Botticelli's, a Crucifixion probably painted in 1502, in similar prophetic terms.[44] The Crucifix divides the picture laterally: the right hand side depicts a scene of wrath and punishment in which burning brands descend from a dark sky and an angel whips a bushy-tailed animal; on the left side the city of Florence appears bathed in light, while in a circle of light stands a figure with an open book; in the middle a beautiful woman embraces the Cross. Florence is here represented three times: under chastisement, as the whipped *marzocco* (lion): repentant, as the woman at the Cross: glorious, in the light of God's open revelation.

One of the most interesting cases of Savonarola's influence was that of Francesco da Meleto who in 1473 had been in Constantinople seeking Jewish prophecies.[45] Inspired by Savonarola's vision of the *renovatio ecclesie*, he set out to determine its date. In his *Convivio de' segreti della Scriptura santa*, written *c.* 1508, Meleto seeks to harmonize all the prophets. He uses Joachim's schemes for the structure of history and proclaims again Savonarola's three-fold scourge leading to the Age of the Spirit, to begin in 1517, when the world would be brought into one sheepfold and a *parvulus ydiota* would finally reveal all mysteries in a new book. Meleto caught the attention of the reformers who paid his expenses for an audience with Leo X. His

Quadrivium temporum prophetarum was written to present to the Pope. In this he set out to prove that the universal reformation would be consummated in 1530. But although the humanists secured him an interview, the authorities were now growing alarmed by the radical reformers. His book was banned and, though in fact it was published with the aid of his humanist friends, Meleto was condemned in a Florentine Provincial Synod and forced to write a retraction. This was partly the result of a fierce campaign by P. Orlandini, a Laurentian and also probably once a Savonarolan, who now in bitter disillusionment wrote against false prophets. The dream of *renovatio* and Angelic Pope was heretical, he declared, and Florence—once famed for scholarship—had fallen mightily in entertaining these nightmares and delusions. When he died he left an *Expugnatio Miletana*.

The repercussions of Savonarola's message were, in fact, going off in a series of minor prophetic detonations throughout these decades in extravagant expressions that alarmed the authorities and alienated the humanists.[46] Already in 1496 Pietro Bernardino was forming his society of the *Unti* (Anointed). By 1498 he had become the *Papa Angelicus* of his sect, preaching a new outpouring of the Holy Spirit and a prophetic programme which echoed Savonarola's closely. For a time he enjoyed a considerable vogue and even found a refuge with the younger Pico, but in 1502 he was convicted and burnt. In 1500 a mad prophet named Brozzi appeared in Florence; in 1508 another hermit was preaching Woe! there; soon after Francesco de Montepulciano was proclaiming the same message of tribulation and renewal in Florentine pulpits. About 1515 a visionary named Theodore disturbed Florence still further by proclaiming himself to be the Angelic Pope. He was pursued vigorously by the authorities and finally imprisoned perpetually at San Miniato.

Theodore's aberrations had been specifically connected with Savonarola and the belief grew that his influence was at the root of all these dangerous dreams. Yet some serious reformers still believed in the core of Savonarola's prophetic message. Thus Contarini admitted to believing in the future *renovatio* and defended Savonarola whilst seeking to dissociate his reputation from the radical prophets.[47] This defence was taken up by the Dominican, Luca Bettini, in his *Oracolo della renovatione della Chiesa secondo la dottrina del R.P. Frate Hieronimo Savonarola da*

Ferrara in which he claimed to have summarized all Savonarola's doctrine.[48] Once again the emphasis was on the role of Florence in the final *renovatio*. God will send *un Papa santo*; evil priests will be replaced by holy men; the whole world will be converted; Florence will be the illumination of Italy and Jerusalem the centre of a paradise on earth. Bettini's lyrical vision still speaks to Botticelli's picture:

> Et così era tutto il mondo in una charità et Giubilatione . . . Sarà allhora tanta quiete et tanta pace che l'uno amico chiamerà l'altro alla chiesa . . . et empierasse il mondo di dolcezza. Dolci saranno le scritture, gioconde le contemplationi, le predicationi tutte soavi . . . Sarà la chiesa in grande amore, pace et tranquillità. Et gli angeli stilleranno tutta dolcezza nella chiesa militante . . . Veranno gli angeli a conversare, a parlare et habitare con gli huomini . . .
>
> (*Op. cit.*, ff, 160 –161 .)

II

In Venice it was mainly a group of religious who pursued the prophetic dream during this period. There still survives in the Biblioteca Marciana a remarkable manuscript compilation which, in its successive layers, demonstrates a continuing interest in the Joachimist political future.[49] First, in the mid-fifteenth century, Domenico Mauroceno, a Venetian patrician, compiled a book of prophetic excerpts and requested a Dominican, Frater Rusticianus, to organize and abbreviate this material. Its core was the *libellus* of Telesphorus into which he inserted picture-sections. The political programme, as set out in his dedicatory letter to Mauroceno, is still the Telesphorean one: the *Antichristus mixtus*—a German pseudo-pope—was at hand; he would crown the false German Emperor, the expected Frederick III, and together they would devastate Italy and persecute the clergy; there would be three other false popes, but all the evil agencies would finally be overthrown by the divinely appointed partnership of the *papa angelicus* and the French Emperor who would bring in the Age of Tranquillity. Rusticianus's picture-additions point up this programme vividly: three pseudo-popes are crowned by devils; Frederick III's army arrives by sea and by land, with eagle ban-

ners flying; the holy monk sits outside his prison as the deputa-
tion which has come to proclaim him Angelic Pope kneels in awe;
the mitred Angelical in turn crowns the King of France with
thorns. The following Angelic Popes are curiously depicted: one
directs the harvest-gathering from a leafy tree; another preaches
to a crowd; a third, a tonsured monk, operates with a hatchet in a
strange garden. The *nova religio* is shown as pious monks receiving God's Word from an angel. In the final pictures, God from a
cloud blesses his *populus sanctus et electus* who will continue in the
nova religio under their Angelic Popes, while the reprobate are
shown roasting in a curious receptacle. The manuscript which we
have is not Rusticianus's original work but a copy made by
Andreas, a monk of St Cyprian's in 1469, from an exemplar at S.
Georgio Maggiore. Some preliminary pages seem to have been
added and these include certain crude and startling pictures by a
priest named Lazarus of Pavia. One shows the Pope and the
Emperor Frederick III locked in a wrestling match in which
Frederick is being worsted. A second shows a huge bull-figure
with a tail and various appendages to represent Antichrist. These
are followed by some pictures and texts from the Pope-
prophecies, while at the end of the Telesphorean *libellus* appears
the Second Charlemagne prophecy. Here the work of Andreas
stops—but not the book. A different hand takes up the pen in
1476, continuing with an anthology of short prophecies, to be
followed by sequences of Pope-prophecies in various hands and
another version of the Second Charlemagne prophecy inserted in
1495. Thus in Venice a continuous current of interest in these
prophetic figures flows through the fifteenth century to the time,
probably during Charles VIII's expedition, when this last text
was copied into the St Cyprian manuscript.

   An illuminating little letter links Venetian interests in prophecy with the Florentine crisis. In 1495 Pietro Delphino, the
Venetian-born General of the Camaldolesi, wrote from Florence
to a monk in Venice reporting a visit of Zanobi Accaiuoli who had
brought his prophecies to read.[50] Amongst them was one of a
future angelic pope and this had reminded Delphino that his
magnificent and learned friend Mauroceno had a *papalista* about
the Angelic Pope which he urged Delphino to study. So now the
General of the Camaldolesi asks the monk to get permission from
Mauroceno to copy it for him. Now Accaiuoli was the humanist

who persuaded Benigno to support Savonarola and possibly later, when librarian to Leo X, he was one of those who encouraged Meleto's approach to the Pope.[51] In 1495 Delphino was in the thick of the Savonarolan controversy and this little episode may indicate that at that stage he had not yet closed his mind to prophetic hopes. Later, however, we find him combating the radical prophets resolutely and bringing pressure to bear on Orlandini, the Camaldolese Prior of St Maria degli Angeli, which is sufficient to turn him from a Savonarolan to a persecutor of the prophets.[52] The ambivalent attitude of those in authority towards the prophecies—half believing the vision but fearing its radical manifestations—is well illustrated by Delphino.

Perhaps the vogue for prophecies in Venice was stimulated by the fabled connection of Joachim with the mosaics of St Mark's.[53] A widely known legend made Joachim appear in Venice to direct the portrayal of the future SS. Francis and Dominic in mosaic and this was extended to diverse images and figures in the walls and pavements of the church. In the sixteenth and seventeenth centuries these prophetic mosaics were a real tourist attraction. Thus in 1506 a visiting Belgian, Jean Lemaire, reports on them,[54] describing in particular two lions, one fat and well-favoured who breasts the waves strongly, leaving only his back paws on the land, the other thin and feeble, stretched on land, with only his back paws in the sea. Thus Joachim was supposed to have prophesied the decline of Venice when she took to the land. But for the learned the study of prophecy was in manuscripts rather than mosaics. In the sixteenth century the Venetian printing press took up the role of disseminating prophecy. It was from the St Cyprian manuscript that the Augustinian, Silvester Meuccio, published his first Joachimist work in 1516. As we have seen,[55] this was followed by a stream of similar works associated with Joachim, both genuine and spurious. Silvester Meuccio's handling of Telesphorus's work in particular reveals his strong sense of its contemporaneity and the interest expressed by his friend, Paolo Angelo, reinforces this. This elusive person, only known to us through his relations with Meuccio and the two tracts he wrote,[56] claimed descent from Byzantine Emperors. In 1530 his second tract, a summary of Telesphorus in Italian, was addressed to Andrea Gritti, the Doge of Venice. He expects immediately, first, schism and Antichrist, then *renovatio* under the Angelic

Popes. The Venetians appear—as the Florentines had done under Savonarola—as the doughty champions of the angelic cause. Angelo's eastern origin is betrayed in his emphasis on the expected union of the Greek and Latin Churches and in the idealized international relations to be established by the *Papa Angelico*, when men will be able to go dryfoot from Europe to Asia because of three bridges to be built. In the conclusion he bases his faith in the '*tempo della renovatione*' on Joachim's writings and affirms that the death of Antichrist will be followed, not, as many think, by the end of the world, but by the end of labour and the coming of the blessed epoch.

The prophetic alliance between the Second Charlemagne and the Republic of Venice probably accounts for the publication of the *Mirabilis Liber* in Venice in 1514.[57] This was a prophetic anthology which contrived to bring all the prophecies into line in support of the French monarchy. It included the captions of all the Pope-prophecies and a section on the Angelic Pope taken from another Joachimist work. The libraries of France and Italy appeared to have been combed in search of material for the purpose of building up to the grand climax of history in the splendid alliance between Gallican King and Angelic Pope. The Pope-prophecies themselves were first published in Bologna in 1515,[58] but later in the sixteenth century a Venetian, Pasqualino Regiselmo, took up the study of these and his extremely popular annotated edition was published in Venice in 1589.[59] In his dedication Regiselmo speaks of the human propensity to be drawn into the investigation of curious matters rather than to pursue solid and useful knowledge. But some visions and mystical arts are worthy of study and among such are the *Vaticinia* of the Abbot Joachim. Yet these have been twisted by a certain *pseudo-magus* and so the author proposes to counter these false images. The false interpreter is certainly Paracelsus whom we shall encounter later. With that mixture of credulity and science characteristic of the sixteenth century, Regiselmo bases his claim to give the true interpretation on his scholarly researches, informing the reader that he has examined eight manuscripts and seven printed editions in order to eliminate textual corruptions and false interpretations. One of his manuscripts was that compilation of Domenico Mauroceno, written more than a century before. In discussing authorship he comes very near the truth about the origin of the Pope-prophecies when he says that some Greeks have recently declared that the originals of these pictures are to be found in Constantinople under the name of Leo. Alas—he dismisses this as a foolish tale and settles for the authorship of Joachim. The interesting point about Regiselmo's interpretation of the prophecies is that he believed their key lay in some secret mathematical principle, so that they did not apply in continuous sequence and therefore extended into the future.[60] Joachim, he argued, had learnt these principles from the Greeks of his native *magna Graecia*. 'Formal arithmetic' is the best road to the interpretation of prophecy, he remarked, citing Pico della Mirandola and declaring also that Joachim used no other road than 'formal numbers'. Thus, late on in the sixteenth century, interest in prophecy was still alive in Venice and we still meet a scholar who defends the mystical approaches to knowledge so dear to the earlier humanists.

The Venetian printing presses were still finding a sale for prophecies at the end of the sixteenth century. The Pope-prophecies were published again in 1593, 1600 and as late as 1646. There was a craze for imitative series at this time and several of these were printed in the 1600 edition in the form of wheels, with the names and symbols of popes between the spokes. The link which Regiselmo had almost established between the Leo Oracles and the Pope-prophecies is suggested again by a parallel interest in the Byzantine original. There was a Latin edition of the Leo Oracles at Brescia in 1596[61] of which the main point was to prove that Turkish rule would end under the present Sultan. Even more striking is a gorgeous manuscript of the Oracles produced in Crete in 1577 by Francesco Barocci.[62] In his dedicatory letter to Iacopo Foscari, consul of Crete, he relates how the latter had found a mutilated Greek version and asked Barocci to translate it. Barocci, like Regiselmo, claims to have lavished much scholarship and labour on his text to remove the errors of those who first transcribed it. Each figure occupies a whole richly illustrated page with the text given opposite in Greek and Latin. There is no culminating hope in Barocci's version, for the final pictures concern Antichrist, leading up to a magnificent double-page Last Judgement. Nevertheless the care expended on this beautiful production is yet another indication of the perennial interest expressed by Montaigne when he wrote: '*Je voudrais bien avoir reconnu de mes yeux ces deux merveilles: du livre de livre de Joachim, Abbé Calabrois, qui predisoit tous les Papes futurs, leur noms et formes; et celuy de Léon l'empereur, qui predisoit les Empereurs et Patriarches de Grece . . .'*[63]

III

The city of Rome which had been rocked by the prophetic visions of Cola di Rienzo in the fourteenth century was in the mid-fifteenth century being transformed into the brilliant Renaissance capital of a restored papacy. Yet wild hairy prophets still rode through its streets proclaiming doom and, though successive popes played a sharp hand in the developing game of political diplomacy, they were periodically haunted by the spectre of prophetic destiny.[64] In 1440 when the mysterious title of Frederick III was at last embodied in flesh a shiver of apprehension went round. To the Germans he might be a good or a bad portent, and Thomas Ebendorfer, winding up his *Cronica Regum Romanorum*, speculates on which he will be.[65] But to the Italians the Third Frederick had only one image, that of the chastiser of Rome and maker of schism. Even the most sophisticated at Rome were not quite sure whether to flick away the prophecies. Aeneas Silvius Piccolomini gives us an amusing sidelight on the state of mind in Rome as Frederick in 1452 approached it for his coronation.[66] Was he that future intolerable scourge who, according to the oracles, would punish Rome and do mighty deeds? Pope Nicholas V was in two minds, on the one hand fearing what might befall, on the other coveting the glory of crowning Caesar. To this may be added the report of a conversation between Pope and Emperor over dinner in which Nicholas tells him frankly that the prophecies cast him in a bad role.[67] To this the Emperor replies that his intentions towards the Church are good, but if God ordains otherwise for him, the divine will cannot be gainsaid. Even Frederick himself could not evade the role decreed for him: only time could tell if he were really the Third Frederick of prophecy.

No doubt the unspectacular departure of Frederick III restored the Roman nerves and, indeed, as a candidate for a part in the drama of Last Things it is difficult to think of any historical character more disappointing than the Emperor Frederick III. When he died in 1493 Stefano Infessura seems to be recording the epitaph of prophecy when he writes in his *Diario della Cittá di Roma: Mortuus fuit imperator Federicus et cum eo perierunt omnes prophetiae.*[68] Yet within a year Rome was shaken by the appearance of a more menacing King-Chastiser in the person of Charles VIII and by the threatening prognostications of Savonarola. Once again the immediate threat passed, but the Romans could never quite dismiss the prophets from mind. There is some evidence that the vision of the Angelic Pope and the *renovatio mundi* attracted a number of churchmen in Rome at this time. The Blessed Amadeus (Joannes Menesius de Silva of Portugal) provided a focal point for many.[69] Born in 1431, he became a Minorite in 1452 and, coming to Italy, founded his own strict congregation of Amadeites, centring on St Pietro at Montorio in Rome, which was given him by Sixtus IV. Later, in the time of Leo X, the congregation became part of the Observantine Franciscan Order. He left behind an *Apocalipsis Nova* which, according to legend, had been dictated to him by the Angel Gabriel. He also left behind him a great reputation, especially in Rome, where, we are told, his book was to be found in many houses, including those of cardinals. The focus of this interest was his proclamation of the Angelic Pope, about whom he prophesied both in words and in a painting. His influence can be traced, not only in Rome, but also in Florence—where Fra Antonio da Cremona and Fra Francesco da Montepulciano were probably both 'Amadei'[70]—and in Venice where Paolo Angelo translated his prophecies into Italian. In the Italian version Amadeus enquires of Gabriel concerning the 'new Pastor' and is told that he is already concealed in Rome, poor and unknown. But his power will increase '*a poco a poco*' until, when he is old, he will be exalted over the earth. Amadeus, in the vision, aspires to see this unknown Angelic and Gabriel replies: 'You have already seen him, but not in majesty.'

In the early sixteenth century the Angelic Pope seemed near and among Roman ecclesiastics a group of humanist theologians—some disciples of the Florentine Platonists—discussed the *renovatio mundi*. One of the most influential of these was Cardinal Egidio of Viterbo, the General of the Augustinian Hermits.[71] The older assessment of this well-known figure in the Rome of Leo X as 'the polished priest of Renaissance circles' has recently been challenged by a deeper study of his sermons and writings.[72] The eloquence of his great address at the opening of the Lateran Council in 1512[73] has been recognized as springing from the passion of the visionary reformer rather than the rhetoric of the skilled orator. The link which connects him with the Joachimist vision is his meeting in Venice with Silvestro Meuccio, the Augustinian editor of Joachim's works. Silvestro describes how the General asked to see those works already published and, when he had read them, urged Silvestro to publish more and especially Joachim's *Expositio in Apocalypsim*. Silvestro clearly saw Egidio as one of the new spiritual men to lead the reform: 'I do not doubt that in days to come our Order will be reformed under your leadership.'[74]

Now Egidio was a Platonist and a disciple of Marsilio Ficino. He was also a student of Hebrew literature, especially the mysticism of the cabbala, and a searcher of the Scriptures. He gathered within his household humanist scholars in Greek, Hebrew and eastern languages. All these currents flowed into his study of history to form a unique philosophy. Between 1513 and 1517 Egidio wrote *De Historia Viginti Saeculorum* in which he sought to show that classical and Christian culture did not stand in opposition, but formed one harmony in the divine purpose.[75] Although showing a scientific spirit in languages, his approach to history was medieval, not concerned with 'facts' but with the divine ideas embodied in historical actions, the history of humanity *sub specie eternitatis*. He believed it possible to read these divine thoughts through number symbolism and concordances. So he took ten Psalms, symbolizing ten periods of history before Christ, to be paralleled by ten periods after Christ. This method is closely akin to Joachim's, though Egidio's pattern is far wider in range, and seeks to establish concords, not only between the Old and New Dispensations of Christianity, but also between secular and sacred history, especially classical and biblical. He believed that, as humanity had moved inevitably towards a first culminating point in the coming of Christianity, so now it was tending towards a second great spiritual unfolding. All the signs of the times, including the movement of overseas expansion, showed that humanity was approaching a future unity in an age of peace. He dedicated his programme for the future to Pope Leo X, whom he confidently expected to bring all things into harmony. The Pope's name, lineage and all the events of his life were

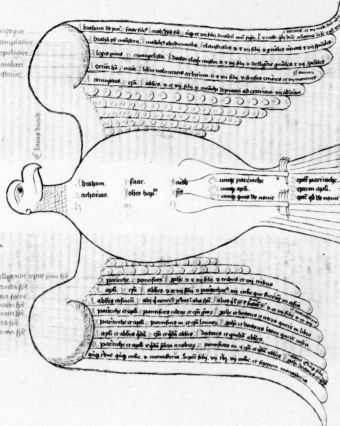

1 *Joachim magnus propheta.* Title-page to *De Magnis Tribulationibus et Statu Sanctae Matris Ecclesiae* published in Venice 1516 (*left*)

2 Eagle from the *Psalterium decem chordarum*, MS. Vat. Lat. 5732, f. 28v (Foto Biblioteca Vaticana)

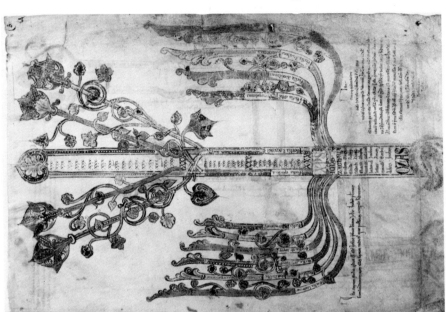

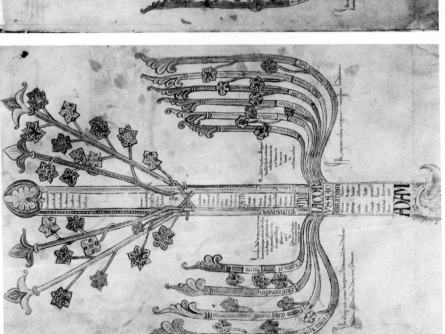

3 Pair of Tree-Eagles from the *Liber Figurarum*, MS. Oxford C.C.C. 255A, ff. 10v, 11r

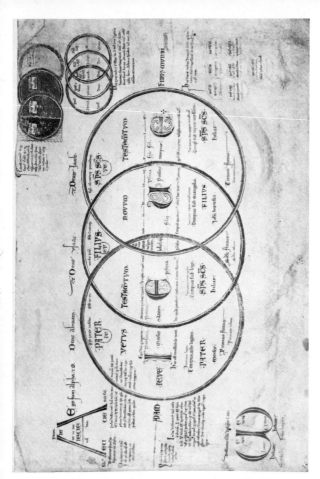

4 Tree-Circles from the *Liber Figurarum*, MS. Oxford C.C.C. 255A, f. 12v (*left*)

5 Trinitarian Circles from the *Liber Figurarum*, MS. Oxford C.C.C. 255A. f. 7v

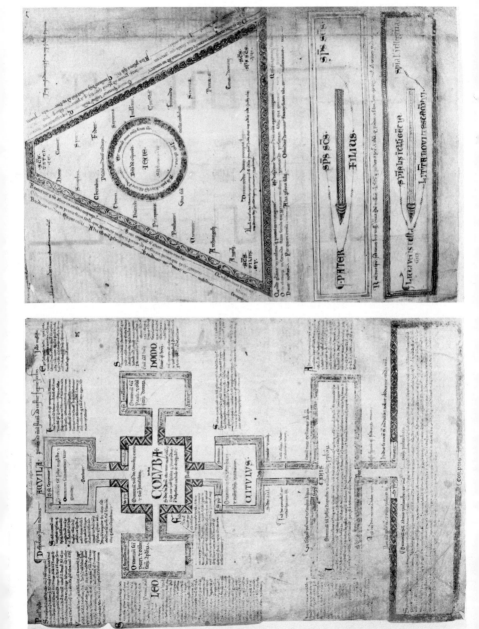

6 *Dispositio novi ordinis* from the *Liber Figurarum*, MS. Oxford C.C.C. 255A, f. 17r (*left*)

7 Psaltery with ten strings and subsidiary figures from the *Liber Figurarum*, MS. Oxford C.C.C. 255A, f. 8r

interpreted prophetically, for Egidio believed that Leo had been elected from the beginning of the world to carry out the work of Chirst in confirming the Christian faith and bringing peace to the Church.

In 1517 Egidio wrote a *Libellus de litteris Hebraicis*, dedicated to Cardinal Giulio de Medici and this was followed in 1530 by *Scechina*,[76] written at the request of the same man, now Pope Clement VII, and addressed to Charles V. Here Egidio moved from the theology of history to an outpouring of hope inspired at once by the clues of prophecy, Jewish mystical studies and the great contemporary signs of the times. His twin stars of destiny were the Medici—under whom classical learning flourished and the Muses were restored—and the great Imperial Charles, called to bring in 'the Kalenda', the Sabbath Age. Interwoven with the mysterious outpourings of the *Scechina* is the theme of imperial power as the divinely appointed agency, with a reiterated apostrophe to Charles to assume his role. The scene is dark—Italy torn by invading armies, the moon of the Church obscured by clouds of heresy—yet how thrilling the more distant prospect! To lift the eyes to the horizons is to see an expanding universe that calls for faith in the future, especially on the part of the Emperor: so many kingdoms and empires, so many lands and seas are subdued by this new Alexander! This vast new world is a theme of such exhilaration that Egidio returns to it again and again. Now is the *decimum saeculum*: it began with Leo X and now, to open the door of the 'celebrated Kalends', the fifth Charles—the Charles with the right number—is summoned. Charles was the new Moses to lead the human race into liberty, the new Caesar to overcome all barbarian tyrannies, the new David to gather all sheep into one fold. He can even be compared with advantage to the Apostles: '. . . they penetrated the known world, thou the unknown; they the part, thou the whole.' Charles' fame must be announced to all the islands (Britain and Hibernia included) and he must open up the new lands which begin to appear in a marvellous vista before amazed eyes. His cosmic task is summed up thus: as Emperor to find, reform and unite the whole world; as advocate of the Church, to cherish, build up and propagate her faith. If he fulfils this role the promise of the future is unbounded: a new earth and a new heaven; a new Asia, Africa and Europe; new seas, new islands . . .

But although the *Scechina* was dedicated to the secular partner
in the great *renovatio*, it was to the Renaissance popes under
whom Egidio served, that the Augustinian looked for the fulfilment of the chief renewing role. It was Julius II that he summoned at the opening of the Lateran Council to bring to fruition
the glorious destiny of the papacy; the *Historia* ends with a
panegyric of Leo X; the *Scechina*, commissioned by Clement VII,
expects the Angelic Pope alongside the World Emperor. These
hopes would seem on the face of it to bear little relationship to the
political aims of Renaissance popes. Yet there was the possibility
that visionary hopes could be accommodated alongside realistic
policies in the papal outlook. In the Lateran Council Cardinal
Baldassare del Rio, as well as Egidio, cited prophecies proving the
world-wide triumph of the Church under Leo, while several
Florentine verses hailed him as the good pastor who will bring in
the Age of Gold. With these voices in his ears, did Leo entertain
the idea that he himself was the Angelic Pope? In 1514, as we
have noted, he authorized a Carmelite preacher who, in a sermon
to the Florentines, identified Leo as the Angelic Pope and cited
the prophecies of Joachim. The reforming group who arranged
for Francesco da Meleto to have an audience with Leo were
clearly hopeful, but Leo, it seems, grew frightened of the radical
implications of prophecy and drew back from contact. Again, as
we have seen, Egidio wrote the *Scechina* at the request of Clement
VIII, although we have no further indication of his official attitude. At any rate these visions had currency value in
Renaissance Rome. It is one of the ironies of history that an
ecumenical expectation was so widespread at a moment when
policies and circumstances were carrying the Church towards
irrevocable divisions.

Also in Rome at the same time as Egidio and probably belonging to his circle was Pietro Columna, or Petrus Galatinus, an
Observantine Franciscan who became a provincial minister.[77] A
theologian and a humanist interested in languages, he spent much
of his life in Rome, where he plunged into Greek and Hebrew
studies. He was, furthermore, an enthusiastic disciple of both
Joachim and Amadeus. His chief published work was the *De
arcanis catholicae veritatis*, but several others survive in Vatican
manuscripts. In a group of these, all written *c.* 1523, Galatinus
expounded his philosophy of history, while in two later tracts,

especially *De Angelico Pastore*, he gathered together his expectations about the future. Reading these, one realizes with astonishment that here was a fully-fledged sixteenth-century Joachite. He states the doctrine of the three *status* in its full Trinitarian form; he adopts Joachim's five/seven number symbolism; he interprets the Alpha and Omega and other biblical symbols in the same way. In spite of his humanist training and interests, his approach to history is Joachim's: every detail in the Old Dispensation prefigures the New, and the overriding intellectual task is to understand this symbolism through the *intellectus spiritualis*. It is surprising that this overt Joachimism—emphasized in marginal captions—was not detected and attacked. Perhaps the fact that most of his works were not printed is significant, but, on the other hand, he shared his views freely with an eager circle of scholars. Galatinus was a great collector of prophecies which were circulated and discussed with his friends. He possessed genuine and spurious works of Joachim and, amongst others, writings of Peter John Olivi, Roquetaillade and St Bridget. He had seen the famous prophecy of St Cathaldus which caused a great stir in Rome and he was particularly committed to the visions of Amadeus. Some of the short prophecies which he used cannot be traced to any earlier source and may well have been produced in his circle.

Galatinus adapts Joachim's programme of the last stages since —he says—Joachim, living in the fifth *tempus* of the Church, could not see the future so clearly.[78] He believes that the *sixth tempus*, now beginning, will be the Golden Age of the Church. It will end in the sharp tribulation of the last Antichrist after which the Sabbath Age of quietitude will last until the *consummatio seculi*. But this last age in Galatinus' expectation is somewhat colourless; it is in the sixth age that the third *status* of the Spirit will begin and here are concentrated all Galatinus' most vivid hopes for the apotheosis of history in a period of limpid understanding and zealous preaching. The programme of this *foelicissimum tempus* follows the usual lines, with the conversion of the Jews, conquest and conversion of the infidels and the gathering of all the world into one sheepfold under the Angelic Pope, aided by the great World Emperor. His concept of the *viri spirituales* brings Galatinus close to Joachim: they will be contemplatives, elevated to the third heaven, yet also preachers descending to the people; they will receive the *spiritualis intellectus* to lay bare all mysteries. In describing this spiritual illumination he constantly uses metaphors and symbols which echo those of Joachim, yet the enthusiasms of a humanist are closely interwoven with those of someone belonging to the mystical, symbolical school. Thus he will turn from the elucidation of prophecies and enigmatic figures to textual criticism which draws on the new scholarship of men like Erasmus. Galatinus no longer assigns to his own Order a leading role as the *viri spirituales*. St Francis and St Dominic were the chief agencies of God in the fifth *tempus*, but St Francis could not have been the Angel 'with the sign of the Living God' since this figure belongs to the sixth age and must therefore be one of the symbols of the Angelic Pope. Although he expects them to be regulars, it is remarkable that Galatinus does not attempt to assign either the Angelic Pope or the twelve *sancti viri* to assist him to any specific order. Of the expected Angelic Pope Galatinus wrote with urgent desire. Many symbols in the Apocalypse point to him, but especially the Angel with the Eternal Evangel—the figure which had been the undoing of Spiritual Franciscans in the mid-thirteenth century. Galatinus interprets the Eternal Evangel as the *spiritualis intellectus* of the Scriptures and in numerous passages proclaims the mystical power of the *Pastor Angelicus* to lay bare all the mysteries of the sacred word, so that the truth of the Scriptures will shine forth in ever-growing splendour until night had passed into mid-day. From the contemplative state the Angelic Pope will descend to assume the government of the Church with five specific tasks to perform: to bring churchmen back to perfect poverty; to liberate the faithful from persecution; to reform the laity and make concords between princes; to convert all infidels; to promote good clergy in the Church. In splendid partnership with him stands the new Zorobabel, the 'athlete' elected by God to realize the vision of political unity in a programme which will begin with reformation of the principalities, proceed to the conquest of the infidel and finally bring all nations under one law.

There is an urgency in Galatinus' writings—*quoniam cito cito appariturus*, he writes, and again, *iam iam in januis esse creditur*[79] —which indicates his desire to find candidates to fill these roles. In 1524 he dedicated his commentary on the Apocalypse to Charles V, coupling him with an unnamed Angelic Pope. Thus the solution of the political prophecy seemed clear, but that of the spiritual role was more problematic, as indicated in Galatinus' successive dedications of his works to Leo X, Hadrian VI and finally Paul III. In this last little tract, *De Angelico Pastore*, he was still looking for this tremendous 'new Moses', buttressing his hopes with passages from Joachim and Amadeus, whose visionary painting of the Angelic Pope he actually claimed to have seen.

Galatinus exchanged prophecies with various scholars and can probably be linked with Egidio of Viterbo. Paolo Angelo, the Venetian, who dedicated his works to Leo X, Clement VII and Cardinal Bernardino da Carvajal, may also have known Egidio through his friend, Silvestro Meuccio. We remember that Francesco da Meleto had friends in the Roman Curia. Rather later a French Joachite, Guillaume Postel, was reading the visions of Amadeus and the works of Galatinus in the Ara Coeli, as also did the Jesuit, Cornelius Lapierre.[80] Thus the picture emerges of a sixteenth-century Rome where prophecies, visions and cabbalistic mysteries were exchanged, discussed and interpreted. This complements, rather than contradicts, the better-known pictures of Renaissance Rome.

But what did those who so ardently looked for the ideal partnership between Angelic Pope and World Emperor make of the Sack of Rome in 1527 by Charles V's German troops? Galatinus was silent, but others, not committed to the cause of Charles V, saw it as confirming rather than destroying the prophecies, for tribulation was part of the prophetic programme and the role of King-Chastiser was well-established. The Florentine Benivieni, now in his eighties, warned Clement VII that this was the second of the three tribulations predicted by Savonarola.[81] In spite of official prohibitions, the prophets had still been busy in the first two decades of the sixteenth century crying Woe to Rome! and thus preparing the minds of popes and ecclesiastics to see these terrible events in an eschatological frame. Whether one read the signs as a manifestation of Antichrist, or the just chastisement which the Second Charlemagne must inflict, all prophets predicted tribulation to Rome, and therefore, when it came, it seems likely that members of the Roman Curia more than half believed that the Sack was an event of cosmic significance. The Pope addressed cardinals and other prelates on the need for reform[82] and Luigi Guicciardini probably gave the common view when he said that Charles V had been the just agent of God's judgement on Rome for her vanity, pomp and luxury.[83]

In the second half of the sixteenth century, when the papacy was turning its attention to reform on a realistic level, the visionary level of the dreamers still existed beside it. In 1564 Benedetto Accolti, the illegitimate son of a cardinal, conspired with others to kill Pope Pius IV.[84] The plot crumbled because the unstable leader was seized with fear. Accolti's confessions reveal the basis of his dream. He believed that Pius had to be removed to make way for one who should come, he whom the people of Rome commonly called the '*pontefice angelico*'. Thus it was the general tradition of the Angelic Pope which drove him to look for '*un papa novo, onto, santo et angelico*' who would be monarch of the world and renovator of the Church. The Pope-prophecies, in fact, continued to excite interpreters all through the century. Paracelsus, who embodied that strange Renaissance mixture of interest in vaticination, astrology and the cabbala, alongside classical and scientific studies, re-stated in 1530 what we may term the Catholic revolutionary position by linking, in his exposition of the *Vaticinia*, sharp denunciation of the papacy with expectation of the angelic series of popes which must supervene.[85] He stressed the revolutionary aspect by insisting that the Angelic Popes would be chosen and crowned by God through his angel, but found it hard to envisage how this blessed regime would be reached. Paracelsus's work provoked a counter-interpretation from Paul Scaliger (or Skalich), who set out to drain all dangerous expectation from the Pope-prophecies by showing that the whole thirty had already been fulfilled, ending with Innocent VIII.[86] Each prophecy was interpreted in terms of an actual pope and this involved Scaliger in applying the portraits of the visionary Angel Popes to fifteenth-century Renaissance popes. He shows much ingenuity and some of the results are amusing, for instance his eulogy of Sixtus IV who now qualified for an angelic portrait. But the visionary expectation was too strong to be thus doused and so we find Regiselmo, the Venetian, countering both Paracelsus and Scaliger in 1589 in his own interpretation of the *Vaticinia*, based, as we have seen, on the theory that the prophecies occur at intervals and therefore some still belong to the future. He is more cautious than Paracelsus in his expectations but still in his interpretation the angelic vision presides over the end of history in the final figures of the sequence.

The extraordinary fascination exercised by these enigmatic prophecies is seen in the proliferation of imitative series in the later sixteenth century.[87] These circulated, not only in print, but in manuscript. In the most extensive collection there are nine such imitative series and these do not include the most famous of all, the prophecies attributed to St Malachy. The sequences are sometimes expressed in the form of wheels with the names of popes and their symbols between the spokes; sometimes in captions and pictures in the style of the original *Vaticinia*. All identify the popes up to a certain point and are then projected into the future. A typical product in print is an edition of 1600 in Venice of the *rotae* of six illustrious men of whom five are named: Joachim, Anselm, Iodochus Palmerius, Egidius Polonus and a Johannes Abbas.[88] Three manuscript anthologies of the end of the sixteenth century illustrate the seriousness with which these prophecies were still studied.[89] One in the Bodleian Library, entirely devoted to Pope-prophecies, is carefully executed in pen and ink and colour wash. There is a tree and also a wheel of popes, but most of the various series are in the style of the *Vaticinia*. The whole forms a strange collection of symbolic pictures in which fantasy runs riot. There are lions, dragons, eagles, serpents, falling towers and churches, armed men, kings and queens, a burning tree, a tree bearing cardinals' hats and many other enigmatic figures. From the last popes named, it seems clear that the various series were concocted between 1590 and 1595 and that the manuscript itself was compiled between 1595 and 1605. A second manuscript in the Bodleian, also of Italian origin but once owned by Laud, is a poor production with ridiculous little pen-and-ink scribbled pictures of a primitive kind. But it has an extensive collection of prophecies, including the vision of Amadeus, and many series of Pope-prophecies. Finally, at Carpentras, a third anthology has been identified. This is clearly a sixteenth-century production but the first part consists of a splendid fourteenth-century copy of the *Vaticinia* which has been cut up and put into a scrap-book. After this large portions of Regiselmo's work are copied out and other prophecies, including the Leo Oracles. All three manuscripts belong to about the same date, and the first two specifically to the pontificate of Clement VIII (1592–1605). What, in the final decade or so of the sixteenth century, sparked off this extraordinary activity in producing Pope-prophecies and collecting them in print and manuscript? Was it just the fun of setting intriguing puzzles in order to play with their solutions? Certainly much of this prophecy lent itself to this game, being *post eventum*, and the angelic theme often seems submerged. But all the series are extrapolated into the future and in some, notably the St Malachy series, the objective of proclaiming the eventual appearance of the Angelic Pope comes through clearly. Again, the theme of the Laud anthology in particular was, I think, the angelic series and the *renovatio mundi*. Even if in attenuated form, some people were still speculating on the possibility of a spiritual revolution.

IV

As we have already seen, the theme of the Last World Emperor continued to attract eager attention. The dismal reputation of Frederick III and the claims of Charles VIII of France, far from discouraging German prophets, only led to a re-focusing of hope on fresh candidates. The *Prognosticatio* of Johann Lichtenberger, published in 1488, was partly astrological—borrowed from Paul of Middelburg—and partly a collection of prophecies, many derived from Joachimist sources.[90] Like some of his contemporaries in Germany, Lichtenberger saw the approaching menace of the Turks as a sign of the final tribulation which must fall on Christian people, but he belonged to the Joachimist tradition in that, beyond catastrophe, he expected the *nova reformatio* which would be inaugurated by the overthrow of the Turks. The chief agent in his programme would be the World Emperor who would carry out the work both of chastisement and renewal in the Church. The great question was where to find a suitable candidate for this role, since the German tradition of prophecy seemed to have run out into the sand. Although sometimes obscured by citation of contradictory prophecies, the real point of the *Prognosticatio* seems to lie in its salutation of Maximilian I and his line as the rising stars in the prophetic firmament. Lichtenberger perceived that the marriage of Maximilian to Mary of Burgundy (descended from the French royal house) made it possible for the first time to unite in one the two prophetic traditions of the German Eagle and the French Lily. It was a Burgundian

World Emperor that Lichtenberger expected to arise as a Second Charlemagne in the region where the first once had his capital. His hint as to who this will be is quite plain: 'And it is said in the book of the kings of the Franks that from the stock of King Charles of France will arise in the last days an Emperor, *"nomine P."*, who will be the monarch of all Europe and reform Church and clergy. After him there shall be no ruler.'[91] Thus for the first time Philip, the son of Mary and Maximilian, comes into the prophecies. At the moment of writing Lichtenberger felt himself to be on the verge of the great crisis of history. The Angelic Pope plays a minor part here, for Lichtenberger's confidence in the future lay in his belief that the consummation of history would be achieved through the union of German and French aspirations.

Others followed this lead. In 1495 Sebastian Brandt prefaced a tract on the recovery of Jerusalem with a frontispiece of Maximilian, King of the Romans, outside Jerusalem and an exhortation to him to take up his proper role.[92] Together with Wilhelm Aytinger,[93] Brandt continued to interpret and publish prophecies designed to show that the Church must be chastised, the Turk overthrown and Jerusalem recovered by the German Emperor, after which he would bring in the Joachimist *renovatio*. In Aytinger's tract Lichtenberger's prophecy of the last great monarch, *nomine P.*, is given, and obviously it is to this quarter that the author looks for the ultimate ruler. But before the end of the century, it would seem, some were already looking beyond Philip of Burgundy. In a late fifteenth-century hand at the back of a manuscript now in Cambridge,[94] the Second Charlemagne prophecy is written out under the heading *Prophetia abbatis Joachimi A.D. 1180*. It begins: '*Carolus philippi filius ex natione illustri lilii.*' Thus we reach the second stage in the appropriation of this prophecy by the Burgundian-Habsburg house: from Philip we have moved to Charles, the grandson of Maximilian.

Round the period of the imperial election of 1519 the prophecies gathered thickly.[95] In 1517 a little German pamphlet by Pamphilius Gengenbach, a Swiss poet, imagines a group of prophets, including Joachim, interviewed by the Emperor and the King of France, leading, of course, to the rejection of the latter as candidate for world empire. The marriage of French and German traditions appears in the pamphlet of Master Alofresant of Rhodes, *Alle alten Prophecien von Keyserliche Maiestat* (1519), in which a galaxy of prophets pronounce their oracles in favour of Charles. The Second Charlemagne prophecy was certainly circulating in favour of Charles V at this time, appearing in a variety of places. Thus it is found in a vernacular version, beginning 'Karolus ein sun Philippi', while in 1519 Sanuto, the Venetian ambassador, sent back to Venice from England an independent English version which substitutes an imperial origin for the Lily descent: 'Charles the son of Philip, of the illustrious Caesarean race.' It seems that prophecy even penetrated the imperial electoral chamber. Some of the speakers in the debate attached great significance to the issue of this election, declaring that the salvation of Europe hung on it and that he who could sustain this office must be of heroic mould and vast strength. Prophecy was invoked and the Elector of Brandenburg declared that the Emperor promised for these times who would excel all others on strength and virtue must be Charles. Though less convincing than Fugger money, no doubt, the asset of the magic name, as against the un-prophetic Francis, perhaps added weight to the scale which turned the election in favour of Charles V.

As Charles's imperial career progressed, the prophetic signs were eagerly read. The Spanish mood on the eve of the Battle of Pavia was one of prophetic hope and on the morrow the whole prophetic programme of world empire was claimed in the official announcement of victory, concluding with the theme-text: *Fiet unum ovile et unus pastor.*[96] An Italian astrologer, Torquatus, purporting to have written his *Prognosticon* in 1480, was probably engaged *c.* 1527 in charting this prophetic progress.[97] The final schism created by the rise of the pseudo-prophets, with their arch-heresiarch, Luther, the conflict with the Turk, the Battle of Pavia, the Sack of Rome—all are 'prophesied' as the essential tribulations to precede the *renovatio*. Now Torquatus looks for the conquest and conversion of the Turk, the renewal of the Church and the union of all political interests under the Emperor. A copy of his *Prognosticon* in the British Museum is studded with notes applying the fulfilment of his 'prophecies' to sixteenth-century events, but there comes a point where these notes change to 'not yet fulfilled'. In particular the note *'nondum impletum renovatio in Ecclesia'* sums up the hope with which such prophecies were read. We have already seen how both Egidio of Viterbo and Petrus Galatinus pinned their hope on Charles as the political partner of the *Papa Angelicus*. The Sack of Rome by the

German army of Charles V in 1527 was a major prophetic event. While, as we have seen, some interpreters might see this, along with the rise of the heresiarch and his 'locusts' from the bottomless pit, as part of the long-expected crisis of Antichrist, others, and particularly Germans, could separate the forces of Antichrist, represented by Protestants and Turks, from the work of chastisement and renewal which belonged to the 'good' Last Emperor.

There was a revival of prophetic propaganda in favour of Charles in the 1530s, sparked off, perhaps, by his expedition against the infidel in North Africa in 1532.[98] The Second Charlemagne prophecy, with its emphasis on the overthrow of the Turks and recovery of Jerusalem, was again in circulation. When the *De Bello contra Barbaros* of Benedetto Accolti the Elder was printed in 1532, the publisher thought the times to be crucial and appended various oracles, one of which brings together in a strange medley the Book of Daniel and the classical Age of Gold, the Joachimist Angelic Pope and the divine Caesar. In the same year Johann Eck published a pamphlet *Sperandam esse in brevi victoriam adversus Turcam* in which he pins his hope on Charles and his brother Ferdinand, calling up the usual prophetic band which includes Joachim. Again, Johann Carion, winding up his chronicle of empires in 1532, passed over from Charles's expedition into prophetic speculation, again citing the stock prophets. The heavens declared their portents and the prophets were all of one mind in expecting the great Emperor. So Carion believed himself to be ending his history on the eve of the *renovatio*. Viewing the prospect from the other side, Martin du Bellay suggests the effects of prophecy on politics. In 1536 he noticed a marvellous concourse of prophecies all promising the Emperor great success, and he observed the effects of these rumours: how Charles lent a willing ear; how the Marquis of Saluzzo changed sides hastily, because one could not go against the oracles of God; how the French were terrified, but Francis I stoutly opposed these superstitions and pursued his designs undismayed.

As late as 1547 a learned man could still believe in Charles's prophetic destiny. Wolfgang Lazius was a Doctor of Vienna and historian to Ferdinand I.[99] He had written four books on Viennese history, twelve on the Roman Empire, two on the genealogy of the House of Austria; finally he made an excursion into the future, gathering together in his *Fragmentum vaticinii cuius-*

dam Methodii prophecies from all possible sources in honour of the Emperor.[100] He saw at this time a consonance between event and prophecy which was most convincing. Here was the final crisis of wickedness in its two-fold, Joachimist form: the infidel and the heretic, the beast from the sea and the beast from the land. The menace of the infidel was obvious and now Lazius was able to produce a formidable crowd of prophetic witnesses to show that Luther was the *pseudo-Papa Germanicus* and his schism was the final one. Then Lazius turned to his real purpose, that of proving that by his double lineage Charles was heir to all the good prophecies. On the one hand he was descended from the Lily, and Lazius of course appropriated the Second Charlemagne and other Lily oracles. On the other hand, Lazius claimed all the Eagle prophecies of the Hohenstaufen. He pillaged many sources and the galaxy of prophets and oracles which he assembled was tremendous. He separated the role of chastiser of the Church into two; in its wickedness it devolved on the Protestant Frederick of Saxony, but for the Emperor he built up a typically Germanic role of chastiser-reformer. Thus to Wolfgang Lazius in 1547 the hope of the world stood in Charles V. The events of his life proved it: he had overcome and imprisoned the Lily, he had brought down Rome and Florence, he had attacked the infidel and contended with the heresiarch. True, the Lily had escaped, the Sack of Rome had unfortunate repercussions, the infidel remained unbeaten, and the heretic increased, but the programme was only half-completed. Lazius did not doubt that the future was in the hands of the Emperor. In his conception of the *renovatio* the Angelic Pope remained a shadowy figure and his faith for the reformation of the Church lay in the Emperor and the Council of Trent, not the Pope. In 1547 he believed the consummation of history and the end of prophecy to be very near: '*infra tempus 1548 annorum totum saeculum congregabitur in unum ovile . . . et fiet unum ovile et unus pastor.*'[101]

The Habsburg monopoly of all the prophecies was not allowed to go unchallenged on the French side. Silvestro Meuccio's edition of Telesphorus's work, published in 1516, set the stage of the Last Things unequivocally, with the bad emperor and pseudo-pope ranged on the German side and the true Emperor and Pope on the French side. The pro-French line favoured in Venice is further indicated by the extensive anthology of prophecies supporting French claims, published in Venice as the *Mirabilis Liber* in 1514 and subsequently re-edited in Paris in 1522 and 1530. For this many libraries had been ransacked for prophecies and the oracles collected represented various stages in the evolution of the Joachimist programme, from Joachim himself to Savonarola. The *Vaticinia* and the Second Charlemagne prophecy were both used. The book named no names and laid down no dates, but was plainly produced in support of the French claim to the Last World Emperorship. In the same period Symphorien Champier (or Campeggio) was also trying to fit the prophecies to the French monarchy. In his *De Monarchia Gallorum*[102] he argued that whereas German rulers had always been enemies of the papacy, the French monarchy had supported it faithfully. The Gallic kings had been hallowed by divine unction, while the Gallic kingdom was the 'vine elect' planted by God according to the prophecy of Isaiah. Finally, the old prophecy declared that from the Gallic kings would arise the last and greatest King who would govern felicitously and hold the final *imperium*. It is not surprising that a French translation of the Telesphorean prophecies, called the *Livre Merveilleux*, was published in 1565 during the reign of Charles IX, the only French king to bear this name in the sixteenth century. It was published again in 1577 and 1588. When in 1580 Giordano Bruno visited France, his visit sparked off a hope that Henry III might prove to be the agent for carrying out the plan of universal reform and peace-making which he envisioned.[103] But the French monarchy supplied no effective candidate for the role of great pacific ruler until the advent of Henry of Navarre. It was at the moment of Henry's conversion to Catholicism that Bruno, returning to Italy, eagerly set about canvassing a universal solution for the problems of politics and religion in a holy alliance of Pope and French King which would bring in a new Age of Gold—a dream which ended in tragedy for him.

The two great figures of medieval political prophecy, the *Rex Romanorum* and the *Rex Christianissimus*, the Eagle and the Lily, still confront each other at the end of the sixteenth century and we shall still meet them, in Protestant dress, in the seventeenth. The search for universal monarchy is not yet dead. The dream of a world united in peace and justice is still fused with a Joachimist theology of history which sees the whole of it as building up to this final age.

5

JOACHIM AND THE CATHOLIC VISIONARIES

I

Angelic Pope and World Emperor seemed to dominate the six-teenth-century prophetic stage, but among the *dramatis personae* of the Third Age there were also the *viri spirituales* of Joachim's vision. For a role amongst these an unexpected candidature was now put forward—that of the Jesuit Order itself. In his concept of two orders to lead the Church into the third *status*, it will be remembered,[1] Joachim distinguished the roles of a more contem-plative hermit order (which had been claimed for the Augustinian Friars) and that of a more active mediating order, charged especially with the work of evangelizing the world. Joachim saw this order typified in 'One like unto the Son of Man, seated upon a white cloud mid-way between heaven and earth' (Revelation 14.14[2]). He looked for the advent of *'quendam ordinem iustorum cui datum sit perfecte imitari vitam Filii Hominis'*. It would be learned in languages to evangelize the whole world and gather in the final harvest. It is well said to be seated upon a white cloud, *'quia nubes quidem corporea res est, nec tamen gravis et ponderosa, sicut terra, sed levis, et conversatio illius non erit ponderosa et obscura, sed lucida et spiritualis'*. These *'felices homines'* will live a life mid-way between the active and the contemplative, above earthly desires and affairs, yet not wholly withdrawn into the contemplative state which is 'in heaven'. In another passage[3] Joachim prophesies that this order will be designated in the name of Jesus; it will appear in the sixth age of the Church and, excel-ling others in spirituality, will be *'praeclarus et Deo amabilis'*. As a piece of real prophecy, there could hardly be a better delineation of the Society of Jesus and the role it conceived for itself.

The early Jesuits had a sense of the drama and urgency of their times which made some of them peculiarly receptive of ideas which issued from so dramatic a sense of history as Joachim's. They saw the world as the battlefield of two mighty 'opposites', under whose banners of good and evil the whole of mankind was encamped. This theme is developed by F. Montanus in his *Apologia pro Societate Jesu*,[4] where he shows, in a chapter on 'opposites', how good and bad are always raised up against each other, reborn ever in the same relationship, Jacob against Esau, Loyola against Luther. The final stage of this battle is now approaching and the Jesuits' own part in the drama of Last Things begins to emerge. This is a two-fold task, for, balancing conflict with the heretic in the Old World, must be set the marvels of universal preaching to the millions of a newly opened world. Against a background of fulfilled prophecy the Jesuits could set their own eschatological role. Thus J. Osorius, preaching on the death of St Ignatius Loyola, hailed him as the Fifth Angel of the Apocalypse at the sound of whose trumpet there fell a great star from heaven.[5] The star is Luther and the army of locusts fighting for him is the pernicious sect of the Protestants. This identification was officially adopted at the Council of Tatra in 1602,[6] while in 1622 a play, in German and Latin, pictured the whole action in dramatic form: the first scene shows the Angel poised with his trumpet, the star falling, the abyss opening to breathe forth locusts, while the rest of the play represents the life of St Ignatius.[7] Again, J. F. Lummius, in his *De extreme iudicio Dei et Indorum vocatione*, expounded the role of the Jesuits in calling the Indies to a glorious future under the fine figure from Isaiah: 'Who are these that fly as a cloud and as the doves to their windows?' He describes the flight of these chosen angels to the Indies, and, drawing on the letters of Fr. Gaspar, a Belgian Jesuit in Ormutius, he shows that prophecy is already being fulfilled.[8]

Thus the frame of mind among some Jesuits, at least, was one likely to be receptive of Joachimist prophecy. It is therefore not so surprising after all to find this connection being made. The claim that the Society of Jesus is indeed Joachim's 'Order designated in Jesus' is openly stated in the sermon by Osorius already cited. He appropriates from Joachim's *Expositio* all the main passages in which this future mediating order is delineated, and one senses his excitement at the striking aptness of the prophecies he quotes.[9] To a remarkable degree, in fact, Joachim's concept of the half-way order found its fulfilment in the Society of Jesus and this idea evidently aroused considerable discussion. Rutilius Benzonius, Bishop of Recanati, recognized in the Jesuits the fulfilment of Joachim's prophecies,[10] while Antonius Zara, Bishop of Petina, quoted from the *Expositio, Liber Concordie* and *Super Hieremiam* to prove the point. A German sermon translated the more trenchant phrases from Joachim; an English Jesuit, Thomas Stapleton, quoted a passage from the *Liber Concordie*, beginning: '*Insurget una nova religio sanctissima*'; in Spanish, J. Nieremberg's *Honor del Gran Patriarcha San Ignacio de Loyola* gathered together all the prophecies of Joachim and many others, translating them into the vernacular. Writing on Joachim's reputation in his history of General Councils, L. Bail commented that his prophecies had been applied to the Jesuit Order, although modesty forbade a general assent to these claims within the Order.

An example of a certain type of 'modesty' is found in the Commentary on the Apocalypse of Blasius Viegas. This contains one quite disproportionate passage in which he disgresses upon Joachim as the prophet of his Order at such length as to underline the importance which this question had now assumed.[11] It begins with a very favourable account of Joachim, stressing those who had praised him and defending him from the calumny of those who had condemned him. Then, expounding Joachim's prophecy of a new order under the figure of the Angel of the Church of Philadelphia, he shows how the Jesuits might apply these words in every particular to themselves. But he will pass no judgement. 'All these are wonderful and marvellous words, so mighty that no one could venture to assume for himself even the least part of them. Yet great is the sanctity of those who apply them to the Jesuit Fathers and strong is their conviction when they see the Society preaching everywhere the evangelical doctrine, obedient in everything to the Pope, practising perfect poverty'—and so on, accumulating proofs; 'when, finally, they see in how small a space of time our smallest of societies has converted the world, establishing itself in almost all the heathen parts, then not without justice do they believe these to be the men whom Vincent and Joachim most wonderfully summoned forth.' 'Yet', concludes Viegas, 'we believe all these things to have been spoken of some other order, we who hold ourselves to be the least and most useless of servants.'

The assumed modesty of this passage deceived at least one Jesuit, P. Deza, who declared his astonishment in a sermon that Viegas did not see how much the prophecies of the Apocalypse stood in their favour.[12] Paraphrasing the opening to the Epistle to the Hebrews, Deza proclaimed: 'In the last days God has spoken to us in His son Ignatius whom he has made the heir of all things.' Here unwittingly he was echoing a similar claim made in the thirteenth century by Angelo da Clareno on behalf of St Francis.[13] But the Jesuit's bold adaptation of New Testament words went altogether too far for the Sacred Faculty of Theology in Paris, which censured him for scandalously, erroneously and blasphemously altering the words of St Paul.[14] By this time the authorities in the Order had been alerted to the dangers of extravagant prophetic claims. We can detect two schools of thought on the validity of such interpretations in a group of Jesuit commentators on the Apocalypse.[15] Those of the 'scientific' school emphasized the historical setting of the work and its literal interpretation as relating to the first age of the Church, or to the first and the last ages. Thus Ribeira, whose great commentary did much to set the study of the Apocalypse on sane, historical lines,[16] believed that the five seals of the Apocalypse described the history of the Church to Trajan, but he could not resist jumping thence to the end of time in his interpretation of the Sixth and Seventh Seals. He was able to work out his interpretations in a past and a future safely removed from his present, but Viegas, who obviously felt the intoxicating power of prophecy, reproached him for being too slavishly bound to the letter. The attraction of the Joachimist method is implied in the strong attack upon it made by the Spanish Jesuit Alcazar in his *Vestigatio arcani sensus in Apocalypsi*. For him the meaning of the profound prophecies of the Apocalypse is buried too deeply to be unravelled like the foolish puzzles which Joachim had contrived on the popes. 'Far from holding that prudent expositors of the Apocalypse ought to follow in the footsteps of the Abbot Joachim,' he concludes, 'it seems rather to me that those who take him as their guide . . . are enslaved to vain errors and illusions.'[17]

The existence of another school of thought is clearly realized by Cornelius Lapierre in his Commentaries on the Apocalypse and the four Major Prophets.[18] He takes Joachim as its prototype, calling him the founder of the method of historic parallels. While careful not to identify himself too closely with this school of interpretation, Cornelius shows a marked preference for those commentators on the Apocalypse who believe that it foretells the whole history of the Church down to the Last Judgement. He is particularly interested in Joachim's concept of new orders and he quotes from Viegas three reasons why the Jesuits might be one of these. It is true that he cautiously pronounces Joachim's prophecy as obscure and uncertain of interpretation, but it is clear that Joachim's vision of new spiritual men in the Last Days moves him. He shows himself much attracted by the hope of a great future age of peace and felicity in the Church under the Angelic Pope to come, and in this the new spiritual men will play a decisive role. Although cautious and critical, this Jesuit is yet attracted to the Joachimist *renovatio* in which the destiny of his own order was involved.

Another Jesuit commentator on the Apocalypse, Benito Pereyra, drew even more deeply on Joachim's thought.[19] He used Joachim's structure of history and clearly saw his own Society as embodying the true spiritual life of the seventh age. Developing the idea of seven adversities and seven prosperities in the Church, he expounded the seventh prosperity as manifested in his own age in the discovery of new worlds and especially in the innumerable people converted to Christianity. He believed passionately that before the end of time the spiritual men must plant the Church in every race on earth. Pereyra's chief interest in Joachim's thought, however, lay in the relation between the life of contemplation and that of active evangelism. He selected long quotations from Joachim's reflections on the tension between these two aspects of the spiritual life, as, for instance, when, in speaking of the 'double gift' which Elisha sought from Elijah, Joachim remarks that it is a rare and difficult thing to have this double gift, to be able, at the same time, to provide for the brethren in the active life and also to enjoy the sweetness of contemplation. Thus some, at least, of the early Jesuits caught an inspiration from Joachim's concept of the mediating order. They felt the sense of standing on the threshold of great developments and, whether combating the heretic or converting the heathen, they recognized the need to be seated on the cloud mid-way between heaven and earth.

It would seem, indeed, that Joachim—whose views had twice been condemned as heretical and who had appeared in several 'catalogues' of heretics—finally takes his place in the *Acta Sanctorum* by virtue of being a true prophet of the Jesuits. Daniel Papebroch, the Jesuit Bollandist, who writes the life of Joachim in the *Acta*, uses his critical scholarship to test legends and dismiss 'figments', yet he still rests Joachim's claim to sanctity mainly on this gift of prophecy.[20] Papebroch is cautious in making a claim for his own order, and yet he enters fully into Joachim's conception of new spiritual men. He sees the 'order designated in Jesus' as combining the activity of Martha with the quietitude of Mary, as resuscitating the *Spiritualis Intelligentia* of the Scriptures from the tomb of a sterile scholasticism, as evangelizing barbarians and combating Antichrist in the heretics. He leaves others to judge if this prophecy is now being fulfilled and in this we see the characteristic Jesuit attitude in which a desire not to claim too high a place mingles with an emotional response which identifies Joachim's vision with its own sense of mission.

This caution was based on experience. The Jesuit leaders had before them many examples of unbalanced prophets and were soon forced to deal with just such a case in their own ranks. The strange history of Guillaume Postel brings together the themes of World Emperor, Angelic Pope and New Men.[21] Postel was a humanist scholar and professor of the University of Paris, interested in linguistic and textual studies, who became enthralled by Joachimist ideas. He met some of the Jesuits in Paris before 1535 and seized on this new order as one of the principal agencies of the eschatological programme. He followed them to Rome, but before doing so sought an interview with Francis I in order to proclaim the stupendous choice before him: if the King would reform Church and State he would become monarch of the universe, if not, evils worse than any previous would come upon him. In Rome Postel was received into the Order as a novice by St Ignatius himself. His ardour and the grandeur of his expectations touched everyone and he was welcomed with high hopes. He planned to give himself to the conversion of infidels, and at first all spoke well of him, but by 1545 doubts about his extravagant fantasies were being expressed. His opinions and writings were scrutinized and he was subjected to discipline. He submitted but could not keep his fantasies under control. Reluctantly—for they admired his enthusiasm—the Jesuits were forced to expel him. This was a tremendous blow, for Postel trusted that here he had found the great instrument of the *renovatio mundi* which he never doubted was to come. It was a pathetic tragedy that, having tried so hard to obey them, Postel should have been shut out of his Promised Land by the sobriety of the 'new spiritual men' from whom he expected so much. He continued to hope for readmission as late as 1562. But the Jesuit authorities had speedily discovered the danger inherent in his seductive ideas when they found them to have infected Jerome le Bas, chosen to organize the new College of Auvergne, and a companion of his. The two Jesuits had been carried away by Postel's promise of a glorious future under the leadership of Pope, French monarch and the Society of Jesus. They were speedily disciplined.

After his expulsion by the Jesuits, Postel focused his chief hope on the French monarchy, asserting that by divine illumination it had been revealed to him that the Gallic King must be the reformer of the Church and the whole world. He bombarded French kings and people with appeals to realize their great destiny and, when Henry II and Francis II in turn were deaf, he threatened them with the fates of Moses and Saul. After another vision *c.* 1551 he drifted into a mystical state in which he came to believe that he had been reborn as the Holy Spirit and that it was his own mission to bring in the Age of the Spirit. He plunged into a frenzy of linguistic and cabbalistic studies and sought to work out his world religion through contacts with Ethiopians, Arabs, Jews and others. He published tracts, wrote letters to influential people and travelled ceaselessly, proclaiming with urgency that all the auguries pointed to 1556 as the fateful date. In despair at French indifference, he turned at one time to the Emperor Ferdinand who, interested in his philological and missionary plans, appointed him to a university chair at Vienna. So Postel sketched out an imperial version of the future: Rome was to be the temporal capital of the world, Jerusalem the spiritual; there would be a general reformation, the earthly paradise would be restored, and the purpose of the world would have been fulfilled. But he was at heart a Gallican and, returning to his true allegiance, was proclaiming a French version of the approaching millennium as late as 1579.

The Joachimist writings are clearly the main source of Postel's inspiration and from Joachim himself he drew the series of mystical threes which he uses. From the French Joachimism of Roquetaillade and Telesphorus he derived his emphasis on the role of the French monarchy in the final age. In his *Concordia Mundi* he builds up on every possible symbol and argument what has been described as 'probably ... the most comprehensive justification for French world leadership in the sixteenth century'.[22] In the great *renovatio* the French King must take the lead because of the corruption of the Roman Curia. Aided by a General Church Council, he must establish a universal monarchy and a universal church. Postel's programme of action is both peaceful and militant. There must be a tremendous world-wide missionary effort, involving attempts to rationalize the Christian faith as well as the study of many languages. Alongside this, however, there must be a great campaign of arms to bring the world under one sway. At the last every man, in all the earth, will understand the truth of God for himself and reach that illumination which is the goal of human experience in the temporal order. Postel's two key phrases are *Concordia mundi* and *Restitutio omnium*, and his constant dream is of an ecumenical Christian order which will embrace all religions. Postel's final world-order follows a Joachimist number symbolism: there will be a trinity of sovereign king, sovereign pope and sovereign judge and beneath this triple authority the world will be ruled in twelve sees. Religious unity will be expressed in one synthesized world religion, social unity through the abolition of private property, and cultural unity in the abolition of separate languages.

It is important to realize that, in spite of his craziness, Postel was attended to, read and admired by many anxious contemporaries who sought to read the signs of the times. The Emperor Ferdinand listened to him and, in spite of their apparent deafness, the French kings could never quite brush him off, granting him asylum at the last. He struck exactly the twin notes of apprehension and exaltation which chimed with the sixteenth-century mood. His warnings were full of foreboding but the tremendous horizons of his vision lifted the heart. Moreover, in a manner typical of his time, he combined national aspiration with a universalism that dreamt of the brotherhood of all mankind. Again typically, he saw the master-plan of Providence accomplished in the achievements and discoveries of his own day:

Today we see clearly that, quite suddenly, Greek, Latin and Hebrew letters, along with all learning, divine and human, have made more progress in fifty years than in the previous thousand ... And we see another great change and marvel when we consider how, during the last ten years, through the efforts of sailors and merchants, the new world, which is greater than our own, has not only been discovered and conquered, but also converted to Christianity ... I do not mention the arts of artillery and printing, discovered among the Latin Christians, the one to consummate the wisdom of the world, the other the power, which has been given to the Christians by Providence ...

(tr. Bouwsma, *op. cit.*, p. 271.)

At last the instruments and conditions were at hand to enable every man on earth to understand the truth of God for himself. So the conversion of the whole human race would carry the drama of history to its climax.

II

We turn now to a group of Catholic thinkers, ranging from the fifteenth to the seventeenth centuries, and of differing backgrounds, but sharing a visionary expectation about the last age of history. Most of them were biblical scholars embodying their prophetic expectations in scriptural commentaries. Giovanni Annio of Viterbo, in his *Glosa super Apocalypsim* (1481),[23] defended the idea of a terrestrial age of bliss against the objection that Christ's kingdom was 'not of this world' and his final victory, a celestial one. He believed that the whole of the Apocalypse concerned the Church militant on earth, not the Church triumphant in heaven. The promised period of Satan bound, Annio argued, must occur within time, since at the end he would be briefly released. So he developed the concept of a 'double resurrection' of the Church, the first of which would be an era of terrestrial bliss when there would be a universal union under one pastor. He expected a great prince, but the real universal monarch would be the Roman pontiff, who would preside over a world government of twelve regions, each ruled by a patriarch, a king and a '*custos angelus*'. This would indeed be the New

Jerusalem, embodying a new heaven, that is, a new state of the Church, and a new earth, a new state of the laity. Although he only once referred directly to Joachim, Annio's phrase *'sequitur ergo tercius status in reformatione ecclesie'* shows that his vision was undoubtedly of the Joachimist Third Age.

In the next generation Berthold Pürstinger, Bishop of Chiemsee, reveals the Joachimist sources of his expectations more clearly in his *Onus Ecclesiae*, written in 1519 and published anonymously in 1524.[24] His work is structured on the pattern of seven ages of the Church which he took from Ubertino da Casale and he draws a good deal on both the genuine and the spurious works of Joachim. He places himself at the end of the fifth or beginning of the sixth age and views contemporary events with the urgency of one who sees prophecies being fulfilled: the locusts to be conjured up by the sixth trumpeting angel are already present in the Lutherans; the prophecies of Cyril are being fulfilled in the intolerable wars of Italy. Following Telesphorus of Cosenza, he expects a first climax of evil to be ended by victory for the Second Charlemagne and Angelic Popes, with an ensuing time of peace, then a second climax of evil in the time of the great Antichrist, succeeded by the final Sabbath of Tranquillity until the Last Judgement. In the end he adopts the true Joachimist framework of three *status* in the world's history and expresses his view of the climax of the third *status* in Joachimist terms of the *intellectus spiritualis* which will shine forth in full glory: *'Tunc enim incipiet regnum Dei et clare splendescet intelligentia sacrarum scripturarum.'*

In the very different setting of Spain we meet Damián Hortolá, a younger contemporary of Pürstinger's, the Abbot of Ville-Bertrand and a trusted agent sent by Philip II to the Council of Trent. He embodied his view of the future in a commentary on the Song of Solomon.[25] While pondering on the mounting crescendo of evil and of tribulation which was rising in waves against the Church in this sixth age and which would reach a climax of iniquity in Antichrist, the constant theme of Hortolá's interpretation of the Song was the beauty and glory of the Church in the seventh age to come. Here he expected all the familiar agencies of blessedness: the *Papa Angelicus*, a pious emperor, an angelic order of world-wide preachers, two orders of 'perfect men', twelve apostolic men—all detected in the various figures of the

Song and the Apocalypse, and interpreted in a style akin to Joachim's. Under the text '*Veni in hortum meum soror mea sponsa*' Hortolá wrote eloquently on the return of the Jews to the true garden of Christ and on the flowing together of all nations into that garden which will follow the universal preaching. Like Annio, he boldly used the symbols of the new heaven and earth and the New Jerusalem descending to earth to describe this last age of history. And again he challenged the pessimists who believed that the *renovatio* belonged to eternity, not history.

Two commentators on the Apocalypse in the later sixteenth century also expected the Golden Age in the seventh age of the Church, between the death of Antichrist and the *consummatio seculi*. Coelius Pannonius (alias Francesco Gregorio) did not base himself directly on Joachim but interpreted many of the Apocalypse figures in a Joachimist sense.[26] Thus the three angels of Revelation 14 typify the three final orders of universal preachers who will convert the whole world and bring in the time of great joy after the death of Antichrist. To the theme of the final Age of Gold and the universal exultation to be experienced then, Pannonius returns several times in passages of lyrical passion. Whether the *aurea etas* will be long or short does not matter compared with the beauty of the natural order at that time and the intensity of joy to be experienced. The second commentator, Serafino da Fermo, a regular canon, drew more directly on Joachim and Ubertino da Casale, adapting the latter's seven ages of the Church and placing his own time in the fifth age.[27] Thus for him the great rejoicing was farther off and he was deeply oppressed by the contemporary manifestations of Antichrist. The great star falling from heaven was Luther, while other falling stars were Zwingli, Melanchthon and the Anabaptists. But, like Egidio of Viterbo and others, he found confirmation that, through all the foreordained tribulation, God's great purpose was working towards the Golden Age in the discovery of new worlds and especially of America. It was necessary for God's Word to go forth into the four corners of the earth and now the fourth has been discovered. He saw the various angels of the Apocalypse as divinely appointed human agencies and envisaged three final orders of preachers. Not until the final age will all peoples flow into the City of God, but already the signs of this appear in the evangelization of new lands. The end is certain, when the Church will enter her state of bliss on earth, when all the poisons of heresies will vanish and great joy will be universal.

In the first half of the seventeenth century a German commentator on the Apocalypse, Berthold Holzhauser, was working out a similar pattern of history.[28] He believed that the fifth state of the Church—one of affliction—had begun with Leo X and Charles V. and would run '*usque ad Pontificem Sanctum et Monarcham illum fortem qui venturus est nostro saeculo et vocabitur auxilium Dei, hic est restituens universa.*' They would inaugurate the sixth age of consolation in which all nations would return to the unity of the Catholic Church. In this age the sixth spiritual gift—*sapientia*—would be poured out on all men; there would be an 'open door' to the '*sensum clarum et apertum Sanctae Scripturae*' which no heretic might close, and a multiplicity of sciences, both natural and celestial, will flourish. Holzhauser paints this vision against a black background of present wars and calamities. Yet even now the triumphs of the Society of Jesus and the spread of the Catholic faith to Asia and the Americas inaugurate the new reign. Although the Angelic Pope has a place, Holzhauser's chief agent to bring it in is the *Monarcha fortis*. Whereas Joachim had seen in the various Angels of the Apocalypse new religious orders to bring in the Age of the Spirit, Holzhauser sees the great Emperor typified in both the 'strong angel descending from the heaven' (Revelation 10:1) and the 'one seated upon a cloud like unto the Son of Man' (Revelation 14:14). He works out the symbolism of these figures in great detail. He expects the Emperor to preside over a General Council which will declare the clear sense of the Scriptures, to break the Turkish Empire, reign over east and west, and give peace and justice to the whole world.

We come lastly to a group of Catholic visionaries who did not lock their utopias away in biblical commentaries but wished themselves to bring the Golden Age nearer by participating in politics. Tommaso Campanella was a Calabrian who drew much of his inspiration from Joachimist sources.[29] At an early stage he tried to push on the inevitable apotheosis of history by taking part in a curious south Italian revolt in 1599 which put him in the hands of the Inquisition for many years. But he was undeterred. Against the atheism of the Machiavellians he pressed his dream of the Golden Age in terms of a world republic under the Church. In his *Monarchia Messiae*[30] he developed the concept of one ruler

and one religion throughout the world and adduced many
arguments for the priest-king, the supreme pontiff, who should
hold both material and spiritual swords. His visionary state embodies just that blend of Renaissance Golden Age and medieval
ecumenism which is so characteristic of this time. In the *saeculum
aureum* wars, pestilences, famines, schisms, and heresies will not
arise. Men will live longer through the new arts of medicine.
Wisdom and knowledge will increase under the one universal rule
and communications will be extended through safe travel. There
will be no barbarians, for the *Pontifex*, the *solum mundi caput*, will
provide rulers for all nations. On the question of this *caput*
Campanella later shifts his ground. In the *Città del Sole*[31] the
head of the ideal city is the Sun, an abstract figure, at once prince
and priest, but later he sought for a political inheritor of the role
of universal monarch. In his *De Monarcha Hispanica*[32] he argued
that this role had descended on the Spanish monarchy, but when,
in 1634, he removed to France, Campanella shifted his prophetic
allegiance to the French monarchy. Spain now represented the
end of the Fourth Monarchy of Daniel, but a Fifth Monarchy
was arising, that of the Most Christian King whose destiny was to
aid the Pope in bringing in the old promise of one fold and one
shepherd.[33] Using every kind of medieval proof, Campanella built
up the case for the final world-empire of the French. It is significant that his dreams were so well received by King and court and
learned men. Even Richelieu appears to have been drawn to his
ideas.[34] His last works show Campanella writing a panagyric of
Louis XIII, propaganda for the French monarchy in Italy, and
an appeal to Richelieu to build the City of the Sun.[35] His final
gesture was a poem to salute the birth of the future Louis XIV
who, he believed, would bring in the Age of Gold.[36]

Perhaps the most striking of these Catholic visionaries were
missionaries in the New World whose dreams were directly connected with the opening up of new horizons. They had a
precedent for seeing the divine plan unfolding in these astonishing developments, for Christopher Columbus himself had
believed in his own prophetic destiny and collected all the prophecies he could find, including Joachim's, in his *Libro de las
profecías*.[37] In later life he increasingly saw his voyages in a
visionary light: 'Who will doubt', he wrote in an undespatched
letter of 1501/2 to Ferdinand and Isabella, 'that this light (i.e. the

resolve to sail westward) was from the Holy Scripture, illuminating you as well as myself with rays of marvellous brightness.'[38] Columbus's account of his fourth voyage (1502–4) in particular belongs to this mood. His voyages, he believed, were the opening of the door through which the missionaries would stream in numbers to convert the whole globe. J. L. Phelan implies that Columbus saw himself in the role of a 'Joachite Messiah'.[39] Without going so far, it seems clear that Columbus's mysticism was nourished on Joachimist prophecy. The climax of history, he declared, would be reached when Sion was rescued and rebuilt, and for this role he cast the Catholic Monarchs, citing Joachim in an unidentifiable prophecy that this Christian lead must come from Spain: 'The Calabrian Abbot Joachim says that from Spain will spring the one who must rebuild the House of Sion.' Thus the discovery of the Indies, the conversion of the Gentiles and the delivery of the Holy City were to be the three climactic events of the Last Age. Through the Holy Spirit Columbus had already accomplished the first and this confirmed his belief that through the agency of Spain the divine plan must be completed.

Columbus took the habit of a Franciscan Tertiary on his deathbed and may well have drawn his visionary mysticism from Spiritual Franciscan sources, for in the late fifteenth century latent influences of this group rose to prominence again in Spain, colouring to some extent the reforms of Cardinal Ximenes de Cisneros, and calling forth in the early sixteenth century such prophetic voices as those of Charles de Bovelles (Bobillus), Fray Melchior and Fray Francesco de Ocaña.[40] In the next generation Gerónimo de Mendieta, a Franciscan missionary in Mexico, took up the theme.[41] He saw the whole progress of the Spanish Empire in the New World as following the providential pattern of the Last Age, and this was the theme of his final work, the *Historia ecclesiastica indiana*.[42] In this divine plan the Spanish monarchy was the great political instrument:

> I am firmly convinced that, as those Catholic Monarchs were granted the mission of beginning to extirpate those three diabolical squadrons of perfidious Judaism, false Mohammedanism and blind idolatry, along with the fourth squadron of heretics . . ., in like manner the business of completing this task has been reserved for their royal successors; so that as Ferdinand

and Isabella cleansed Spain of these wicked sects, in like manner their royal descendants will accomplish the universal destruction of these sects throughout the whole world and the
final conversion of all the peoples of the earth to the bosom of
the Church.   (tr. Phelan, *op. cit.*, p. 13.)

Cortés was the new Moses, called to lead the enslaved Indians out
of the bondage of the Aztec rulers into the Promised Land of the
Church.[43] Calculating (incorrectly) that Cortés was born in the
same year as Luther, Mendieta saw them as 'prophetic opposites',
Cortés restoring in the New World what Luther was destroying
in the Old. The advent of the first twelve Franciscan 'apostles' in
Mexico City in 1524 was an event of vast prophetic significance—
and here there are clearly overtones of the Joachimist twelve
spiritual men to usher in the third age in concord with the twelve
Patriarchs and Apostles of the first and second.[44] Mendieta
believed that Cortés had been inspired by the Holy Spirit when,
at their entry into the city, he took off his cape for them to walk
over and knelt to kiss their feet. Here he acted 'not as a human-
being but as an angelic and divine being', for this signified, in
concord with Christ's entry into the Old Jerusalem, the transformation of Mexico City into the New Jerusalem.

Thus Mendieta would seem to have interpreted the inner
meaning of New World history in the prophetic terms of a dawning third age in the Joachimist tradition. He does not directly cite
Joachim, but his method of extrapolating the concords between
the Old and New Testaments into this present age is similar to
Joachim's, and, like other Franciscan missionaries in the Spiritual
tradition, he saw in the great evangelizing sweep the re-enactment
both of the Israelite entry into the Promised Land and the first
Apostolic preaching to the Gentiles. In the New World was the
unique opportunity for the Spiritual Franciscans, frustrated in
the Old World, to put into practice their great ideal of evangelical
poverty. This would be possible because the Indians had so little
acquisitiveness in their nature. Mendieta claimed that the Holy
Spirit had enabled him to understand the Indians. They were a
Gens Angelicum,[45] reborn in the innocence of Adam before the
Fall, amongst whom the terrestrial paradise could be re-created.
They should be ruled paternally by the friars and preserved from
the contamination of grasping Europeans. It was the role of the

great World Ruler to break the chains of economic exploitation in which the Indians were bound and build the most perfect Christian order the world had known. Then Nature would flourish and the Indians, rejoicing in their new faith, would 'spend their time marching in processions and praising God in spiritual canticles'. The kingdom of the Last Age would have been established on earth.

But Mendieta was writing his *Historia* in the 1590s, when the Golden Age seemed past. He had thought that the Emperor Charles V and the first two viceroys, ideal fathers of the Indians, would actualize the vision. The Mendicants had been given great ecclesiastical power in the new empire and—looking back—Mendieta could see the period 1524–1564 as truly a golden age of the Indian Church. But all this changed: the power of the friars was challenged and reduced by a secular episcopacy and the conflict between regular and secular clergy seemed to be re-enacting the old Spiritual battle. At the same time exploitation of the natives grew heavier, epidemics of disease raged, while a policy of 'hispanization' superseded the earlier ideal of fostering an indigenous Christianity. In bitter letters Mendieta reproached King PhilipII: 'God intended the Indies to be ruled by the friars, for their salvation depended on this, but now the exploitation of transitory silver mines was given precedence over the exploitation of the eternal and spiritual silver mines of Indian souls.'[46] He now emphasized in his pattern of concords an inevitable 'time of troubles': as in the Old Testament, after the golden age initiated by Moses, the Jewish People fell into Babylonish captivity, and as in the Apocalypse the period of tribulations occurs, so from 1564 onwards until the time in which he stopped writing in 1596 is the new period of Babylonish captivity, the tribulation expected by the Spiritual Franciscans. But, although Mendieta nostalgically idealized the reign of Charles V, it seems that he still expected the messianic kingdom in the future, after the time of troubles. His mystical vision of the universal monarchy of the Spanish Hapsburgs is symbolized in the parable of the Great Supper. His millennial kingdom of the future is located somewhere in the Indies[47]—a magic island vision of an innocent paradise. In the meantime, the battle is joined between the City of God and the City of Mammon. Mendieta concludes his *Historia* with a prayer that God will raise up the messianic King of Spain (perhaps the future Philip III) to destroy the Antichrist of avarice and inaugurate the millennial kingdom when the Indian Commonwealth would become a terrestrial paradise on the model of the enchanted island of Antillia.[48] But the scene looks black; Spain seems to be taking on the character of Babylon; now is the time for the King to decide whether he will rule over the celestial City of Friars and Indians or over the City of Man. If he fails, God may turn against his Chosen People of the New Testament as once against the chosen race of the Old.[49] Historically, perhaps the best comment to be made on Mendieta's hopes and fears is the fact that his *Historia* was not allowed to be published until 1870.

Franciscan visions in Spain and Mexico can be paralleled by Jesuit ones in Portugal and Brazil.[50] There was in sixteenth-century Portugal a strong current of messianic expectation, for the Portuguese, like the Spanish, saw themselves as a nation with a divine mission to evangelize the world.[51] This hope was popularized in the widely circulated prophetic verses known as the *Trovas* of Bandarra. These drew on the Joachite Roquetaillade, as well as other Spiritual prophets, and promised to Portugal the revealing of a 'hidden king' and a Fifth World Monarchy of peace. These hopes focused first on King Sebastian, born in 1554, and suffered a crushing blow when he was killed in 1578 and Portugal fell under Spanish rule for sixty years. But there soon arose an 'Arthurian' myth of a resurrected Sebastian who was the 'hidden king' of Bandarra and would appear in due course to deliver Portugal from the Babylonish captivity of Spanish rule and inaugurate the Fifth Monarchy under her. During the 'captivity' Jesuits, both in Brazil and Europe, played an important part in fostering the prophetic hope of Sebastianism and from their ranks came one of the most striking exponents of a messianic future—Antonio Vieira, born in Lisbon in 1608 and dying in Brazil in 1697.

Vieira did not long wait for a miraculously resurrected Sebastian. Instead, he espoused the cause of the House of Braganza and when Lisbon revolted against Spain in 1640 he went from Brazil as one of a delegation to declare its allegiance to Don João IV. From this point he plunged into a life of ceaseless activity, advising the king, preaching to the court, the cardinals at Rome, Queen Christina of Sweden and others, acting in diplomatic negotiations, travelling incessantly and at one time converting masses in the Amazon region. Through all this there runs a passionate conviction that history has been leading up to this appointed time and that now is the day of the Fifth Monarchy, the world-wide reign of God, the final Portuguese empire. He believed that the restoration of 1640 had confirmed the prophecies, that Don João was the true hidden Sebastian and that now Portugal under the House of Braganza should move forward on the traditional programme of destroying Mohameddanism, delivering Jerusalem and establishing one empire in the world. He set out his philosophy of the future in the *Historia do Futuro*, begun in 1649.[52]

Vieira believed that the study of the future was possible and allowable because God was progressively lifting the veil from hidden things and revealing new knowledge. Like Postel he rejoiced in the new discoveries, advancement of the sciences, developments in the art of navigation and so on. All this progress was part of the divine plan, but the chief clues to it were still to be sought avidly in the Scriptures. Progress in knowledge was designed by God to lead men to a higher understanding of scriptural truth. Thus his second great work, written concurrently with the *Historia*, was the *Clavis Prophetarum*.[53] His hope is unshakeable: God would not have permitted the present flowering of the sciences, human and divine, or allowed Vieira himself to lift the veil on his designs, if the plenitude of time were not come. The messianic kingdom dawning must be an earthly one and must be established, not by a return of Christ to earth, but by a divinely chosen human agent. Since God has inspired the Portuguese to explore the seas and call new nations to the Gospel, it is clear that he has elected Portugal as the chosen nation. Here Vieira draws prophecies, biblical clues, classical and historical information, into one grand synthesis to prove his point. Above all, the astonishing achievements of Portugal set the seal on their divine election, for how otherwise would so small a nation have conquered so vast an empire? So he bends all his mental energies to the task of using the methods of modern exegesis to search out the vital moment when the prophetic programme will start.

The essence of Vieira's vision was the participation of men in God's design: *Gesta Dei per homines*. God allows prophecies to be unveiled in order to invite men to collaborate in making the future. Hence Vieira's immensely practical activity and involvement in great projects: negotiations for creating world-wide commercial companies; campaigns to improve the economic position of new Christians in the Indies and Brazil; currency schemes, navigation, the cultivation of sugar—all were brought into the sweep of his future. Even war had its place, for the King of Portugal must recover the empire which rightfully belonged to her before he could become the great protector of all converted peoples, redeeming them from exploitation and slavery. In the final state of peace and justice, Pope and King will rule together over the one sheepfold.

Vieira's first hope was Don João whom he identified as the true Sebastian, the hidden King of Bandarra, and for whom he drew up a splendid genealogical tree, compared with that of Christ himself. In the early days of his reign there were, in fact, a number of Jesuits who hailed the King in these terms in their sermons and writings, but as time went on this hope became less credible. The King's death was a terrible blow to Vieira who turned afresh to Bandarra and worked out a new exposition in which the temporary death of Don João becomes part of the divine plan and his resurrection is assured. But by 1665 Vieira is hailing Alfonso VI as the true 'hidden King' promised by prophecy and focusing—like many others—on the year 1666 as the fateful date. Thus we slip into a familiar pattern: as each crucial date passes, the will o' the wisp hope dances ahead. The date will be 1670, then 1672, then, basing himself on the prophecies of Roquetaillade, Bandarra and Nostradamus, 1679. Here he was encouraged by other prophets, notably a Franciscan, P. Tenorio, who announced the imminent conversion of the whole world. In 1681 Vieira returned for the last time to Brazil and in 1684 two comets seem to have rekindled his hope. He was reading prophecies on the future felicity of Portugal by Antonio Lopes Bonaventura when he heard of an heir born to the reigning Don Pedro. Recovering all his exuberance, he plunged into a frenzy of number calculations and proclaimed: 'In the cradle at Lisbon sleeps the future emperor of the world'—but the baby died. Then another heir was born and the calculations were re-done. A long *Apologia*, written in 1688, shows that Vieira was still exercising all his agility of mind to maintain his tottering edifice of prophecy and in 1695 he reaffirmed his belief in the Fifth Empire as the most perfect state of Catholicism. He had started work again on the *Clavis Prophetarum*, at the request of the King and the Jesuit General, when he died in 1697.

Vieira stood in the Catholic tradition of messianic expectation. He read Hortolá and the two Jesuits, Cornelius Lapierre and Benito Pereyra. In religious circles, both in Rome and Portugal, ' his work was viewed with great interest and the Jesuits insisted that he try to complete the *Clavis Prophetarum*.[54] Various imitative works from Jesuit pens appeared after his death. It is true that there had been a sentence of the Inquisition against him, but in the eighteenth century this was expunged. When the Society of Jesus was suppressed in 1773 many Jesuits in confusion turned back again to prophetic hopes such as Vieira's, and there was a new wave of messianism. The last great proponent of this view among the Jesuits was Manual de Lacunza y Diaz (1731–1801) who finished his chief exposition of it, *La Venida del Mesias en gloria y majestad*, in 1790.[55] Thus the currents of expectation which we have been tracing among Catholic visionaries were continuing to flow at the end of the eighteenth century.[56]

6

JOACHIM AND
PROTESTANTISM

The sixteenth-century radical reformers had many roots in their medieval past. This point is receiving increasing attention today and the continuing influence of Joachimist ideas well illustrates it. But the reformers used their church history negatively as well as positively, so, before turning to the radical visionaries, we will look briefly at this negative aspect. There was a tradition of Protestant church history in which Protestant scholars ransacked the annals of the Roman Church for weapons to turn against her. The history of Joachimism provided two splendid pieces from this armoury. One was Joachim's own pronouncement at Messina that Antichrist was already born in Rome.[1] It was used with obvious effect by the Germans, Mathias Flacius Illyricus and Johann Wolf, and the English, John Foxe and John Bale.[2] Here is the latter's version of the story:

Antichrist detected by Ioachim abbas.

Whils kynge Richarde was yet in the lande of Palestyne, he sent to the Ile of Calabria for abbas Ioachim, of whose famouse learnynge and wonderfull prophecyes he had hearde muche. Among other demandes he axed hym of Antichrist, what tyme and in what place he shulde chefely apere. Antichrist (sayth he) is already borne in the cytie of Rome and wyll set hym selfe yet hyghar in the seate Apostolyche. I thought (sayd ye king) that he shuld have bene borne in Antyoche or in Babylon . . . Not so (sayth Joachim) . . . Whan thys was ones knowne in Englande and in other quarters of the kynges dominyon, the prelates begonne to starkle. Yea Walter Coustaunce . . . with other . . . prelates . . . cast their heades togyther, impugnynge thys new doctryne with all power possyble. And though they brought fourth many strange argumentes in aperaunce (saith

Roger Hoveden) yet could they never to thys daye brynge their matter to a full conclusion but left it alwayes in doubt.

Bishop Jewel translated Joachim's famous remark thus: 'Antichriste is longe sithence borne in Rome, and yet shal be higher avaunced in the Apostolique See,'[3] and there were a number of other versions in German, French and English.[4] The other weapon was supplied by the scandal of the Eternal Evangel which was used as evidence of the corruption of the Roman Church. Edward Stillingfleet, the Irish bishop, among others, used it in his *Discourse on the Idolatry of the Church of Rome*[5] and John Donne elaborated on it in a sermon at St Paul's in 1628:[6]

About foure hundred yeares since, came out that famous infamous Booke in the Roman Church, which they called *Evangelium Spiritus Sancti* . . . in which was pretended, That as God the Father had had his time in the government of the Church in the Law, And God the Son his time, in the Gospel, so the Holy Ghost was to have his time; and his time was to begin within fifty yeares after the publishing of that Gospel, and to last to the end of the world . . . By this Gospel, the Gospel of Christ was absolutely abrogated . . . for it was therein taught, that onely the literall sense of the Gospel had been committed to them who had thus long governed in the name of the Church, but the spirituall and mysticall sense was reserved to the Holy Ghost, and that now the Holy Ghost would set on foot. And so (which was the principall intent in that plot) they would have brought all Doctrine and all Discipline, all Government into the Cloyster. . . . He that first opposed this Book was *Waldo*, he that gave the name to that great Body . . . who . . . put themselves in the gap, and made themselves a Bank, against this torrent, this inundation, this impetuousness, this multiplicity of Fryars and Monks . . . And so they kindled a Warre in Heaven, greater than that in the Revelation . . . For here they brought God the Son into the field against God the Holy Ghost, and made the Holy Ghost devest, dethrone, disseize, and dispossesse the Sonne of his Government.

More generally, the great Protestant compilers of historical anthologies saw Joachim and his disciples as prophetic voices denouncing the Roman Church as Babylon. Flacius picks out various supposed prophecies of Joachim which are damaging to the papacy but also emphasizes his expectation of reformation which is now being fulfilled. Flacius had certainly seen the application of Joachim's third *status* to the Reformation, but he was only mildly interested in it; his use of Joachimism is mainly negative. Johannes Wolf's mighty collection includes a large amount of Joachimist material. From Joachim's *Liber Concordie* he takes an interesting set of passages, as also from the main pseudo-Joachimist works. He reproduces the whole of the Pope-prophecies, with a survey of the various interpretations. Throughout his volumes there are numerous references to Joachites such as Arnold of Villanova, Olivi and Roquetaillade. There are long extracts from Telesphorus's *libellus* which he must have known in Meuccio's edition, for he fastens eagerly on the picture of the *Papa Angelicus* in the habit of an Augustinian hermit, applying it to Luther himself. A great deal of his material is negative: he can, for instance, cite thirty authorities to prove that the Roman Church equals Babylon, of whom Joachim is the nineteenth. But towards the end of his work he begins to put together a potpourri of prophecies which go beyond the prophecies of schism and tyrant to those of *renovatio mundi* under the Angelic Pope. The identification of Luther as an 'angelic' type had earlier appeared in the edition of the Pope-prophecies produced by the Lutheran pastor of Nuremberg, Andreas Osiander,[7] where the figure of the monk with sickle and rose, originally intended for Celestine V, as prototype of the Angelic Popes, was applied specifically to Luther. But, for the rest, Osiander treats the prophecies as a blast against the papacy and does not recognize the angelic series. Both Luther and Melanchthon commented on this application of prophecy[8] but neither seems to have taken the idea of Luther as the *Papa Angelicus* of prophecy seriously.

Among British writers, besides Bale and Foxe who were in touch with Flacius during exile, we find John Knox using Joachim—'a man sometymes of great authoritie and reputation among the Papistes'—as a prime witness for identifying Rome with New Babylon.[9] In his *Answer to a Letter of a Jesuit Named Tyrie*, Knox says that he will refute Master Tyrie from Catholic writers, but in order not to cause him too much pain he will limit himself to two, of whom one is Joachim. He then quotes several passages from Joachim's *Expositio* with great effect.[10] In concluding his appeal to Joachim, Knox rubs in the point that he had learned the truth about the Papists, not from Luther, but from the Papists themselves. For, he says, God's mercy towards his little flock showed itself in that, when a universal corruption was spreading, he raised up one or two to admonish the present age and future posterity: 'that at least God might have some testimonie that ye veritie of God was not altogether buryed in the earth.' The famous Pope-prophecies were imported into England in disguise and published by Walter Lynne as an attack on the papacy under the title of *The Begynninge and Ende of Poperie*.[11] A little later, William Perkins in Cambridge showed in his *Idolatrie of the last times* that, like Knox, he had read Joachim's *Expositio* for himself.[12] But he used Joachim in the entirely negative sense of fastening on his interpretations of Babylon and its members. He was not at all interested in a doctrine of the third *status*.

The real Joachites among the Protestants were the visionaries who felt that they must interpret their religious experience in terms of a revolutionary new era of history. Among the early radical reformers the line of demarcation between Catholic and Protestant was not at all clear-cut. Thus Postel was in touch with Melanchthon and Bullinger at one time, though he repudiated connections with David Joris,[13] and there was considerable coming and going between Italian humanists and reformers at Geneva and Basle. Among Italians of the mid-sixteenth century the combination of humanist expectation, evangelical regeneration and Joachimist philosophy of history produced some unusual revolutionaries. When belief in the 'new man' was married to the expectation of a new era in history, a distinctive attitude emerged. Among those who visited Basle was the humanist Curione, who combined in his view of history pessimism about the present state of man with optimism about the future Christian perfection to be attained.[14] He pinned his faith on a 'middle Advent' of Christ which would be the reform and renovation of the Church, as prophesied by Joachim and Cyril, and which he believed to be already dawning.[15] It would bring all peoples into one religion, including those of the newly-discovered Americas and the Jews. But especially it would be an advent of light upon earth. For Curione 'light' meant a mixture of humanist understanding and evangelical truth. As it took God six days to make the world, it had taken six thousand years to perfect true religion, but the dawn of the seventh age was inevitable. Man was the crown of the Creation on the Sixth Day and it was the *verus homo*, or *sanctus populus* whose emergence would crown the sixth age and make the seventh. It was the humanist's dream of the perfect man which Curione placed within the old medieval framework of history. It is certain that Christ must come in judgement, but, Curione asserts with equal certainty: '*ventura prius aurea secula.*'[16]

In Basle Curione shared hopes with the Savoyard humanist and biblical scholar, Sebastian Castellione, who maintained in his preface to his translation of the Bible that the Age of Gold announced in the Scriptures must be awaited with expectation.[17] In the Basle group we also find Bernardino Ochino, one-time General of the Observantine Franciscans, but finally an exiled preacher in Germany, England and Switzerland.[18] It is possible that his emphasis on the third stage of history now about to dawn, when the evangelical faith would be diffused throughout the whole world and all men would live in Christian liberty under the law of love, owed its inspiration to copies of works by Joachim and his disciples known to have been in the Sienese convent from which he started. A generation later the Florentine Francesco Pucci was influenced by Curione from whom he took the idea of an intermediate advent of Christ to establish the reign of felicity.[19] Although he never repudiated the authority of the papacy, Pucci found that judgement upon the sins of the Roman Curia had long since been pronounced by Joachim and Bridget. He expected a General Church Council, illumined by revelation and reason, to bring in the perfect society which would cure all ills in Christian love and unity. In this the Roman Curia would be abolished. His two final institutions of a 'new order' and a 'supreme pastor' remain very much in the Joachimist tradition.

In their break-away from an over-intellectualized dogma and search for a more imaginative vision of the work of the Holy Spirit in history some recognized Joachim, the antagonist of Peter Lombard, as their fore-runner. The most interesting example of these is Servetus. He twice referred to Joachim in his polemic against metaphysical views of the Trinity,[20] but it was in his whole philosophy of history, in his conception of divinity as a continuing activity working within the process of history that he came closest to Joachim's thought, fusing, as Cantimori has said, the Joachimist vision of Christian history with the passion of the reformer in order to refute scholasticism.[21] The reign of Christ, begun in the new liberty of evangelical truth, was indeed the Third Dispensation of history, the Age of the Spirit, the humanist Age of Gold. In his *Christianismi Restitutio* Servetus worked out the pattern of history in many number symbolisms, but it is in the significance of threes in history that he found his chief clue to its meaning.[22] He developed various sequences of threes which reach a climax in the three-fold sending forth of the Holy Spirit. The first was at the Creation and the second at Pentecost, but, like Noah's dove, even at the second time it found no permanent resting-place. The third coming was even now to be expected: *Tertia est nunc spiritualiter et interna missio.* Antichrist, the Roman Church, must first be fought and overcome, but Servetus believed that the days were near when the reign of Antichrist would end and the new reign of Christ in the Spirit be inaugurated.

One of the radical Protestants who openly acknowledged his respect for Joachim was Thomas Müntzer and he did so, significantly, in the context of the interpretation of the Scriptures by concords. In a letter of 1523[23] he says that his enemies ascribe this teaching to the Abbot Joachim calling it mockingly an eternal gospel. But, he continues, for me the witness of the Abbot Joachim is of great importance. He acknowledges, however, that he has only read the (pseudo-Joachimist) *Super Hieremiam* and states emphatically that his own inspiration comes directly from God, not from Joachim. The question is whether Müntzer had not picked up more of Joachimism than this implies.[24] He may well have derived thence firstly, the method of interpreting the Scriptures by concords in a pattern of threes, secondly, his belief that in the third 'state' of enlightenment the Holy Spirit would unlock the Scriptures and lead men into further truth, thirdly, the conviction that the new age of enlightenment would be brought in by the activities of men themselves. He believed that he himself was directly inspired by the Spirit to inaugurate the new kingdom of God and certainly his '*bund*', his society of the elect, has overtones of Joachim's *novus ordo* in its role of changing the social order on earth. In his Prague manifesto he put forth a programme for the new Church of the Spirit in which the elect would be directly instructed by a seven-fold outpouring of the

Spirit, superseding all previous religious authority. It has been suggested[25] that one can trace a current of Joachimist influence from heretics in Bohemia and perhaps Erfurt through to Müntzer and his circle. The evidence is slender, but around Müntzer there were traces of Joachimist thinking. In Nuremberg Johann Herrgott, who was probably an adherent of Müntzer's, wrote a pamphlet which opens with a clear statement of Joachim's three *status*:[26]

> Three transformations have been seen in history: the first was instituted by God the Father in the Old Testament; the second transformation was instituted by God the Son in the world with the New Testament; the third transformation will be brought about by the Holy Spirit; with this future transformation the world will be changed from the evil in which it finds itself.

In Zwickau Müntzer was associated with Nicholas Storch and his followers. They were described as 'Picards', a mysterious sect which in Bohemia showed Joachimist traits, and certainly their intention of forming in Zwickau an elect society with twelve Apostles and seventy-two disciples echoes Joachim's number-symbolism in prophesying the future order of the third *status*.[27] An influential thinker who joined the radical cause of Müntzer was Martin Cellarius (Borrhaus) who believed in a progressive revelation of God's truth and looked for a final state of illumination and peace yet to come.[28] He, in turn, influenced Giacopo Brocardo who, as we shall see, was a complete Joachite. Thus there certainly seem to have been Joachimist ideas 'in the air' among the followers of Müntzer.

In seeking to assess the extent of a distinctively Joachimist influence on the Protestant radicals, it is necessary to remember that a general millennial expectation constitutes no such proof, since this could obviously be derived directly from the Apocalypse. More particularly, where the emphasis is placed on the Second Advent as the final event of history, with a millennium to follow as an extra-historical state beyond, such a belief actually runs counter to the Joachimist philosophy of history. The true mark of a Protestant Joachimism is the third historical *status*, with its assignation of historical roles matching those of the Old and New Testaments which represent the first and second *status*. This Third *status* may be ushered in, as some of the earlier Spiritual Franciscans had conceived, by an intermediate or second 'coming' of Christ, not in the flesh, but in a new outpouring of the Spirit which is to be clearly distinguished from the final Advent in judgement at the end of this last era of history. But even rejecting loose ascriptions to Joachimism and using a tighter set of categories, there are still some significant examples of Protestant visionaries who saw their own experience of bursting into a new age as part of a three-fold pattern of history on the Joachimist model. David Joris may have received his Joachimist inspiration from Postel's works which he certainly discussed and studied.[29] Characteristic of his thinking was the pattern of threes in history. He called himself the third David, in succession to the first, the historic David, and Christ, the second David. While admitting Christ to be greater, Joris believed that he himself was the chosen instrument of the Spirit in the third age to break the tyranny of 'dead-letter' faith in the Bible and reveal its spiritual secrets, or—in the Old Testament figure—to smite off the head of Goliath and liberate Israel. The three Davids were the focal points of Joris's three ages of history, as expounded in his *Wonderboek* in 1542.[30] His characterization of the three ages culminates in a third surprisingly close to Joachim's thought: the first had been polygamous; the second was monogamous; now, the dawning age of the Spirit would be celibate. A rather similar echo of Joachimism is found among the High-German Anabaptists who called Old Testament time yesterday, New Testament time today, and future time tomorrow.

Melchior Hofmann[31] was one who developed the three-fold pattern in terms of Church history: (i) apostolic times to the time of the popes, (ii) the period of the unlimited power of the popes, (iii) the period of the Spirit, already prepared by Hus and now beginning, in which the papacy would be deprived of all power and the Letter transformed into the Spirit. Hofmann used concordances between the Testaments in a Joachimist way. He saw himself and his followers as the Israelites sent into the wilderness and as the Woman clothed with the Sun in the Apocalypse fleeing, as the bride of Christ, into the wilderness. He fastened particularly on the role of the two witnesses in the Apocalypse and came to think of himself as either Elijah or Enoch in the final age. As Rome was the spiritual Babylon, so he expected Strasbourg to be the spiritual Jerusalem from which 144,000 heralds of world regeneration would go forth. There is probably a confused echo of Joachimism in the following words on the final climax:

> And now in this final age the true apostolic emissaries of the Lord Jesus Christ will gather the elect flock . . . and lead the Bride of Christ into the spiritual wilderness. . . . For in the New Covenant the Third Day, that third lunar festival, that is, the spiritual Feast of Tabernacles, will be in the spiritual wilderness; and the last appearance of all that is lunar.

Less directly linked to Joachimism, we find Bernard Rothmann,[32] in his *Restitutio mundi*, expounding a similar pattern of history in terms of two Falls and two Restitutions. Man had fallen under the Old Covenant and been restored in Christ, but there had been a second Fall under the New Covenant from the second century onwards. Now the second restitution, begun under Luther and Hofmann, must be extended to all. This would be a restitution not for the learned, but for the common man. Dietrich Philips expounded the history of the Church in terms of Origins, Fall, and Restoration, believing that the last era had now begun in the New Jerusalem which had already descended from heaven to earth. In all these examples we see how a three-fold pattern of history expressed, better than the traditional two-fold one, the faith and burning zeal of reformers who believed they had been called to be the active agents in inaugurating a wholly new era of history. In G. William's words: 'With the overriding conviction that they were living at the opening of a new age, the Radical Reformers began to alter their conception of the redemptive role of Christ.' Thus, he says, 'the Trinitarian scheme of Joachim of Flora (*sic*) was especially pervasive' among Reformation eschatologies.[33]

The most complete Joachite among these Protestants appears to be Giacopo Brocardo, a Venetian who was educated as a humanist, experienced a prophetic vision which led to his conversion in 1563, and later fled north from the Inquisition.[34] His works divide sharply into '*opere retoriche*', before the great crisis in his life, and '*opere profetiche*' afterwards.[35] The last of the first group belongs to 1558, the first of the second, which includes works of exegesis on the Apocalypse, Leviticus and Genesis, appeared in 1580. We find him in Heidelberg, England, Holland, Bremen, Nuremberg, but he apparently threw in his lot chiefly with the Huguenots, under the protection of the influential courtier Ségur-Pardaillon.[36] As he describes the illumination which led to his conversion, it appears in the direct Joachimist tradition of a gift of spiritual understanding to interpret the hidden secrets of the Scriptures. His exposition of the Apocalypse[37] starts at once with the three *status* of history, of which the third, belonging to the Holy Spirit, will be the Sabbath of 'opened prophecy'. In using the seven world-ages, he reckons the sixth as that of the new prophets and the seventh as that of Christ's Second or 'middle' Advent. This is clearly distinguished from the Third, as an advent in spirit only, a crucial revolution in human history but not its end. He distinguishes seven divisions in the *status* of the Son—in which the seventh 'begun to shyne as the mornynge doth' when Luther renewed the preaching of the Gospel—and seven seasons to the *status* of the Holy Spirit. Of these latter, the first was from the preaching of Luther to the preaching in Switzerland, the second and third covered the preaching in England and Denmark and elsewhere and the fourth 'commeth to the French troubles'. These four seasons were marked by four new prophets corresponding to the four Angelic Popes. The fifth ran 'even unto the universall slaughter of the Gospellers', and the sixth would last until 'the conflicte of hostes, when in thicke cloudes in the sky Chryst shalbe present to turne his Judgement agaynst ye Papistes'. In spite of these last words, Brocardo clearly saw this as the second of three advents and believed he was already living in the third *status* and the seventh age.

Brocardo acknowledged the source of this view of history quite openly. In the sixth age, he says, a preparation began to be made: 'Chryst sendeth the Abbot Joachim and many others whom Theleasphorus recordeth, who sayth that the Lordes comming is to bee looked for, and that there must needes be an innovation or renewing, to weete of the Gospell.' The new prophets, of course, did not know everything; they told some things truly, some not, and they could not open all the mysteries of God's Book. Yet 'stronge was the Voyce of the Abbot ioachimus wrytinge and foretellinge many thinges . . .' Joachim is the key prophet of the sixth age and the chief medieval influence on Brocardo's thought.

This is made clear not only by the number of direct references to Joachim but also by Brocardo's use of characteristic symbols from Joachim which he adapts in his own way. Thus he uses the 'wheel within a wheel' to show, as does Joachim, the co-existence of all three Persons of the Trinity in all three *status*. A second symbol adapted from Joachim is that of the trumpet, used to express the preaching of the Gospel in all ages. A third, drawn from Joachim's *Liber Concordie*, is that of the sacrifice of Elijah on Mt Carmel. But it is in the fascination of letters that Brocardo most shows the influence of Joachim's ways of thought. Joachim, says Brocardo, had used the forms of letters (i.e. the Alpha and omega) in the *Psalterium* to demonstrate the mystery of the Trinity, but he, Brocardo, is determined to discover these same mysteries in a comparison of all three alphabets, for the Hebrew represents the work of the Father, the Greek the work of the Son, and the Latin that of the Holy Ghost. Here he finds a figure embodying at once the unity and the diversity of the Trinity in which Joachim might have revelled: 'The Alphabets are doubtless dystinct, as there is a distinction of the three persons in Divinity: but because there is one meaning in these three tongues, we understand God the Father, ye Son and ye holy Ghoste in one essence . . .' He then shows by a study of the orders in the several alphabets the relationship of the Persons. Thus Brocardo shares much of Joachim's thought on the Trinity, but there is one notable difference in his treatment: a new emphasis on the work of the Son as central to the mystery of the three Persons. Here was a Protestant reorienting Joachim's thought on the Trinity to accord with an evangelical Christology.

The detailed exposition of the Apocalypse by this Protestant Joachite makes fascinating reading. Under the figures of the Seven Churches of Asia he gives an interesting account of the state of Protestantism in various parts of Europe. In the later chapters, the Pope is, of course, the Antichrist and the Church of Rome the Babylonish Whore. The bottomless pit is the Inquisition and the locusts which rise from it, the Jesuits. The Seven Angels with trumpets stand for things spoken by the new prophets, such as Joachim, Savonarola, and Luther, while the Angel with the Eternal Evangel is the preaching touching the Lord's Second Coming ('middle Advent') foretold by Joachim. The two following Angels preached the same Gospel 'and drewe all men to a newnesse of life as every man may perceave by the Booke of Theolosphorus'. It does not really please this Protestant to find the blessedness of the Sabbath Age symbolized in the silence of the Seventh Seal-Opening, so he interprets the silence as the time from Savonarola to Luther—and then writes with exultation of the 'voice of many waters' as the voices of the preachers now ringing everywhere: 'as wee see now in Germany, Fraunce, Italy and in many other Countryes that an innumerable number of People doth speake the selfe-same worde of God.' Proclamation, not contemplation, is Brocardo's ideal state.

Brocardo's vision of the third *status* is of a *respublica christiana* to embrace all peoples. It contains no Angelic Popes or last World Emperor and is, indeed, the kind of utopia which would appeal to French, Dutch and English Calvinists. It was to be inaugurated by a General Council of 'true catholicks and gospellers' who would guide men into open prophecy and erect a Church of all Christian people. Brocardo showed unexpected loyalty to his origins in placing this Council in Venice, an idea that would not appeal so much to his northern friends. A *Dux Evangelicorum* would lead the reforming armiês. The first heaven and earth, i.e. the popish ecclesiastical state, would pass away and the new heaven and earth would represent the new *status* wherein Satan would be cast away and the City would need neither sun nor moon in the shape of an ecclesiastical hierarchy, for the Holy Ghost would instruct in full open revelation. Brocardo saw the diffusion of the Gospel throughout the world symbolized in Christ's bright garment which he compared to Aaron's with bells and pomegranates:

> (These) signifie the last age of the worlde, wherein Christes Garment is more inlarged and comprehendeth the whole world, when everywhere there shal be little Belles and Pomegarnates, that is, Churches, and the preaching of the Gosple shalbe in the whole worlde. No other religion, no other lawe, and rule to heare then that of the Gosple shall be heard.

> Then shall be the kyngdom of God in the state of the Holy Ghost untyll that when the Saboth is fynished in this worlde, hee bryngeth us in his thyrde comming to Heaven.

There is some evidence to suggest that Brocardo's ecumenical dream may have influenced the aspirations towards Christian unity in Henry of Navarre's circle, and even, perhaps, Sully's

Grand Dessein. The Calvinist nobleman, Ségur-Pardaillon, who became Brocardo's patron, was employed in 1583 by Henry on diplomatic missions to England, Denmark, Germany and elsewhere to try and build up a great Protestant alliance. J. A. De Thou (Thuanus), writing only a little later, maintained that Ségur-Pardaillon had been much attracted by Brocardo's prophetic vision of the third *status* and had adapted it to a political scheme for unity between the Protestant powers which he presented to Henry of Navarre.[38] In this he apparently looked for the overthrow of the papacy and the re-establishment of religious unity through a general European synod called by a '*princeps*' who would be the '*caput concordiae Christianae*'. Now Brocardo's *respublica Christiana* was based on a series of councils of all evangelical people and, although his *Dux Evangelicorum* was not necessarily to be seen as a monarch, it seems likely that Ségur-Pardaillon saw Henry in this role as the *dux* who would gather all Europe into the unity of one Protestant state.

It is difficult to know what weight these dreams carried in official quarters, but it is clear that Henry of Navarre became a new focus for all the old oracles. In Paris the famous Nostradamus was the centre of a group which sought the future from oracle and star. One of the group, the Sire de Chavigny, tells us that Nostradamus was the first to apply Joachimist prophecies to Henry IV. In 1603 Chavigny dedicated *Les Pléiades* to Henry.[39] There are, of course, seven prophetic *Pléiades* and the first is none other than a French translation of our old Second Charlemagne prophecy, written for Charles VI, applied in turn to Charles VIII and the Emperor Charles V, and now, with name or initial omitted, appropriated for Henry IV. The following *Pléiades* set forth the well-known prophetic future: great wars and tribulations, the overthrow of thrones and the multiplication of heresies, but after these things will come '*un règne meilleur et une saison plus douce*'. Thus the Joachimist hope of renewal emerges once more, but it now carries a Protestant overtone, for '*il n'y a rien plus doux à l'homme . . . que de vivre avec liberté . . ., telle que preschent par tout les nouveaux Evangelistes du iourd'hui.*'[40] We get a vivid impression from the writings of Agrippa d'Aubigné of how all over Europe men speculated on the rising sun of Henry of Navarre.[41] D'Aubigné himself returned to France to tender his loyalty, noting how the prophets and diviners forecast universal empire for the French monarch, reunion of all Christians and reduction of the papacy to a mere bishopric. He reports that the Duke of Saxony likened Henry to King David and sent a gold chain to the author of a book entitled *Carolus Magnus Redivivus*.[42] He concludes: 'Je m'en vins à la Cour, gros de ces ouvertures, pour estre compagnon de tant de belles esperances.'

From Pucci and Postel through to Brocardo, Campanella and others in the early seventeenth century, there is a current of visionary hope that the *respublica Christiana* might really come into being in Europe. In 1581 an anonymous *Forma d'una Republica Catholica* which is almost identical with Pucci's *De Regno Christi* envisages a General Council as the basis of a universal republic.[43] Among Henry of Navarre's entourage, besides Ségur-Pardaillon, we find Pierre de la Primaudaye putting forward his *Advis sur la necessité et forme d'un S. Concile pour l'union des Eglises chrestiennes en la foye catholique*.[44] The Calvinist leader, François de la Noue, put forward with passion in his *Discours Politiques et Militaires* (1584)[45] a detailed plan to unite all Europe against the Turk, thus proposing the destruction of the infidel as the means for recovering the unity of the European republic. As we have seen, the dream of a world Church under an Angelic Pope had long been associated with the political dominion of a World Emperor, and thus it was natural, in the Protestant counterpart, to make the transition from a universal Church Council called to restore religious unity to a political scheme for a 'united states of Europe'. These ideas were particularly at home in the France of Henry IV and thus Sully's *Grand Dessein* seems to spring naturally from a soil in which the political ambitions of an aspiring French monarchy mingled with prophetic hopes of the type that Brocardo and others were disseminating.

Pursuing a somewhat similar line, Frances Yates[46] has shown that the strange phenomenon of the Rosicrucians was connected with the dream of a world reformation which, she argues, was focused at one time on the expectation that the Elector Frederick of the Palatinate, the 'Winter King' of Bohemia, would lead a great Protestant alliance against the Habsburgs and bring Europe into peace. The alchemical aspects of Rosicrucian dreams carry the imagination on to a different plane from Joachimism, but there are certainly some points of cross-reference. Paracelsus, a forerunner of the Rosicrucian movement, interpreted the Pope-prophecies and imitated them.[47] Dr John Dee, claimed by Dr Yates as a source of Rosicrucianism, was interested in Joachim's number symbolism.[48] It seems probable that a figure of circles in a Rosicrucian work by Franckenberg, *Raphael oder Arztengel*, was drawn from Joachim's *figura* of the Wheels of Ezechiel.[49] More generally there was an obvious affinity between Joachim's *intelligentia spiritualis*, based on a combination of study, meditation and illumination, and the Rosicrucian 'Enlightenment', while both latter-day Joachites and the so-called Rosicrucians hailed the Renaissance advances in learning as signs of the new dawn.

At the political level we find Rosicrucian dreams supported by prophecies in the Joachimist tradition. In 1604 Simon Studion dedicated to the Duke of Württemberg a work entitled *Naometria* in which he used number symbolism to forecast the future.[50] His chief interest was in a secret Protestant alliance, of great consequence for the future, which went back to a supposed secret meeting in 1586 between representatives of Queen Elizabeth, Henry of Navarre and various Protestant princes, and which had now taken the form of an alliance between James I, Henry IV and the Duke of Württemberg. This seems to have been a figment of the imagination but the *Naometria* was used by Johann Valentin Andreae, perhaps the chief initiator of Rosicrucianism, in his *Turris Babel* in 1619.[51] Studion had proposed the date 1620 for the end of Antichrist in the destruction of the papacy and Mohammedanism, and this was to be followed *c.* 1623 by the millennium. In using this prophecy Andreae links it with those of Joachim, Bridget, Lichtenberger, Paracelsus and Postel. The Bohemians, who 'tried to marry Frederick of the Palatinate to the world', were inspired, it is suggested, by a Rosicrucian dream which, in its political expectation of world reform, owed something to the Joachimist prophetic programme. Even after the tragedy of the Winter King was over, prophecies of his return were circulating. In 1625 Philip Ziegler who, it has been said, 'fused Rosicrucian ideas with the Joachite Age of the Spirit',[52] came to seek James I's help for a restoration. More particularly these hopes were focused on the prophecies of Christopher Kotter, Nicholas Drabnik and Christina Poniatova who promised the collapse of Antichrist and the return of the reign of light.[53] Comenius, who fell under the influence of Rosicrucian ideas, attached great importance to these prophecies which he brought to England and published in his *Lux in tenebris* in 1657.[54] Possibly that strange figure Quirinus Kuhlmann drew his inspiration from the same sources.[55] Once again we meet here the Joachimist three ages, with Kuhlmann himself as the prophet of the third, and his own interpretation of the Scriptures as the third Testament. But he saw the future in a historical perspective: the Church of God was to be built through six days, represented by Wycliffe, Hus, Zwingli, Luther, Calvin, and the final Reformation still to come, so that on the Seventh Day it would have rest. In expounding his apocalyptic view of history he used the prophecies of Kotter and his two fellow visionaries, as well as a certain J. Kregel, applying them no longer to the House of Palatinate but to events yet to come. In 1679, in Rotterdam and London, he announced the imminence of crisis: *The General London Epistle of Quirinus Kuhlmann, A Christian, To the Wiclef-Waldenses, Hussites, Zwinglians, Lutherans and Calvinists. Being an Explication of a Vision and Prophecy of John Kregel. Wherein the Reformation from Papacy is fundamentally asserted and the Union of Protestants convincingly urged: Together with a postscript relating to the present Popish Plot.* 'The Seventh Day of the World has found its beginning', he declares. After the fall of the papacy an earthly Community of Saints will precede the Paradisical Community. Eastern Christians, Jews and Turks will be brought in and all Christian sects will form one communion. Kuhlmann was passionately concerned to retrieve the Scriptures from corruption and make them available to all nations:[56]

> I can no longer bear these dark evasions of a corrupted Text, but shall retrieve the Scriptures ... by the help and assistance of the Dictator himself ... I shall restore the Text itself, both Hebrew and Greek, not by mine own knowledge, but by the Grace of God alone ... for a pattern to all other Peoples and Nations and Languages that so our universal work may come to be of universal use.

Thus an ecumenical dream of a great Protestant confederation and reformation was still being disseminated by prophets late in the seventeenth century. These, as we have noted, turn to England quite often. We must now look more carefully at the English prophetic scene in the sixteenth and seventeenth centuries.

As we have noted, Bale and Foxe were both in touch with the great Protestant compilers of medieval prophetic material on the Continent. Walter Lynne, who published part of the Pope-prophecies, may have had contact with Osiander of Nuremberg, while his contemporary, George Joye, translated Osiander's *Conjectures of the ende of the worlde* in 1548. Bernardino Ochino spent six years in England (1547–1553) at the invitation of Cranmer.[57] Paul Grebner, whose prophecies circulated in seventeenth-century England, was said to have visited England and presented them to Queen Elizabeth, while Jacopo Brocardo was also in England at that time.[58] He may have been in touch with a group interested in prophecy, for his exposition of the Apocalypse was translated for publication by a James Sanford whom we also find contributing dedicatory verses to Stephen Batman's *The doome warning all men to the Judgements*.[59] This itself contains a curious prayer for Queen Elizabeth which links her, to form a sequence of three, with her namesakes, the wife of Aaron and the wife of Zacharias. A marginal note gives this sequence an interpretation which is clearly Joachimist:

> The first in the old Testament Gods Kingdome.
> The first in the new testament Christes kingdome.
> The firste after the bewraying of Idolatrous Churche. The Kingdome of the holye Ghost.
> Looke next for the coming to judgment, that these three victories maye be in one kingdome.

Thus from the 1540s onwards there would appear to have been in England a current of interest in prophecy which drew much inspiration from continental sources, often in the Joachimist tradition. Occasionally we can track prophetic material in scholars' libraries. Edward Stillingfleet's fine library, for instance, probably contained several Joachimist works.[60] John Bale had a most interesting and unusual collection of medieval prophetic material, of which a good deal can be linked with Joachimism.[61] It would seem that he actually saw the Lollard precursors of the Reformation in a Joachimist context, for, in publishing his *A Brefe Chronycle concernynge the Examynacyon and death of . . . Syr Johan Oldecastell*, Bale ends it with a section headed *Prophecyes of Joachim Abbas*, which sets out the doctrine of the three *status* and culminates in a statement on the Age of the Spirit which must have appealed to the Reformers:[62]

> In the latter dayes shall apere a lawe of lyberte.... More
> clerely shall menne than be lerned.... The holy ghost shall
> more perfyghtlye exercise his domynyon in convertynge
> peoples by the preachers of the latter tyme, than by the
> Apostles.... The churche of Rome shall be destroyed in the
> thyrde state, as the synagogue of the Jewes was destroycd in
> the second state. And a spirituall churche shall from thensforth
> succede to the ende of the worlde.

Frances Yates and others have pointed to the aspirations of the
Elizabethan age which turned medieval imperialist dreams in a
nationalist direction. 'The religious use of the imperialist theme is
strongly characteristic,' she says, and 'Tudor imperialism is a
blend of nascent nationalism and surviving medieval imperialism.'[63] This dream was fed partly on historical parallels—with
Constantine and Arthur, for instance—but it also needed the
thrust of a forward prophetic vision. Dr John Dee[64] based his
expectation of England's destiny as the 'one Mysticall City
Universall' on historical parallels with Arthur, Edgar and the
Byzantine emperors, but also on his own prophetic illumination
from God. He does not consciously invoke the Joachimist structure of history, although elsewhere, in another context, he cites
Joachim the Prophesier on the beauty and prophetic power of
numbers.[65] Where, however, these dreamers use a prophetic
structure of history to project their visions into a dawning future,
they are, in effect, using a Joachimist framework, though by no
means always aware of it. Their Golden Age is essentially human
and terrestrial, the apotheosis of history *after* the fall of the great
Antichrist and *before* the Last Judgement which we have seen to
be the characteristic note of Joachimism. Sometimes the key is
found in the concept of the three *status*, sometimes in the millennium of Satan bound, but most often it is on the Joachimist
interpretation of the Seven Seal-Openings which culminate in the
Sabbath Age on earth that their expectation is founded.

John Bale's *The Image of Bothe Churches*[66] antedates the
upsurge of directly nationalist expectation. His emphasis was on
the prophetic past rather than the future. Nonetheless, in showing, from an impressive array of medieval and earlier sources,
how God's providence has shaped history to his grand design,

Bale was always looking forward to its culminating age yet to come. He probably took his framework of the Seven Seal-Openings directly from Joachim, whom he actually cites eight times,[67] and, like Joachim, he identifies the silence in heaven at the opening of the Seventh Seal as the bliss of the final Sabbath Age on earth, when—after the fall of Babylon and the binding of Satan—peace will reign and God's word will be held in estimation.[68]

> In the tyme of this swete silence shall Israell be revived, the Jews shal be converted, the heathen shal come in again. Christ will seke up his lost shepe . . . that they may appere one flock, lyke as they have one shepeherde.

He is insistent that this sabbath—as distinct from the eternal one—will be 'in the pleasaunte land of the lyvyinge' and proclaims that 'in this latter tyme wyl the true christian churche, when all the worlde shall confesse his name in peace, be of hyr full perfyghte age.'[69]

John Foxe's providential view of history already points to some kind of apotheosis under Elizabeth. In dedicating his first English edition of the *Actes and Monuments* to her, Foxe compares the end of the sufferings of the Reformed Church to the end of the early persecutions by Constantine. Elizabeth is the new Constantine. Foxe's latest work, *Eicasmi seu Meditationes in sacram Apocalypsim*,[70] shows him preoccupied with the prophetic future, although because it remained unfinished we do not know exactly how he envisaged the final age of history. But he draws on Joachim, not only negatively (in the condemnation of the Roman Church), but positively, in his interpretations of the Apocalypse, and leaves us with a sense of history rising to a positive climax before the end, rather than dissolving into failure. This hope centres on the new preaching of the Gospel. Twice Foxe gives lists of the new evangelists raised up by God to renew evangelical doctrine,[71] ranging from Arnold of Villanova to those '*saniores*' of his own day. In particular he sees this *renovatio* symbolized in the resurrection of the two witnesses of Revelation 11.3–12, and he links these with the new opportunities of his day which, like Postel, he finds embodied in such signs as the development of printing and the new illumination of doctrine.

Although obviously not sharing the Elizabethan sentiments of

Foxe and Dee, John Napier, known as the inventor of logarithms, approached the Apocalypse in his *Plaine Discovery*[72] from the same viewpoint as an interpretation of history leading up to his own day and thence forward into a positive new age. This last age he conceived as beginning *c.* 1541 'in the mouths of Luther, Calvin and other his ministers'. Now is the time for the blowing of the seventh trumpet when Christ's kingdom 'shall bee spread and enlarged over all. And this can no other wayes come to passe, but by the preaching of the Evangell, which was of newe opened up and preached at the coming of the first Angell, whome the Text saith to have the *Evangelium aeternum*.'[73] Thus Napier, like Foxe and Bale, looked for the seventh age in history as one of further illumination and the universal preaching of the true faith.

The special role of England in bringing in the seventh age is directly enunciated in Thomas Brightman's *Revelation of the Revelation* which, although only published at Amsterdam in 1615, seems to have been written within Elizabeth's reign. He stands clearly in the Joachimist tradition in proclaiming that *after* 'this storme (of Antichrist) has blowne over, there shall followe presently gawdy dayes'.[74] Comparison at a number of points shows Brightman sometimes obviously using Joachim's *Expositio* as his source, sometimes following Joachim's interpretations closely. Thus the various angels of the Apocalypse are symbols of God's human agents. The four *Animalia* are also human servants of God and Brightman links them with a scheme of four ages of the Church in which the Lion extended to Constantine, the Ox to Wycliffe, the Man to the Reformation revival of the Gospel, and now the age of the Eagle is expected, embodying the whole dimension of the *spiritualis intellectus* with which Joachim had endowed this figure:[75]

> Wee doe as yet looke for Eagles to come into the World . . . when as the Gospell shalbe fully restored and brought to his due and glisteringe beautie . . . Then . . . they shall search out with a mervailous sharpenes of witt, whatsoever part it is of the truth of God that shall lye hidden to that day . . . they shall soare aloft, havinge all there conversation in the heavens.

The right and left feet of the descending angel of Revelation 10.2 are good medieval teachers, and Brightman's list of these includes two Joachites.[76] The angel's 'little book' signifies the restoration of the gift of prophecy now, in the time of the sixth trumpet, when 'a more full prophecy and more plentiful knowledge shined forth'.[77] Once again he finds this fulfilled in Reformation history and the development of printing.

Thus for Brightman the chief personalities and events of his own time are pre-figured in the Apocalypse as actors and happenings in the final drama of the sixth age which will usher in the seventh. The Son of Man seated upon a cloud (Revelation 14.14) is a worthy prince, perhaps a German reforming ruler.[78] But England seems to hold the central role. The angel with the sickle (Revelation 14.17) was Thomas Cromwell, and the second angel Thomas Cranmer. The harvest was begun to be reaped in Germany in 1521 but the vintage harvest will be reaped in 'our owne Realme of England'. A peculiar position of importance is accorded to Elizabeth who is an angel pouring a vial of wrath on the popish bishops.[79] Like the Joachites Brightman believed himself to be standing on the threshold of the final act in the drama: 'And indeed we waite now every daye, while the Antichrist of Rome and the Turks shal be utterly destroyed. Till this victory be obtained the Church shal be still in her warfaring estate, she must keepe in Tents.'[80] His final age embodies all the traditional features: the destruction of the Turks, the gathering of the whole world into one sheepfold, the reign of tranquillity everywhere. It is emphatically planted in history: '. . . not that Citie which the Saintes shall enjoy in the Heavens . . . but that Church that is to bee looked for upon earth, the most noble and pure of all others that have ever bene to that tyme.' And again: '. . . then shall be indeed that golden age and highest top of holy felicity and happinesse, which mortall men may expect or think of in this earthly and base habitation.'[81]

Hugh Broughton, who was Brightman's contemporary, also holds the two essential Joachimist concepts that history is moving towards a positive climax and that God will bring this in through human agencies. Thus, to him, the seven angels of Revelation 15.6 represent 'what God by men will doe on earth'.[82] The opening up of the new world is a sign of God's will at work: 'Now God driveth us to both (East and West) Indians, not for Pepper and Tobacho: but in tyme to show his name.'[83] Equally the growth of knowledge and illumination over the last hundred years is a sign of progress towards the climax: 'All reformed Countries flow with learned men.' The rider who is called faithful and true (Revelation 19.11) is already at work, as a marginal note points out: 'This is made famous in 1588 and 1605 for our Albion.'[84] Thus Broughton shares the belief in a special role for England in the prophetic future.

His main emphasis, however, is on the ecumenical dream of the New Jerusalem on earth as the city of enlightened learning, evangelical truth and universal citizenship. Into it must be brought all tongues and tribes. In particular, he believes passionately in the imminent conversion of Jews and Turks and writes eloquently against obscurantist scholarship which hinders their entry. 'A city so long and so broad would hold an infinite companie of men.' If envious men had not obstructed the 'opening up of both Testaments in Ebrew and Greeke Jewes and Turkes had seene the xii tribes over our gates . . . and had taken Chambers in the large building of our square Jerusalem'.[85] The pearls of the gates, that is, the words of the New Testament, which, when buried in Latin 'had lost their gaynesse', will now be brought back to their pristine beauty. The pure gold of the streets represents the 'open lawes' and rules of faith now being made 'agreeable to the soules frame'.[86] Broughton's passion for pure texts makes his New Jerusalem a scholar's paradise and he ends with a plea for help in preparing material for the Jews and a threat that he will 'leave all hinderers, as murtherers of soules, out of Jerusalem the holy Citie'.[87]

Carrying forward the theme of national aspiration from Elizabeth to the Stuarts, James Maxwell in 1615 published a remarkable collection of *Admirable and notable Prophesies*[88] drawn from twenty-four famous Roman Catholic witnesses to 'the Church of Rome, Defection, Tribulation and Reformation'. To these he attaches a large number of other oracles, drawn from a range of sources which demonstrate his wide researches. Altogether Maxwell's small book forms a commentary on the whole history of prophecy from Hildegard to Nostradamus, but the Abbot Joachim holds pride of place and Maxwell has collected an impressive amount of material in his praise.

Maxwell's viewpoint is extremely interesting, for he shares the full reformer's zeal for proving the iniquities of Rome, yet he is so steeped in medieval prophecy that he accepts all its categories of future reformation. Thus, although the prophecies of denunciation, tribulation and chastisement are fully represented, the thrust of the book is towards the future *renovatio* which he still sees focused on the two medieval figures of the Angelic Pope and the Holy Last Emperor under whom Christians will enjoy a golden peace. Here we seem far away from a Protestant *respublica Christiana*. Maxwell, in drawing so much on pseudo-Joachimist prophecies, gives an exceptionally Catholic tone to his vision of the future. Indeed, the value of the Catholic past to Protestants is directly affirmed: 'And though that the Iurie bee called from Rome (i.e. his twenty-four witnesses), yet the verdict thereof is very likely to find credite with the reformed (for few of them bee of the opinion that no good thing can come from Rome).'[89] Yet it becomes clear that his real devotion is to the house of King James VI and I. Though cautiously, his commentary on the prophecies points to a particular quarter whence the world may see the Angelic Pope and Holy Emperor emerging:

> The Good Bishop or Pope that should thus reforme the Church is commonly called Pastor Angelicus, Angelicall Pope, and who knoweth but that he may even be a Pastor Anglicus, a Pastor or Bishop sent forth from the Countrie of England. . . . And as there is in no other Countrie or Nation of the world to be found so many learned and eloquent Preachers, nor so many complet Divines, for Iudiciousnes, Ingeniousnes and Moderation . . . as there is in England, so it may well be that God will honour this same Island with the reformation of the Church of Rome and her daughters.   (*Op. cit.*, p. 84.)

And again, commenting on a pseudo-Joachimist prophecy beginning *Flores Rubei*, he interprets this as red roses sending forth sweet waters to purify the Church and hopes that these refer to a 'rosie Prince', that is, the Rose of England which, he believes, will be called to propagate the Gospel and reform the Church.[90] To support this claim Maxwell traces the royal line back to Constantine and announces an unpublished treatise which he describes thus:

> A Discourse of Gods especiall providence for . . . the Monarchie of great Brittaine: wherein is shewed by divers probabilities, olde Predictions and Prophecies, that from thence is likely to spring the last Imperiall Monarchie, which

sould subvert Mahometisme and Iudaisme, convert both Jewes
and Gentiles . . . and restore both Church and Empire to the
integrity they once had in the happy days of Constantin . . .:
therein likewise . . . is laid open the vertuous inclination . . .
and happy education of Prince Charles, with a brief note of his
most noble descent from forty-nine Emperours, of Romaines,
Greeks and Germans, besides Kings . . .   (*Op. cit.*, Preface.)

Surely this is a pointer to Charles I as the Last World Emperor?
The power of ancient prophecy could not be better demonstrated than by the way the ghost of the Second Charlemagne
stalks on through the seventeenth century with the same aquiline
nose, large eyes and high forehead, once delineated for the young
Charles VI of France. Wherever the prophecies of Paul Grebner
originated, they continued to excite study and argument. An
anonymous pamphlet of 1651[91] declares that supporters of the
Stuart cause have resurrected and published from a paper in
Trinity College, Cambridge, a misleading version of Grebner's
predictions which include the Second Charlemagne prophecy.
This they have applied to the young Charles (whom the author
calls the young King of Scotland), prophesying that he will erect
the universal fifth Monarchy. The author demolishes the whole
fabric of interpretation. 'He (the young King of Scotland) may, I
confesse, in person and bulke be greater than Charles the Great,
but not in Warre and Achievements.'[92] In the process of proving
that none of the oracles apply to Charles, King of Scotland, the
author betrays a considerable knowledge of old prophecies, citing
the pseudo-Joachimist commentaries on Sybil Erithera and Cyril
the Carmelite, and invoking the Abbot Joachim himself, as well
as many later prophets. Especially he stresses the ubiquity of the
Last World Emperor prophecy:

> To say the truth, there is scarce a Prophet or Man of any
> Nation in Europe, who hath been indued with Prophetick
> Spirit but he in some part of his works, or other, hath hinted at
> such a Person, Emperor or King, nay some have not been
> wanting to affirme his name as you may see in the Chronicles
> of Magdeburg, testified by Carion in his third Booke: 'Ex
> sanguine Caroli Caesaris et Regum Galliae Imperator orietur
> Carolus dictus, dominabitur is in tota Europa, per quem et

Ecclesiae collapsus status reformabitur et vetus Imperii gloria
restituetur.'   (*Op. cit.*, p. 59.)

One of the writers responsible for disseminating the Second
Charlemagne prophecy in the seventeenth century was David
Pareus, a Protestant theologian of Heidelberg[93] who, wishing to
emphasize the future destruction of Rome, incorporated it into
his commentary on the Apocalypse, with the note that the prophecy had been found in an old manuscript 'in the house of
Salezianus and lately sent to me'.[94] Thus we find the old text in
an English translation of Pareus's work published in 1644. His
interpretation of the Apocalypse was as a 'propheticall drama',
not of the past, but of things to come and he appears to have
exercised some influence on English prophetical expectation. Milton knew his commentary,[95] while Pareus's use of the Second
Charlemagne prophecy had considerable publicity. It appeared in
a 1682 pamphlet of prophecies[96] and in 1689 in the *Wonderful
Predictions of Nostradamus, Grebner, David Pareus and Antonius
Torquatus Wherein the Grandeur of their Present Majesties, The
Happiness of England and Downfall of France and Rome Are
plainly Delineated With a Large Preface shewing That the Crown of
England has not been obscurely foretold to Their Majesties William
III and Mary* . . . In his preface William Atwood declares that
'David Pareus, one would think, had seen the Person of the
Prince of Orange in a Divine Dream', yet, in fact, his prophecy is
still the same old Second Charlemagne:

There shall arise a King out of the Nation of the most
Illustrious Lilies, having a long Forehead, high Eye-brows,
great Eyes and an Eagle's Nose: He shall gather a great Army
and destroy all the Tyrants of his Kingdom . . . Rome and
Florence he shall destroy and burn with Fire . . . The greatest
Clergyman who hath invaded Peter's Seat, he shall put to
Death; and in the same year obtain a double Crown. At last
going over the Sea with a great Army, he shall enter Greece
and be named the King of the Greeks: The Turk and
Barbarian he shall subdue . . . And none shall be found able to
resist him, because an Holy Arm from the Lord shall always be
with him. And he shall possess the Dominion of the Earth.
These things being done, he shall be called the Rest of Holy
Christians.

The traditional political version of the third age, however, meets its counterpoint in England in the mid-seventeenth century when some of the more radical and visionary sectarians turn to the idea of a dawning Age of the Spirit and in so doing come closer again to the vision of Joachim himself. It has been calculated that of some 112 ministers producing new works in the period 1640–1653, nearly 70 per cent believed in an imminent spiritual kingdom of glory on earth.[97] England in the 1640s appeared to be on the verge of a new dispensation in history. At this period, according to M. Fixler, John Milton himself believed that God had purposed in these last days an outpouring of the Pentecostal Spirit and had designed a special role for England, saved from past miseries and reserved for 'greatest happiness to come'.[98]

> Now once again by all concurrence of signs, and by the generall instinct of holy and devout men . . . God is decreeing to begin some new and great period in his Church, even to the reforming of Reformation itself: what does he then but reveal Himself to his servants, and as his manner is, first to his Englishmen . . . Behold now this vast City; a City of refuge, the mansion house of liberty . . . What could a man require more from a Nation so pliant and so prone to seeke after knowledge?

He commented on the free discussion as a healthy system of national renewal, betokening the 'casting off the old and wrinkl'd skin of corruption to outlive these pangs and wax young again, entring the glorious waies of Truth and prosperous vertue destin'd to become great and honourable in these latter ages.' So Milton held that God covenanted with England 'to doe some remarkable good to our Church or State' and that this spiritual condition would last until the actual Second Coming of Christ.

If a new dispensation, then what more appropriate than to see it as a third, the Age of the Holy Ghost. This concept particularly fitted the thought of William Saltmarsh who saw the divine pattern of history 'folded up in' three dispensations of 'Law, Gospel and Spirit, or of letter, graces and God, or of the first, second and third heavens'.[99] The design of God, he believed, had been to lead out His people 'from age to age, from faith to faith, from glory to glory, from letter to letter, from ordinance to ordinance, from flesh to flesh and so to Spirit, and so to more Spirit and at

length into all Spirit'.[100] In tracing this progress of the people of
God towards the goal of history, Saltmarsh used many biblical
figures in the same way as Joachim, as, for example, the crossing
of Jordan to typify the passage of the spiritual Israelites into the
Promised Land. As the ministry of the Gospel was more glorious
than that of the Law, so that to come will exceed the ministry of
the Gospel in its gifts. The present ministry through Christ's
people runs through the channels of Arts, Sciences and Language
acquired by natural power, according to any appearance of the
Spirit of God. It marks progess in the long passage from 'lower
ministrations to higher', but is still not that ministry of 'more
Spirit' which will embody the final glory of life in the flesh, and
must still be distinguished from the 'last and more full and rich
ministration and most naked', which belongs to the presence of
God beyond time.[101]

Here we meet a doctrine of progess—not of Man's achieving,
but of God's ordaining—which is very close to the Joachimist
belief in progressive revelation. Yet Saltmarsh shows no knowledge of Joachim and there remains here a problem as to whether,
as has been suggested.[102] Saltmarsh did derive his three-fold
dispensation from this most likely source, or whether the new
experience of the age could spontaneously have engendered a
similar concept of history through the working of a similar type of
biblical exegesis. In the absence of direct evidence the other way,
one must conclude that the parallels with Joachimism here spring
from a particular type of religious experience and hope common
to both Joachites and Puritans rather than the direct influence of
the one on the other.

The same conviction concerning a third dispensation in history
now about to dawn is central to William Erbery's thought. This
third dispensation 'which we are now entering upon' will be a
discovery of God differing from the previous two of Law and
Gospel, yet: 'tis mixt of both, for both were glorious and the
glory of both . . . is joyned together in this third.'[103] There is a
clear parallel here with Joachim's belief that just as the Spirit
proceeded from Father and Son, so the third age must grow out
of the first two. Again his biblical exegesis parallels Joachim's at
many points. His new age is clearly within history, brought about
by human agencies and involving the transformation of secular as
well as religious institutions. 'In this third dispensation God in

the Saints restores all things . . . things spiritual and civil also, renews the forms of Kingdoms, of outward Government and Order, as well as things in the Spirit.'[104] Where Maxwell still saw his age of tranquillity in terms of World Emperor and Angelic Pope, Erbery centres his expectations on the Saints and the Nation, affirming that:

> these wars and wranglings will shortly cease in the Nation, in which God will so appear with power and glory that all Nations about us shall be broken, or brought in with us at last to the Government of Jesus. That is, when God alone shall reign in Men and Men reign in righteousness, and Righteousness arise in truth, then shall the Royal Law and Rule of Christ in love be followed: That Men and Magistrates shall do to all as they would be done unto, or rather, do to Men as God would.   (*Op. cit.*, p. 192.)

We have already encountered the problem of how a further dispensation of new knowledge could be squared with the orthodox Christology of a once-for-all revelation. The Spiritual Franciscans of the thirteenth century fastened on the concept of three Advents of Christ. With the same sense that a new stage in history was beginning, some Puritans, including both Saltmarsh and Erbery, postulated the same concept of an intermediate advent. Alternatively, they speak of three resurrections: the first of Christ in His Flesh; the second, the spiritual resurrection of the saints to rule in the new dispensation; the third, the general resurrection of the dead.

Among a number of other Puritans of this time who expected a new dispensation within history, we may cite Robert Maton who uses all the old ideas—the conversion of the Jews, the one shepherd and one sheepfold, the concept of an intermediate resurrection—and proves from the Bible that the words 'My kingdom is not of this world . . .' do not literally mean another world, but 'such an alteration over the whole frame of nature and such a change of government on the Earth, that this time shall then as well be accounted the time of another world as the time before the Flood is now taken for the old world by us.'[105] Again, John Brayne in *The New Earth, or the True Magna Carta of the past Ages, and of the Ages or World to come*, uses the figure of the three tabernacles in the Transfiguration story (Luke 9.33):[106]

The service of God under Moses and under the law is meant under the tabernacle for Moses. The service of God under Christ and grace is meant by the tabernacle for thee or Christ. Which administrations falling, in the hiding of the Church, are again to be restored in our dayes by that Elias, in that tabernacle attributed to him.

This is strikingly reminiscent of Joachim's writings and, in particular, the figure of the returning Elias was to Joachim the harbinger of the third age.

Yet none of these writers shows any direct use of Joachimist sources. Only in the case of William Dell do we have open references to Joachim. Of particular interest is the long passage he quotes and translates from the pseudo-Joachimist *Super Hieremiam* which, of course, he attributes to Joachim.[107] Here the locusts loosed from the bottomless pit are interpreted as *Scholastici et Magistri*, leading to a great diatribe against the idols of carnal learning. The significant thing is that Dell carries the quotation on from denunciation to prophecy of the true illumination to come when the preaching of the Cross has destroyed 'all Philosophical Doctrine and Humane and secular learning'. At that time 'the children and youth and men of all ages, sorts and conditions shall be taught no other Doctrine . . . than that which is found in the Scriptures . . . and that not according to any humane and philosophical understanding, but according to the teaching and mind of the Spirit.' I have not met this passage quoted by any other writer of the period, so one may presume that Dell selected it for himself straight from the work. He had already expressed, in a sermon of 1646, his vision concerning the new spiritual Church now being born. Its hall-mark is that 'where Christ sends the Ministration of the Spirit, there many young people are brought to Christ, as being most free from the forms of the former age.'[108] He believes that 'the Lord must build this spirituall Church and set it up in the world . . . and cause it to increase till it fills the world.'[109] Thus Dell certainly seems to be translating the *spiritualis intellectus* of Joachim's third *status* into Protestant terms, even echoing the Joachimist idea that the third age would be particularly characterized by boys. His conclusion, too, carries a Joachimist overtone: 'Goe and tell the Foxes that we will walk without feare in the world both today and tomorrow, and the third day we shall be perfected.'[110]

It is clear that many Protestants, of varying shades, drew on medieval prophecy, oracle and myth, and that they used these materials both negatively and positively. The strength of the Joachimist element in this inherited tradition lay in its affirmation of a coming new age in history which would be one of illumination and liberty. For some this seemed to chime so much with their own experience that the new Age of the Spirit became their faith, while adjusting the concept to their central Christology by thinking in terms of a 'middle advent' or 'middle resurrection' of Christ. The point of focus was the vision of the new age. This might still be seen in terms of the old symbols of Angelic Pope and World Emperor; it might be embodied in schemes for a universal Church Council and a new *Respublica Christiana* constructed on Protestant lines; it might be focused on nationalist aspirations in the 'chosen nation' concept; it might express the highly personal leadership of revolutionary prophets such as Müntzer and Joris, or the excitement of seventeenth-century English visionaries when history seemed about to pass into the hands of the Saints. All have certain themes in common: an expectation of immediate catastrophe in the near future, coupled with an optimistic attitude towards the future beyond; an ecumenical belief in the possibility of a *concordia mundi*, both ecclesiastical and political; an affirmation of 'progress' towards the light, as seen in the recent development of learning, printing, geographical discovery, illumination of the Scriptures and evangelical preaching. Their affirmation was basically one about further revelation from God, not about the innate capacity of men to progress; furthermore, it would seem that they expected change to stop in the final stage of immutable beatitude. Nonetheless, their ideas could become a seedbed for future hopes:[III] a new illumination of the Spirit, a reign of peace, an ecumenical gathering into one sheepfold, a blossoming of the gifts of men, a richer yield from the earth, all these expectations, detached from their eschatological setting, could be translated into purely human hopes within history, that is, into a doctrine of human progress.

EPILOGUE

At the end of the seventeenth century serious thinkers and sober men still believed in prophecy. Isaac Newton, when he had finished *Principia*, turned to the prophetic secrets of the Apocalypse. Daniel Papebroch, the scholarly Jesuit, believed that Joachim had in truth prophesied the future advent of his own order.[1] Although the Enlightenment gradually eroded these beliefs, the concept of the third age, an Age of the Spirit, the climax of history yet to come, was too powerful an image to drop out of the imagination. Even when the Renaissance excitement over the opening up of new avenues of knowledge—avenues spiritual and mystical as well as intellectual and scientific—had been doused by the rigour of the new mathematical sciences, a further illumination, another 'newness of spirit', always seemed to be just ahead. On the other side, the vision of a new society in the tranquillity of world unity was still nourished on political prophecy. In various forms right down to the present century this vision recurs, sometimes consciously linked with Joachimism, sometimes not. Here it is only possible to end with a few scattered examples.

In the second half of the eighteenth century another Jesuit, Manuel de Lacunza y Diaz (1731–1801), also born in Latin America, took up the theme of Vieira.[2] He took his final vows in 1767 and it may have been the suppression of his Order in 1773 which—as with other Jesuits at the time—turned his mind towards prophecy and the future. Exiled in Imola, he studied the Book of Daniel and the Apocalypse. His great work, *La Venida del Messias in gloria y majestad*, was finished in 1790 but was not published until after his death. Like Vieira, he built up an immense structure of learning to show that there must be an intermediate resurrection and coming of Christ after the destruction of Antichrist. This would be the millennium within history in which all nations would be converted and participate in the terrestrial bliss. The end of the world would separate it from the bliss of eternity. One of Lacunza's concepts, that of two orders as agencies of the new age, links him closely to Joachim and there are other ideas that he seems to have taken from Joachim or Joachites, such as Olivi, Ubertino da Casale or Roquetaillade. We have no direct evidence, however, that he knew their works. More likely is his use of Cornelius Lapierre, Pereyra and Vieira from his own order and the Franciscan, Galatinus. But from whatever immediate source Lacunza drew his vision of a glorious reign of Christ in history, he seems to belong to the tradition of prophetic expectation which we have been tracing. The upheavals of the late eighteenth century—especially the French Revolution— threw many members of religious orders into confusion and drove them towards apocalyptic expectations. Vieira and Lacunza were both seen as relevant, and right on throughout the nineteenth century there appeared prophetic works from Catholic religious in the same vein. Thus in 1861 the Jesuit, Henri Ramière, cites both Vieira and Lacunza in his *Espérances de l'Église*, and as late as 1890 Abbé Chaubauty writes *Études . . . sur l'avenir de l'Église Catholique selon le plan divin ou la régénération de l'humanité et la rénovation de l'univers*.

German philosophers of the Enlightenment also found Joachim to their taste. Lessing's grand vision of a progressively illumined human race seems to have taken a significant lift when he came on the evidence of the thirteenth-century Joachites and their Eternal Evangel. In his *Uber die Erziehung des Menschengeschlechts* (*On the Education of the Human Race*) he asks: 'Is the human species never to arrive at this highest step of illumination?' and answers: 'No! It will come! It will assuredly come! the time of the perfecting . . . the time of a new eternal Gospel which is promised us in the Primer of the New Testament itself!'[3] And then he continues:[4]

Perhaps even some of the enthusiasts of the thirteenth and fourteenth centuries had caught a glimpse of a beam of this new eternal Gospel, and only erred in that they predicted its outburst as so near their own time. Perhaps their 'Three Ages of the World' were not so empty a speculation after all, and assuredly they had no contemptible views when they taught that the New Covenant must become as antiquated as the old had been. . . . Only they were premature. Only they believed that they could make their contemporaries, who had scarcely outgrown their childhood, without enlightenment, without preparation, men worthy of their Third Age. And it was just this which make them enthusiasts. The enthusiast often casts true glances into the future, but for this future he cannot wait. He wishes this future accelerated, and accelerated through him. . . . For what possession has he in it if that which he recognizes as the Best does not become the best in his lifetime?

Lessing's sympathy for those far-off enthusiasts communicated itself to the Saint-Simonians. One of them, Eugene Rodrigues, translated Lessing's essay into French and used it in his *Nouveau Christianisme*. In this he sets forth his belief in the evolution of Christianity towards a *renovatio mundi* which will be embodied in a completely new social order. He actually expresses this progression in a three-fold movement from the Law of Fear, to that of Grace, to that of Love. '*L'heure est arrivée où cette doctrine du secours du Saint Esprit . . . doit briller d'un éclat inconnu jusqu' à présent.*'[5] At the end of his visionary sketch of the new order Rodrigues appends Lessing's work.[6] Clearly he, too, was attracted to the Joachites, for in his introduction he says that Lessing had summoned forth 'à grand cris' the third and definitive religious era of mankind, but his voice had fallen on deaf ears and he remained a dreamer, like those visionaries of the thirteenth and fourteenth centuries whom Lessing had not succeeded in rehabilitating. But now the moment has come: let all unite to demand *un nouveau Christianisme*.[7]

From Rodrigues we follow the theme to Auguste Comte who in his Saint-Simonian phase was actually Saint-Simon's secretary. Although the three stages of Comte's final philosophy of history are far from those of the medieval mystics, he specifically cites Joachim as one of his predecessors. In Part III of his *Système de Politique Positive*, which is entitled *Dynamique Sociale ou Traité Général du Progrès Humain*, he recalls the regeneration attempted by St Bernard and then goes on:[8]

Au treizième siècle une tentative plus radicale, préparée par le pieux utopiste que Dante installa dans son paradis comme doué de l'esprit prophétique, s'accomplit sous le digne prédécesseur de Saint-Bonaventure au gouvernement des franciscains. Son livre, aujourd'hui méconnu, mais alors organe des meilleurs aspirations, s'efforca de faire noblement prévaloir la troisième personne de la trinité, pour inaugurer le règne du coeur, en écartant une loi provisoire qui représentait l'ascendant de l'esprit.

It is curious, but perhaps mere chance, that neither Lessing, Rodrigues nor Comte actually names Joachim or the Joachites, yet the references are plain enough, and Comte in particular knows enough, not only to pick up Dante's reference, but to connect John of Parma with the book of the Eternal Evangel. What they have all fastened on is the essence of Joachimism, its Trinitarian pattern of threes. But they know it in the over-dramatized version of the 'scandal of the Eternal Evangel' and— in Comte's formulation especially—Joachim's *spiritualis intellectus* has been transformed into '*le règne du coeur*'.

Finally, from Comte to George Eliot, who read Comte and assimilated some of his thought. Her novel *Romola*, set in Savonarola's Florence, contains a specific reference to Joachim as the source of Savonarola's doctrine:[9] 'The warning is ringing in the ears of all men; and it's no new story; for the Abbot Joachim prophesied of the coming time three hundred years ago, and now Fra Girolamo has got the message afresh.' It is significant that George Eliot ferreted out Savonarola's connection with the Joachimist tradition, for only recently have historians been emphasizing it. Her interest in the prophetic theme, however, goes further, for in the *Proem* she twice speaks of the dream of a *Papa Angelico* and, when describing Charles VIII's entry into Florence, she refers to the Second Charlemagne theme.[10] Was this simply a case of a good piece of research in Florentine libraries? It has been suggested to me that she was endeavouring to express in the personal development of Romola three stages which might represent Comte's idea of stages in the development of the human race. At any rate, at the end of her *Proem* she seems to be using the myth of the Angelic Pope as a vision of the future:[11]

The sunlight and shadows bring their old beauty ... and men still yearn for the reign of peace and righteousness—still own *that* life to be the highest which is a conscious voluntary sacrifice. For the Papa Angelico is not come yet.

Another German philosopher who was excited by the discovery of Joachimism was F. W. Schelling. In the thirty-sixth lecture of his *Philosophy of Revelation* he developed the prophetic expectation of an approaching third age of the Spirit in a mood of high excitement, while, it has been said, 'many a listener to his Berlin lectures of 1841 had the impression that he was watching the rise of a new stage of consciousness and the birth of a new religion.'[12] Like Joachim he used 1 Cor. 13.12, as a key text and saw St John as the apostle of the future. Indeed, he used a Trinitarian pattern of progress which has clear overtones of Joachim: corresponding to Moses, Elijah and John the Baptist who consummates the Old Testament, stand Peter, Paul and John, representing three stages in the Christian Church, all reflecting the Trinity. Peter was the apostle of the Father, Paul of the Son, while John is the Apostle of the Spirit who is leading into the full truth of the future. The first stage was that of Catholicism, the second of Protestantism, but the third will be the perfect religion of mankind.[13] It was in a footnote to this passage that Schelling afterwards wrote of his excitement and surprise when he discovered in Neander's *History of Christian Religion and the Church* that Joachim had anticipated his vision.[14]

At the political level Professor Paul Alexander has demonstrated the relationship between nineteenth-century German aspirations towards unification and the study of Last World Emperor legends.[15] In the second decade of the century F. Rückert published his poem on Barbarossa which revived the old legend of the sleeping Emperor in Mt. Kyffhauser and this inspired W. von Giesebrecht. In the preface to the second edition of his *Geschichte des deutschen Kaiserzeit* (1873) he looks forward to a time 'when the resurrected names of Emperor and Empire will exert their magical power on millions of people'. Then in the 1870s and 1880s there came a spate of academic studies of medieval prophecy and oracle, culminating in F. Kampers' *Kaiserprophetien und Kaisersagen im Mittelalter* which appeared when Germany was celebrating the twenty-fifth anniversary of the Empire in 1895/6. Although Döllinger's cool and sceptical essay can be cited 'as a warning against the prevailing spirit of excitement', there is little doubt that many German intellectuals of that period were fascinated by these old dreams of world empire almost to the point of treating them as presages of the future. Here the mind is inevitably carried forward to the twentieth-century myth of the 'Third Reich' and its tragic consequences.

It is strange that Joachim of Fiore should have caught the imagination of W. B. Yeats, and still stranger to find the twelfth-century Cistercian biblical scholar in the setting of a romantic fairy tale. Among the early stories of Yeats is one called *The Tables of the Law*, written, as he says, 'when I had left Dublin in despondency' and first published in 1925.[16] How did Yeats get on to Joachim? It is difficult to say, but one remembers the Joachimist material of Bale and Stillingfleet, some of which found its way into the Marsh Library, now in St Patrick's Cathedral, Dublin.[17] From whatever source, Yeats gleaned some correct and some incorrect facts about Joachim and then created a complete fantasy. He got Joachim's abbacy wrong but he knew that Joachim wrote the *Expositio in Apocalypsim* and he understood the doctrines of the three *status* and the *spiritualis intelligentia* which would triumph over the Letter. He knew that extreme Franciscans had produced the *Evangelium aeternum* and that Alexander IV had condemned and destroyed it. In his story a strange fanatic shows the narrator a beautifully adorned copy of this book which had escaped destruction and been handed down secretly through the Renaissance period and onwards. Its revolutionary significance is symbolized by the fact that in the small chapel where they sit the marble Tables of the Law have been replaced by empty ivory tablets: 'It has swept the commandments of the Father away . . . and displaced the commandments of the Son by the commandments of the Holy Spirit.' The appearance and contents of the book, as described by Yeats, are utterly fantastic, bearing no relation to the original Eternal Evangel produced by Gerard of Borgo San Donnino in the thirteenth century. Yeats's version commemorates all the disruptive artists of history who have created anarchy, and culminates in the *Lex Secreta*, 'the true inspiration of action, the only Eternal Evangel'. Thus, although Yeats knows that Joachim acknowledged the authority of the Church and submitted his writings to the Pope, he sees him as a master who taught hidden and anti-authoritarian secrets to the initiated, revealing 'that hidden substance of God which is colour and music and softness and a sweet odour'. It is fascinating that Yeats—who could hardly have known the *Liber Figurarum*—should have recognized Joachim as an artist and felt in him the compelling, overthrowing power of art which he expresses in the story as the theory 'that the beautiful arts were sent into the world to overthrow nations'. In the story the fanatic dedicates himself to discovering and propagating the secret law which finally destroys him. The narrator recoils in horror from its deadly attraction. Curiously, this story is linked with another, *Rosa Alchemica*,[18] with a similar theme of the evil fascination exercised by secret knowledge, this time of alchemy, and the bare escape from its destroying power which, once again, the narrator makes. This brings to mind the possible connections between Joachimist prophecy and Rosicrucian alchemy in the seventeenth century which we have already noticed.[19] Was Yeats caught momentarily by the fascination of that search for knowledge which quickly crossed the frontiers into hermeneutics, alchemy, prophecy, magic? He seems to have known that here he was following the Renaissance scholars for he calls the Eternal Evangel 'that terrible book in which the freedom of the Renaissance lay hidden'. Unlike the Renaissance adepts, his narrator drew back, as from a deadly poison. Why?

Roughly contemporary with Yeats an artist with less inhibition was also feeling his way towards a new breakthrough in knowledge. There is no evidence yet that Kandinsky, the apostle of abstract art, had any direct knowledge of Joachim's philosophy of history, yet he came remarkably close to the twelfth-century visionary both in belief and in use of symbol to express it. Like Joachim, Kandinsky felt that the inner meaning of history was a spiritual progression which was now about to reach its climax in a third illumination. Kandinsky's own spiritual experience appears to have resembled Joachim's in that it combined a sense of the organic growth of wisdom through the past ages of history with sudden moments of illumination. In his reminiscences he wrote:[20]

Today is the great day of one of the revelations of this world . . . Here begins the great epoch of the spiritual, the revelation of the spirit, Father-Son-Spirit . . . Art is like religion in many respects. Its development does not consist of new discoveries which strike out the old truths . . . Its development consists of sudden illuminations . . . This illumination shows new per-

spectives in a blinding light, new truths which are basically
nothing more than the organic development, the organic growing of earlier wisdom which is not voided by the later but as
wisdom and truth continues to live and produce. The trunk of
the tree does not become superfluous because of a new branch:
it makes the branch possible. Would the New Testament have
been possible without the Old? Would our epoch of the
threshold of the 'third' revelation be conceivable without the
second? It is a branching of the original tree-trunk in which
'everything begins'. And the branching out, the further growth
and ramification ... are the necessary steps to the mighty
crown—the steps which in the final analysis create the green
tree.

This passage is strikingly akin to Joachim's thought in the role it
assigns to 'given' illumination and in its rapid transition to the
tree-image to express the organic growth of wisdom through the
three stages of the Old and New Testaments and the 'third
revelation' (of *spiritualis intellectus* in Joachim's language). Kandinsky's stress on the living oneness of the tree also echoes
Joachim's thought on the Trinity.

Kandinsky saw the new art of his time 'not as the abnegation of
all earlier art but only as a vitally important division of an old
trunk into two main branches from which other branches grow
that are essential for the formation of the green crown'.[21] He
came to regard his present understanding of art as essentially
Christian, sheltering within itself the necessary elements for the
reception of the 'third' revelation, the revelation of the Holy
Spirit. What was needed was to create the conditions to

enable men as a whole to feel the spirit of things, to experience
this spirit even if unconsciously, just as today the outward form
of things is experienced unconsciously by mankind in general
which explains the public enjoyment of representational art.
Thus will mankind be enabled to experience first the spiritual
in material objects and later the spiritual in abstract forms.
And through this capacity, which will be the sign of the 'spirit',
the enjoyment of abstract, i.e. abstract art, comes into being.

(*Op. cit.*, p. 42.)

Finally, Jung discovered the Abbot Joachim as a significant

psychological phenomenon. Although a little uncertain in his dates, Jung places the Abbot in the context of 'an epoch noted for its spiritual instability' when 'everyone felt the rushing wind of the pneuma'.[22] He sees Joachim as 'one of the most powerful and influential voices to announce the coming of the new age of the spirit'[23]—or third aion, as Jung also calls it. He concedes that one must not impute extreme ideas to Joachim himself and yet Jung is caught, like Yeats, by what he conceives as the anarchic implications of a Third Dispensation and does, in fact, impute more to Joachim than the evidence will warrant:

> One must ask oneself what psychological impulse could have moved him and his adherents to cherish such bold expectations as the substitution of the everlasting gospel for the Christian message or the supercession of the Second Person in the Godhead by the Third to reign over the new era. This thought is so heretical and subversive that it could never have occurred to him had he not felt supported and swept along by the revolutionary currents of the age. He felt it as a revelation of the Holy Ghost whose life and procreative power no church could bring to a stop. . . . Just as Joachim supposed that the status of the Holy Ghost had been secretly begun in St Benedict, so we might conjecture that a new status was secretly anticipated in Joachim himself. Consciously he thought he was bringing in the status of the Holy Ghost . . . but unconsciously —and this is psychologically what probably happened— Joachim could have been seized by the archetype of the spirit. His activities were founded on a numinous experience which is characteristic of all those who are gripped by an archetype.
>
> (*Op. cit.*, pp. 84–5.)

Jung actually discovered one of Joachim's Trees, apparently in the Zurich Central Library, although the original of the reproduction which he gives is clearly the Tree-Circles in the Dresden manuscript. He obviously felt the attraction of this organic image and his use of it raises again in the mind the question of whether Kandinsky had seen any of the Joachimist Trees.

Thus it is not the devout biblical exegete who has lingered longest in the historical memory, but the imaginative, artistic apostle of a bold new spirit, a spirit which 'bloweth where it listeth'. The Abbot who submitted all his writings to the authority of the Pope has become transformed into a symbol of anarchy and revolutionary change. As such he still fascinates. Roger Garaudy, Professor of Aesthetics in the University of Poitiers, in 1972 referred to the 'first great revolutionary movements in Europe' as 'all more or less imbued with the ideas of Joachim of Fiore' and quoted Friedcrich Schlegel as declaring that 'modern history began with the revolutionary desire to bring in the Kingdom of God.' Elaborating the theme, he says:

> What characterizes this Christian revolutionary tradition from Joachim of Fiore to John Huss, from Thomas Münzer to the theologies of hope and political theologies of our own day, is that the Kingdom of God is not conceived as another world in space and time, but as a different world, a changed world, a world changed by our own efforts . . . . This means that human history is where all the issues are settled. ('Faith and Revolution', *Ecumenical Review*, xxv (1973), pp. 66–7.)

Even very lately Joachim has been made the subject of an experimental opera, while a recent prophecy by Dr George Macleod re-states the essential Trinitarian theme of Joachimism in terms of the Church's history:

> In its first three hundred years, the Church was small, faithful, joyous and persecuted by the state. That was the 'Age of the Father'. Then came the Emperor Constantine who, instead of persecuting, began to promote the Church and to patronise it. The church became the servant of the State, the beginning of 'Christendom'—the Age of the Son. Now all that is ended. . . . The Crown Rights of the Redeemer are forgotten. It is the end of our time—and, suddenly, there is a 'rumour of angels'. It is like the end of the Old Testament. The Age of the Spirit breaks through! (Reported in the *Baptist Times*, 2 May, 1974.)

NOTES

STANDARD ABBREVIATIONS USED IN NOTES

AS   *Acta Sanctorum*, May, vol. vii, Day 29, *Joachimus Abbas*

AFH   *Archivum Franciscanum Historicum*

AK   *Archiv für Kulturgeschichte*

ALKG   *Archiv für Literatur u. Kirchengeschichte des Mittelalters*

PL   Migne, *Patrologia Latina*

MGHS *Monumenta Germaniae Historica. Scriptores*

MOPH *Monumenta Ordinis Fratrum Praedicatorum Historica*

RS   *Rolls Series*

PREFACE

1 *Ecumenical Review*, xxiv (1972), p. 406.

2 According to F. Russo, *Gioacchino da Fiore e le fondazioni Florensi in Calabria* (Naples, 1958), pp. 139–207.

3 Rome, Bibl. Corsin., 41. F.2, ff. 1–115.

CHAPTER 1

All abbreviated forms in notes are extended in the bibliographies and list of abbreviations.

1 B. Smalley, *The Study of the Bible in the Middle Ages* (Blackwell, Oxford, 1952), pp. 286–7.

2 St Augustine, *Serm.* 81, 8, trs. P. R. Brown, *Augustine of Hippo* (Faber, London, 1967), p. 298.

3 See bibliography to ch. I for Joachim's main writings and for the principal works on him. Abbreviations used in footnotes are there extended.

4 Rupert of Deutz, *De Trinitate et Operibus Eius*, *Patrologia Latina* (PL), vol. 167 (Paris, 1854); Anselm of Havelburg, *Dialogi*, PL, vol. 188 (Paris, 1855).

5 The evidence for Joachim's early life and the meeting at Veroli is given in Reeves, *Influence of Prophecy*, pp. 3–4, 21. See also B. McGinn, 'Joachim and the Sybil', *Citeaux Com. Cist.*, ii (1973), pp. 97–138.

6 The chief authorities on whom Joachim draws are St Jerome, St Augustine (among a number of works the *De Civ. Dei* and *De Trinitate* are frequently

cited), and St Gregory (especially the Homilies and Dialogues). He also uses St Ambrose occasionally. Historical materials are drawn from Cassiodorus, Paul the Deacon, Eusebius and Bede. He cites Virgil and Origen. Obviously the Benedictine Rule and the *Carta Caritatis* are basic sources, while he refers to St Bernard's works specifically in the *Psalt*. Of special interest are Joachim's references to Petrus Alphonsi and the mysterious *Secreta secretorum* (*Expos.*, ff. 35v–36v; see below, p. 19), and the possible influence of Pseudo-Dionysius Areopagita, *Coelestis Hierarchia* (see *Figurae*, p. 60).

7 B. Hirsch-Reich, 'Joachim v. Fiore u.das Judentum', *Miscellanea Mediaevalia*, iv, pp. 239–43.

8 On Joachim's debt to Petrus Alphonsi, see *Figurae*, pp. 40–5.

9 *Psalt.*, f. 227r–v. See *Figurae*, pp. 51–3, for a fuller account of this experience.

10 *AS*, pp. 97–9.

11 *Expos.*, f. 39r–v.

12 *Psalt.*, f. 227r–v.

13 *Lib. Conc.*, f. 19r.

14 *Psalt.*, f. 243r.

15 *AS*, p. 93.

16 The material in the next four paragraphs is more fully treated, with full references, in *Influence of Prophecy*, pp. 16–20, 395–6; *Figurae*, pp. 1–12, 38–9, 46–7.

17 F. Russo, 'Il libro delle Figure attribuito a Gioacchino da Fiore', *Miscellanea Francescana*, xli (1941), p. 334.

18 *Expos.*, f. 170v.

19 For the following two paragraphs, see *Figurae*, pp. 5–19.

20 *Lib. Conc.*, ff. 8r–v, 26v–27r; *Expos.*, f. 34v; *Psalt.*, ff. 266v–267v, 269r.

21 Ibid., f. 82v.

22 The following is a selection of references: *Lib. Conc.*, ff. 18v, 42r, 61r, 116r–v; *Expos.*, ff. 12v, 18v, 25r, 83r–v; *Psalt.*, f. 268v; *Lib. Fig.*, Pls. XX, XXI.

23 The following is a selection of references: *Lib. Conc.*, ff. 56v–57r, 70r–v, 80r *seq.*, *Expos.*, ff. 12r–v, 18r–20r, 25r, 50r, 93v; *Psalt.*, f. 268v.

24 Genesis, 48:11–20. The following are only the chief references: *Lib. Conc.*, ff. 27r–29v, 30v; *Expos.*, ff. 32v, 49v–50r; *Quat. Evang.*, pp. 120, 179.

25 On the significance of Elijah for Joachim, see *Figurae*, pp. 196–8.

26 The symbolism of Elijah's career is worked out in *Lib. Conc.*, ff. 97r *seq.*

27 *Lib. Conc.*, ff. 7r, 101r *seq.*

28 *Lib. Conc.*, ff. 8v–10r, 20r, 56v–58v, 70v; *Expos.*, ff. 18v, 21v–22r, 28r–29v, 37v, 62r–63r, 141r; *Psalt.*, 244v–247r, 266v–267v.

29 For a fuller treatment of the concept of new spiritual men and full references, see *Influence of Prophecy*, pp. 141–4.

30 *Expos.*, ff. 175v–176r.
31 *Lib. Conc.*, f. 92v.
32 Ibid., f. 56r.
33 Ibid., ff. 89r, 132v.
34 Ibid., f. 95v.
35 Ibid., f. 112r.
36 *Psalt.*, f. 268r.
37 But A. Crocco, *Gioacchino da Fiore e il Gioachimismo* (Naples, 1976), p. 28, no. 2, has recently judged the two hymns ascribed to Joachim to be apocryphal partly on the ground that they appear in a later hand on additional pages in this MS. For a tentative list of Joachim's authentic works, see *Influence of Prophecy*, Appendix A, pp. 511–18.
38 See *Figurae*, pp. 75–98.
39 *Lib. Conc.*, f. 26v.
40 *Psalt.*, f. 262r.
41 See *Figurae*, pp. 33–8.
42 *Lib. Fig.*, Pl. XXII.
43 Ibid., Pls. V, VI.
44 On Alphonsi and Joachim's debt to him, see *Figurae*, pp. 40–5.
45 *Lib. Fig.*, Pl. XI.
46 Ibid., Pl. XIX.
47 Ibid., Pl. XII.
48 Ibid., Pl. XIII.
49 For the evolution of this figure see *Figurae*, pp. 51–61, 199–209.
50 *Lib. Fig.*, Pl. XIV, cf. Apocalypse, 12:3.
51 'Benedict of Peterborough', *Gesta Henrici II et Richardi I*, *RS*, ii, pp. 151–5; Roger Howden, *Cronica*, *RS*, iii, pp. 75–9. For a discussion of the authenticity of these accounts, see *Influence of Prophecy*, pp. 8–10; *Figurae*, 86–8. See also E. R. Daniel, 'Apocalyptic Conversion: The Joachite Alternative to the Crusade', *Traditio*, xxv (1969), pp. 128–154.
52 *Expos.*, f. 134r.
53 For a fuller account of this material and its preservation, see *Influence of Prophecy*, pp. 11, 112.
54 Ralph of Coggeshall, *Chronicon Anglicanum*, *RS*, pp. 67–79.
55 Title-page to *De Magnis Tribulationibus et Statu Sanctae Matris Ecclesiae*, pub. Venice, 1516, see Pl. 1.
56 *Psalt.*, f. 229r.
57 *Lib. Fig.*, Pl. XXVI (a).
58 *Psalt.*, f. 332v.
59 On this controversy and the condemnation of 1215, see *Figurae*, pp. 212–23.
60 But a fragment was apparently discovered by A. Maier in a MS. once in the

papal library at Avignon, see Maier, 'Zu einigen Handschriften der Biblioteca Alessandrina in Rom u. ihrer Geschichte', *Rivista di storia della Chiesa in Italia*, xviii (1964), pp. 1–12.

61 Naples, Bib. Naz., MS. Brancacciana I.F.2, f. 288r–v and repeated on f. 331v; Rome, Bib. Casanatense, MS. 1411, f. 191r. The text was published and discussed by C. Ottaviano, *Sophia*, iii (1935), pp. 476–82).

62 See quotations and references in *Influence of Prophecy*, pp. 34–6.

63 *MGHS*, xxvi, pp. 148–9; see *Influence of Prophecy*, pp. 40–1.

64 Paris, Bib. Nat., MS. Lat. 11864, ff. 151v–152v.

65 For a full account of these MSS. and discussion of their dating, see *Lib. Fig.*, Tables and Introduction, pp. 13–31.

66 Bloomfield, Reeves, 'The Penetration of Joachism into Northern Europe', *Speculum*, xxix (1954), pp. 777–80, where the arguments for *c.* 1213, rather than *c.* 1246, are set out.

67 On the scandal of the Eternal Evangel see below, p. 33 and *Influence of Prophecy*, pp. 59–70.

CHAPTER 2

1 *Expos.*, ff. 175v–176r.

2 Reeves, 'The Abbot Joachim's Disciples and the Cistercian Order', *Sophia*, xix (1951), pp. 355–71.

3 Gerard de Fracheto, *Vitae Fratrum*, *MOPH*, i (1897), 13.

4 L. Wadding, *Annales Minorum* (Rome, 1731), iii, p. 380.

5 For this and the following references to Dominican sources, see *Influence of Prophecy*, pp. 147, 162–4.

6 *AS*, 7 Mar., p. 667.

7 Salimbene, *Cronica*, *MGHS*, xxxii (abbreviated *Salimbene*), p. 236. On the origins of Joachimism in the Franciscan Order, see *Influence of Prophecy*, pp. 184–90; Bloomfield, Reeves, *Speculum*, xxix, pp. 786–93; E. R. Daniel, 'A Reexamination of the Origins of Franciscan Joachitism', *Speculum*, xliii (1968), pp. 671–6.

8 Salimbene, pp. 238 *seq.*

9 See the bibliography to this chapter for works dealing in general with the conflict in the Franciscan Order.

10 Clareno, *Historia*, *ALKG*, ii, p. 263.

11 On the Eternal Evangel, see *Influence of Prophecy*, pp. 59–70.

12 But it is now claimed that a large part survives in a Dresden MS., Sächs. Landesbibl., A.121, see B. Töpfer, 'Ein Handschrift des Evangelium aeternum des Gerardino v. Borgo San Donnino', *Zeitschrift für Geschichtswissenschaft*, vii (1960), pp. 156–63.

13 William of St Amour, *De periculis novissimi temporis*, ed. E. Brown, Appendix to O. Gratius, *Fasciculus Rerum expetendarum* ... (London, 1690), pp. 18–41; ibid., two sermons, pp. 43–54; E. Faral, 'Les *Responsiones*

de Guillaume de St Amour', *Archives d'Histoire Doctrinale et Littéraire du Møyen Age*, years 25, 26 (1950–1), pp. 337–94.

14 *De Periculis*, p. 27. Not an exact quotation, cf. *Super Hier.*, f. 1r; also *Lib. Conc.*, f. 41v.

15 Jean de Meung, *Roman de la Rose*, Société des Anciens Textes Français, iii (Paris, 1921), p. 216, l. 11801–4; also pp. 217–19; *OEuvres complètes de Ruteboeuf* (Paris, 1959), pp. 254, 325, 426.

16 Clareno, *Historia*, *ALKG*, ii, pp. 271–83.

17 Salimbene, p. 456.

18 D. West, unpublished study; see by the same author two articles: 'The Reformed Church and the Friars Minor: The Moderate Joachite Position of Fra Salimbene', *AFH*, lxiv (1971), pp. 273–84; 'The Present State of Salimbene Studies', *Franciscan Studies*, xxxii (1972), pp. 225–41.

19 See *Influence of Prophecy*, pp. 52–3, 90–1, 175–8, 185.

20 H. R. Patch, 'The Bridge of Judgement in the *Fioretti*', *Speculum*, xxi (1946), pp. 343–4. The authenticity of Joachim's poem has recently been questioned (ref. *supra*, p. 178, n. 37), but this needs further consideration.

21 Bonaventura, *Omnia Opera*, ed. Quaracchi, i, *Commentaria in quatuor libros sentiarum Mag. P. Lombardi*, p. 121.

22 *Collationes in Hexaemeron*, ed. Quaracchi, vol. v; ed. F. Delorme (Florence, 1934). See *Influence of Prophecy*, pp. 179–181, for references.

23 Ratzinger, *Bonaventura* (Munich & Zurich, 1959), pp. 16–96, 106–120. For comment on Ratzinger's argument, see B. McGinn, 'The Abbot and the Doctors: Scholastic Reactions to the Radical Eschatology of Joachim of Fiore', *Church History*, xl (1971), pp. 30–47; R. Daniel, 'St Bonaventure a Faithful Disciple of St Francis?', *Studia de Vita, Mente, Fontibus et Operibus Sancti Bonaventurae* (Grottaferrata, Rome, 1974), pp. 171–87.

24 See, for example, *Collationes*, ed. Delorme, pp. 185, 192–3; ed. Quaracchi, pp. 408–9.

25 *Collationes*, ed. Quaracchi, pp. 437–44; see Ratzinger, *Bonaventura*, p. 49.

26 See Apocalypse, 7:2–4 and 3:7–8. For the identification of St Francis as the Sixth Angel by Bonaventura and others, see *Influence of Prophecy*, pp. 176–7 and S. Bihel, 'S. Franciscus Fuitne Angelus Sexti Sigilli (Apoc. 7:2)?', *Antonianum* ii (1927), pp. 59–90.

27 *Collationes*, ed. Delorme, pp. 265, 269.

28 ed. F. Tocco, *Le due prime tribolazioni dell'ordine dei minori* (*Rendiconti della Reale Accademia dei Lincei*, xvii) (Rome, 1908), pp. 97–131, 221–36; remainder ed. F. Ehrle, *ALKG*, ii, pp. 125–55, 256–327.

29 H. Grundmann, 'Die Papstprophetien des Mittelalters', *AK*, xix (1929), pp. 77–159.

30 *ALKG*, i, pp. 522–3.

31 Ibid., i, pp. 563–4, 555, 567–8; ii, p. 155.

32 L. Oliger, 'Documenta inedita ad historiam Fraticellorum spectantia', *AFH*, iii (1910), p. 265; iv (1911), pp. 697–708; vi (1913), pp. 276–88;

Vanzolini, *Scelta di curiosità* . . ., vol. 55 (Bologna, 1865), p. 22; Tocco, *SF*, pp. 502–6, 515.

33 Oliger, *loc. cit.*, iv, p. 697.

34 Tocco, *op. cit.*, p. 515.

35 Weinstein, *Savonarola*, pp. 43–56; M. B. Becker, 'Florentine Politics and the Diffusion of Heresy in the Trecento', *Speculum*, xxxiv (1959), pp. 60–75.

36 Weinstein, *Savonarola*, pp. 57–62.

37 See bibliography to this chapter for recent books on Olivi.

38 See quotations and references in *Influence of Prophecy*, pp. 196–200.

39 *Postilla super Apocalypsim*, MS. Rome, Bibl. Angelica, 382, ff. 7v–8r.

40 Tierney, *Papal Infallibility*, pp. 71–130.

41 *ALKG*, iii, pp. 534–40.

42 On Bernard Delicieux see references in *Influence of Prophecy*, pp. 201–2.

43 B. Gui, *Manuel de l'Inquisiteur*, ed. G. Mollat (Paris, 1926), pp. 108–74 (Latin and French); P. a Limborch, *Historia Inquisitionis cui subjungitur Liber Sentiarum Inquisitionis Tholosanae 1307–1323* (Amsterdam, 1692), pp. 298 *seq.*

44 Limborch, *op. cit.*, pp. 298, 300–1, 304, 306, 308, 311–2, 316, 322–3, 325–6.

45 Ibid., p. 298.

46 See *Influence of Prophecy*, pp. 207–9 for a fuller account of Ubertino.

47 Published Venice, 1485.

48 *Arbor*, f. cc^r.

49 Ibid., f. cciii ^{r}.

50 Ibid., f. ccvi^v.

51 Ibid., f. ccix^r.

52 See *Influence of Prophecy*, p. 219, for references.

53 Ibid., pp. 219–23; Pou y Marti, *Visionarios*, pp. 36 *seq.*

54 Pou y Marti, *Visionarios*, pp. 100, 198–200. Fuller evidence for these groups will be given in the introduction to a forthcoming edition of the *Breviloquium* by H. Lee and M. Reeves.

55 See *Influence of Prophecy*, pp. 221–2; Pou y Marti, *op. cit.*, pp. 483–512.

56 See *Influence of Prophecy*, p. 219.

57 Ibid., pp. 220–1; Pou y Marti, *Visionarios*, pp. 165 *seq.*

58 Arnold of Villanova's relations with the House of Aragon will be dealt with more fully in the forthcoming work cited in n. 54.

59 *ALKG*, i, p. 558 (cf. Hebrews 1:1–2; Phil. 2:6–9).

60 On Giovanni delle Valle, see *Influence of Prophecy*, p. 229 and the references there given.

61 Ibid., pp. 220–33, on Ubertino and St Bernardino.

62 For the sources on the Apostolic Brethren, see *Influence of Prophecy*, pp. 242–8.

63 Salimbene, pp. 255–93.

64 Gui, *op. cit.* (n. 43), pp. 20–2.

65 Ibid., pp. 22–3.

66 *ALKG*, ii, p. 131.

67 See references in *Influence of Prophecy*, p. 247.

68 Ibid., pp. 248–50, for the sources on Guglielma of Milan.

69 F. Tocco, 'Guglielma Boema e i Guglielmiti', *Atti della R. Accad. dei Lincei*, ser. v, Cl. di Scienze Morali, Storiche e Filologiche, viii (Rome, 1903), p. 26.

70 For Prous Boneta, see W. May, 'The Confession of Prous Boneta Heretic and Heresiarch', *Essays in Medieval Life and Thought Presented in honour of Austin Patterson Evans* (New York, 1955), pp. 3–30.

71 H. Grundmann, *Religiöse Bewegungen im Mittelalter* (Hildesheim, 1961), chs. IV, V, VI.

72 edn. in *Analecta Augustiniana*, iv (1911–2), pp. 279–83, 298–307, 321–8, and by R. Arbesmann, *Augustiniana*, vi (1956), pp. 37–145.

73 *Expos.*, ff. 176r, 120r–v.

74 See *Influence of Prophecy*, pp. 258–9, 478, for references.

75 Ibid., pp. 259, 476–8.

76 Ibid., p. 478.

77 Ibid., pp. 254–6 on John Erghome.

78 The so-called Prophecies of John of Bridlington were published by T. Wright, *Political Songs and Poems*, *RS*, i, pp. 123–215; see especially p. 204.

79 *Pars Historialis* (Nuremberg, 1484), iii, ff. ccliiii^v–cclv^r.

80 For a fuller account of this group, see *Influence of Prophecy*, pp. 262–7.

81 This compilation survives in MS. Lat. Cl. III, 177 in the Bibl. Marc., Venice. See *Influence of Prophecy*, pp. 173, 343–6.

82 Published under the title *Expositio magni prophete Joachim in librum beati Cirilli de magnis tribulationibus et statu sanctae matris ecclesiae* (cited as *Libellus*).

83 *Libellus*, f. 22r.

84 Ibid, 2nd edn., f. iiii.

85 *Super Hier.*, Dedicatory Letter.

86 *Libellus*, f. 21r.

87 *Super Hier.*, Dedicatory Letter.

88 *Le Chandelier d'or du Temple de Salomon* (Lyon, 1643), pp. 151–2.

CHAPTER 3

1 *Lib. Fig.*, Pl. XIV; *Figurae*, pp. 146–52. See also R. Daniel, 'Apocalyptic Conversion: The Joachite Alternative to the Crusades', *Traditio*, xxv (1969), pp. 127–54.

2 *Expos.*, f. 134r–v.

3 *Lib. Conc.*, ff. 17v, 92v, 134v; *Lib. Fig.*, Pls. XV, XVI.

4 *Lib. Fig.*, Pls. XV, XVI.

5   See Cohn, *Millennium*; E. Sackur, *Sibyllinische Texte*. See also P. J. Alexander, *The Oracle of Baalbek. The Tiburtine Sibyl in Greek Dress* (Dumbarton Oaks, 1967); 'Medieval Apocalypses as Historical Sources', *Amer. Hist. Rev.*, lxxiii (1968), pp. 997–1018; 'Byzantium and the Migration of Literary Works and Motifs', *Medievalia et Humanistica*, N.S. ii (1971), pp. 47–68; J. Wortley, 'The Warrior Emperor of the Andrew Salos Apocalypse', *Analecta Bollandiana*, lxxxviii (1970)', pp. 43–59.

6   *Super Hier.*, ff. 11v, 15v, 18v, 45v–46v, 58v, 62r.

7   *Supra*, p. 35.

8   *De Oneribus*, ff. 38v–44r; *Super Esaiam*, ff. 3r, 15r, 19r–20r, 27r, 29r, 35r, 37r–40v, 42v, 46v–47v, 49v, 59r.

9   For references and further discussion of Frederick II's attitude, see *Influence of Prophecy*, pp. 309–10.

10 Ibid., pp. 310–1, for references to the Swabian group.

11 *MGHS*, xxiv, p. 207.

12 See list of references in *Influence of Prophecy*, p. 312, n. 1.

13 ed. O. Holder-Egger, *Neues Archiv der Gesellschaft für ältere deutsche Geschichtskunde*, xxx (1904–5), pp. 383–4.

14 ed. H. Grundmann, *Alexander v. Roes, De Translatione Imperii u. Jordanus v. Osnabrück, De Prerogativa Romani Imperii* (Leipzig, 1930), pp. 30–1.

15 Descent through Constance, daughter of Manfred, who married Peter of Aragon. On Frederick's friendship with Arnold and role as protector of Fraticelli, see the forthcoming study cited *supra*, n. 54, p. 181.

16 ed. K. Lanz, *Chronik des edlen En Ramon Muntaner* (Stuttgart, 1844), p. 331.

17 *Dantis Alagherii Epistolae*, ed. & trs. P. Toynbee, 2nd edn. (Oxford, 1966), Epistle V, 'To the Princes and Peoples of Italy', pp. 47–62; Epistle VI, 'To the Florentines', pp. 66–81.

18 Dante, *Divina Commedia, Inferno*, i, 101–11; *Purgatorio*, xxxiii, 43–5; *Paradiso*, xvii, 76–90.

19 *Paradiso*, xii, 140–1: '. . . il Calabrese abate Gioacchino di spirito profetico dotato'. This echoes the Antiphon to Vespers in which Joachim's Order commemorated their founder.

20 *Paradiso*, xviii.

21 *Lib. Fig.*, Pls. V, VI.

22 *Supra*, p. 19

23 *Lib. Fig.*, Pl. XI.

24 Tondelli, *Lib. Fig.* I, p. 223.

25 *Expos.*, f. 101r.

26 J. N. Hillgarth, *Ramon Lull and Lullism in Fourteenth-Century France* (Oxford, 1971), ch. II.

27 ed. C. Langlois (Paris, 1891), pp. 98–9.

28 See H. Grundmann, 'Die Liber de Flore', *Historisches Jahrbuch*, xlix (1929), p. 71.

29 The fundamental work on Roquetaillade has been done by J. Bignami-Odier, *Roquetaillade*, from which the material in the following two paragraphs has been drawn.

30 For Telesphorus's *libellus*, see bibl. On Telesphorus, see E. Donckel, 'Die Propheziung des Telesforus', *AFH*, xxvi (1933), pp. 29–104; *Influence of Prophecy*, pp. 325–30, 423–4.

31 MS. Rome, Vatican Lib., Reg. Lat. 580, f. 52r.

32 See *Influence of Prophecy*, pp. 330–1, 341–6, 355–7, 361–3, 368, 370, 378, 380, 386, 391–2.

33 M. Chaume, 'Une prophétic relative à Charles VI', *Revue du Moyen Âge latin*, iii (1947), pp. 27–42.

34 For references and further discussion of Cola di Rienzo, see *Influence of Prophecy*, pp. 318–19, 420–1; Burdach, *Vom Mittelalter*, II, Pt. iii.

35 For Gamaleon references, see *Influence of Prophecy*, p. 332.

36 *Vita*, pp. 83–4.

37 *Expos.*, f. 170v.

38 *Lib. Conc.*, f. 92v.

39 Ibid., ff. 56r, 122v, 132v. See also f. 89r for the exaltation of Joseph as a figure of the Papacy.

40 Ibid., f. 95v.

41 *Super Hier.*, ff. 3v, 10r, 38r; *Super Esaiam*, ff. 15r, 20v, 28v, 58v; *De Oneribus*, ff. 38r, 39r–v.

42 Ed. J. Brewer, *Opera Inedita*, *RS*, p. 86.

43 *Compendium studii philosophiae* (ref. as in previous footnote), p. 402.

44 Salimbene, pp. 492–3.

45 *Oraculum Cyrilli*, p. 292.

46 A. Messini, 'Profetismo e profezie ritmiche italiana d'inspirazione Gioachimito-Francescana nei secoli XIII, XIV et XV', *Miscellanea Francescana*, xxxvii (1937), p. 51.

47 Grundmann, *AK*, xix (supra, n. 29, p. 180 for full reference).

48 See full description in Reeves, *Popular Prophecies*, from which the material in the next four paragraphs is taken.

49 Limborch, *Hist. Inquis.* (full ref. *supra*, n. 43, p. 181), pp. 304, 315–16; *ALKG*, iv, pp. 9, 11–12, 100, 113–14, 120, 122.

50 Grundmann, *AK*, xix, pp. 120–4; *Influence of Prophecy*, p. 412; *Popular Prophecies*, pp. 117–19.

51 For the material in this paragraph, see Bignami-Odier, *Roquetaillade, passim.*

52 Quoted *Influence of Prophecy*, p. 418.

53 For references, see *Influence of Prophecy*, pp. 419–20.

54 *Liber coelestis revelationum*, see J. Jørgensen, *St Bridget of Sweden*, tr. I. Lund (London, 1954), i, 300 *seq.*

55 Petrus de Aliaco, *Concordantia astronomie cum theologia* . . . (Venice, 1490, unpag.), cap. lix.

56 See bibl. for Telesphorus' *libellus.*

57 *Libellus*, ff. 9r–14v.

58 Ibid., f. 14r, cf. *Lib. Conc.*, f. 95v.

CHAPTER 4

1 M. Ficino, *Opera* (Basle, 1576), i, p. 944, quoted *Influence of Prophecy*, p. 429.

2 Cited A. Chastel, 'L'Antéchrist à la Renaissance', *Cristianesimo e ragion di Stato*, *Atti del II Congresso Internazionale di Studi umanistici*, ed. E. Castelli (Rome, 1952), p. 178.

3 See references in *Influence of Prophecy*, p. 430.

4 *Diario della Città di Roma*, ed. O. Tommasini (Rome, 1890), pp. 264–5.

5 On St Cataldus, see refs. in *Influence of Prophecy*, p. 358, n. 1.

6 Ibid., p. 347, n. 2, for refs.

7 See E. Garin, (i) *Giovanni Pico della Mirandola. Vita e Dottrina* (Florence, 1937), p. 147; (ii) *Italian Humanism*, pp. 83–110.

8 P. O. Kristeller, 'Lodovico Lazzarelli e Giovanni da Correggio due ermetici del quattrocento ...', *Bibl. degli Ardenti della Città di Viterbo. Studi e Ricerche ...* (Viterbo, 1960), p. 17.

9 E. Garin, *La Cultura*, p. 190; Garin, *Italian Humanism*, pp. 107–110.

10 Garin, *Italian Humanism*, p. 83.

11 Chastel, *loc. cit.*, n. 2, pp. 177–8. See also P. O. Kristeller, *Studies in Renaissance Thought and Letters* (Rome, 1956), p. 235; Garin, *op. cit.* (i), pp. 167–189.

12 Kristeller, 'Marsilio Ficino e Lodovico Lazzarelli', *op. cit.*, n. 11, pp. 221–47; *op. cit.*, n. 8, pp. 20–7.

13 For these examples and the prophetic background to Charles VIII's expedition, see *Influence of Prophecy*, p. 355.

14 Ibid., p. 355, n. 5, for full refs.

15 Ibid., p. 357, for refs. to this paragraph.

16 Ibid., pp. 358, 434, for refs.

17 Ibid., pp. 252, n. 5, 434, for ref. and quotation.

18 S. Krauss, 'Le Roi de France, Charles VIII, et les espérances messianiques', *Revue des études juives*, li (1906), pp. 87–95.

19 The fullest and most recent study of Savonarola's prophetic background is by Weinstein, *Savonarola.*

20 Ibid., pp. 129–136.

21 *Divina Commedia, Inferno*, canto xv, l. 76.

22 For the following examples, see Weinstein, *Savonarola*, pp. 43–65.

23 For refs. see *Influence of Prophecy*, pp. 430, 358.

24 *Op. cit.*, (n. 1), i, pp. 960–1.

25 Weinstein, *Savonarola*, p. 143.

26 Ibid., p. 144.

27 Ibid., p. 145.

28 See P. Villari, *La Storia di Girolamo Savonarola* (Florence, 1882), vol. II. *Documenti*, p. xi.

29 *Trattato delle revelatione della reformatione della Chiesa* . . . (Venice, 1536), f. 17r.

30 Weinstein, *Savonarola*, pp. 186–7.

31 Quoted ibid., p. 159.

32 Ibid., pp. 185 *seq.*, on Savonarola and the Laurentians.

33 *Oracolo de novo saeculo* (Florence, 1497), sig. c. vii^v. See Weinstein, *Savonarola*, pp. 194–7, 202–4.

34 Chastel, *loc. cit.*, n. 2, p. 183.

35 G. Benignus, *Propheticae Solutiones* (Florence, 1497), sig. c. i; see also sigs. a.ii^v–iii^r, b.vi^r–vii^r.

36 See Weinstein, *Savonarola*, pp. 205–6, 212–20.

37 *Opere novissimamente revedute* . . . (Venice, 1524), *Frottola pro Papa Leone in renovatione ecclesie*, ff. 205v–207v.

38 J. Schnitzer, *Quellen u. Forschungen zur Geschichte Savonarolas* (Munich, 1902), 'B. Redditi, Breve Compendio e Sommario della verita predicata e profetata dal R. P. fra Girolamo da Ferrara', pp. 37–84, especially p. 49.

39 D. Weinstein, 'The Apocalypse in sixteenth-century Florence: the vision of Albert of Trent', *Renaissance Studies in Honor of Hans Baron*, ed. A. Molho & J. A. Tedeschi (Florence, 1971), pp. 313–31.

40 G. Tognetti, 'Un Episode inedito di repressione della predicazione post-savonaroliana', *Bibl. D'Humanisme et Renaissance*, xxiv (1962), pp. 190–9; Weinstein, *Savonarola*, pp. 342–9.

41 On the Medici and prophecy, see Weinstein, ibid., pp. 350–3.

42 Printed by B. Varchi, *Storia fiorentina* (Florence, 1858), pp. 307–28.

43 F. Saxl, *Journal of the Warburg and Courtauld Institutes*, v (1942), p. 84. On the interpretation of this picture, see H. Ulmann, *Sandro Botticelli* (Munich, 1893), pp. 148–9.

44 Weinstein, *Savonarola*, pp. 336–8.

45 For refs. on Meleto, see *Influence of Prophecy*, pp. 437–8; also Weinstein, *Savonarola*, pp. 354–7.

46 For the examples in this paragraph, see Weinstein, *Savonarola*, pp. 324–34, 357–8; *Influence of Prophecy*, p. 438.

47 Weinstein, *Savonarola*, p. 361.

48 Published Venice, 1536.

49 MS. Venice, Bibl. Marc., Lat. Cl. III. 177.

50 Printed in E. Martène & V. Durand, *Veterum Scriptorum et Monumentorum* . . . *Amplissima Collectio* . . . (Paris, 1724–33), iii, cols. 1152–3.

51 *Supra*, p. 93.

52 Weinstein, *Savonarola*, p. 366; J. Schnitzer, *Peter Delphin. General des Camaldulenserorden, 1444–1525* (Munich, 1926), p. 364.

53 On these mosaics, see *Influence of Prophecy*, pp. 96–100.

54 *La Légende des Vénitiens, OEuvres*, ed. J. Stecher (Louvain, 1885), ii, pp. 361–3.

55 *Supra*, pp. 54–56.

56 (i) *Epistola ... ad sanctissimum ... patrem ... Clementem ... Papam septimum ... In Sathan ruinam tyrannidis ...*, pub. 1524; (ii) *Profetie certissime, stupende et admirabili dell' Antichristo et innumerabili mali al mondo*, pub. 1530. On Angelo, see *Influence of Prophecy*, pp. 432–3, 445–6; F. Secret, 'Paulus Angelus, Descendant des Empereurs de Byzance et la Prophétie du Pape Angélique', *Rinascimento, Anno* XIII (1962), pp. 211–24.

57 Described in more detail in *Influence of Prophecy*, pp. 379–80.

58 On the sixteenth-century editions of the *Vaticinia*, see *Influence of Prophecy*, pp. 452–60.

59 *Vaticinia sive Prophetiae Abbatis Ioachimi et Anselmi Episcopi Marsicani* (Venice, 1589), in Latin and Italian, preceded by a life of Joachim by Gabriele Barrio.

60 Ibid., notes to Figs. XV and XXX.

61 *Vaticinium Severi et Leonis Imperatorum in quo videtur Finis Turcarum in praesenti eorum Imperatore ...* (Brescia, 1596).

62 MS. Oxford, Bodleian Lib., Barocci 170.

63 *Essais* (Paris, 1598), Livre i, ch. 11, 'Des Prognostications', p. 36.

64 E. Garin, *Filosofi italiani del Quattrocento* (Florence, 1942), p. 501; S. Infessura, *op. cit.* (ref. n. 4), pp. 264–5; *Influence of Prophecy*, p. 367 and refs. in n. 1, pp. 447–8.

65 Ed. A. Pibram, *Mittheilungen des Instituts für oesterreichische Geschichtsforschung*, Ergänzungsband III (Innsbruck, 1890), pp. 43–9.

66 *Historia rerum Friderici III imperatoris*, ed. J. Schilter, *Scriptores rerum Germanicarum* (Strasburg, 1687), p. 45.

67 J. Trithemius, *Chronicon Hirsaugiense* (St Gall, 1690), ii, p. 423.

68 Infessura, *op. cit.* (ref. n. 4), pp. 292–3.

69 On Amadeus see *Influence of Prophecy*, pp. 233–5, 440–1, 461. See also A. Morisi, *Apocalypsis Nova. Ricerche sull'origine e la formazióne del testo dello pseudo-Amadeo* (Rome, 1970).

70 Weinstein, *Savonarola*, pp. 342, 348.

71 On Egidio (Giles) of Viterbo, see refs. in *Influence of Prophecy*, pp. 268–70.

72 See F. Martin, *The Problem of Giles of Viterbo* (Louvain, 1960), p. 5.

73 J. Hardouin, *Acta conciliorum* (Paris, 1714), ix, cols. 1576–81.

74 *Expos.*, Dedicatory Letter.

75 Unpublished. Two MSS. are in the Bibl. Angelica, Rome. A summary

was published by L. Pelissier, *De 'Historia Viginti Saeculorum' Aegidii Viterbiensis* (Montpellier, 1896).

76 *Scechina e Libellus de Litteris Hebraicis*, ed. F. Secret (Rome, 1959).

77 For references and further discussion on Galatinus, see *Influence of Prophecy*, pp. 234–8, 366–7, 442–5.

78 *In Apocalypsim . . . Commentaria*, MS. Rome, Vat. Lib., Lat. 5567, f. iiiir.

79 Ibid., f. iiiir.

80 *Infra*, pp. 119–20.

81 Ref. *supra*, n. 42.

82 L. Pastor, *History of the Popes*, trs. R. F. Kerr (London, 1910), x, p. 16.

83 *Il sacco di Roma* (Paris, 1664), pp. 4 *seq*.

84 For refs. on the Accolti plot, see *Influence of Prophecy*, pp. 450–1.

85 For further discussion and sources on Paracelsus, see ibid., pp. 454–6.

86 Ibid., pp. 456–8, on Scaliger.

87 See 'Popular Prophecies', pp. 127–31.

88 *Vaticinia seu Praedictiones Illustrium Virorum Sex Rotis . . . cum declarationibus et annotationibus Hieronymi Ioannini* (Venice, 1600).

89 (i) MS. Oxford, Bod. Lib., Ital. c. 73 (*olim* Phillipps 1726); (ii) MS. Bod. Lib., Laud Misc. 588; (iii) MS. Carpentras, Bibl. Imguimbertine, 340.

90 For refs. and further discussion on Lichtenberger, see *Influence of Prophecy*, pp. 347–51.

91 *Prognosticatio* (Strasbourg, 1488), unpag., ii, cap. 16.

92 *De origine et conversatione bonorum Regum et laude civitatis Hierosolymae cum exhortatione eiusdem recuperande* (Basle, 1495).

93 W. Aytinger, *Tractatus de revelatione beati Methodi* (Basle, 1498).

94 MS. Cambridge, Univ. Lib., Kk. VI. 16, f. 185v.

95 See *Influence of Prophecy*, pp. 360–3, for refs. covering the material in this paragraph.

96 See M. Bataillon, *Érasme*, pp. 243–4.

97 Published in Latin edns. in 1534, 1535 & 1544, and in German in 1535.

98 See *Influence of Prophecy*, pp. 367–9, for material in this paragraph.

99 For refs. and fuller treatment of Lazius, ibid., pp. 369–72.

100 Published Vienna, 1547, unpag.

101 Ibid., sig. Hv[r].

102 *De Monarchia Gallorum Campi Aurei: Ac Triplici Imperio, vid. Romano, Gallico, Germanico: una cum gestis heroum ac omnium Imperatorum* (Lyon, 1537).

103 See his *Spaccio della Bestia Trionfante*, written in 1585, ed. G. Gentile, *Opera Italiane*, ii (Bari, 1927), pp. 225–6. On Bruno, see F. A. Yates, (i) 'Considérations de Bruno et de Campanella sur la monarchie française', *L'Art et la pensée de Léonard de Vinci*, *Actes du Congrés Léonard de Vinci* (Paris, 1954), pp. 6–7; (ii) *The French Academies of the Sixteenth Century* (London, 1947), pp. 229–33.

CHAPTER 5

1 *Supra*, p. 29.

2 *Expos.*, ff. 175v–176r.

3 Ibid., f. 83v.

4 *Apologia pro Societate Jesu* (Ingolstadt, 1596), p. 259.

5 *Tomus Quartus Concionum de Sanctis* (Venice, 1595), p. 153; cf. Rev. 9:1–3.

6 Cited J. Nieremberg, *Honor del Gran Patriarcha San Ignacio de Loyola* (Madrid, 1645), pp. 1–4.

7 *Sanctitas Ignatii Loyolae* (Ingolstadt, 1622).

8 *De extremo iudicio Dei et Indorum vocatione* (Antwerp, 1567), cap. vi.

9 *Op. cit.*, p. 166, quoted *Influence of Prophecy*, pp. 277–8.

10 For this and refs. in the rest of this paragraph, see *Influence of Prophecy*, pp. 278–9.

11 B. Viegas, *Commentarii Exegetici in Apocalypsim* (Evora, 1601), pp. 196–200.

12 *Trois tres-excellents predications prononcées au jour et feste de la beatification du glorieux patriarche . . . Ignace fondateur de la Compagnie de Jesus* (Poitiers, 1611), pp. 110–11; cf. Rev. 10:1.

13 *Supra*, p. 46.

14 *Censure de la Sacrée Faculté de Théologie de Paris sur trois sermons prétendus, faicts en l'honneur de P. Ignace . . .* (no place of pub., 1611), pp. 5, 9–10.

15 See E. Allo, *St Jean*, pp. ccxxviii–ccxxx, on the different schools of interpretation.

16 F. Ribeira, *Commentarius in Apocalypsim* (Salamanca, 1591).

17 *Vestigatio arcani sensus in Apocalypsi* (no. pl. of pub., 1614), p. 76.

18 Cornelius Lapierre or Lapidus (Cornelis Cornelissen van den Steen), *Commentarius in Apocalypsim* (Lyon, 1627); *Commentaria in Quatuor Prophetas Maiores* (Antwerp, 1622).

19 *Disputationes super libro Apocalipsis* (pub. Lyon, 1606; edn. used here, *Opera Theologica*, i (Cologne, 1620). For refs. in this paragraph, see *Influence of Prophecy*, pp. 283–5.

20 *AS*, pp. 141–2.

21 On Guillaume Postel, see Bouwsma, *Concordia Mundi* and *Influence of Prophecy*, pp. 287–9, 381–4, 479–81, where full refs. for material in the next four paragraphs are given.

22 Bouwsma (tr.), *Concordia Mundi*, Cambridge 1957, pp. 219–26.

23 *Glosa super Apocalypsim de statu ecclesie ab anno . . . MCCCCLXXXI usque ad finem mundi* (Louvain, undated, unpag.). For refs. in this paragraph, see *Influence of Prophecy*, pp. 463–4.

24 *Onus Ecclesiae temporibus hisce deplorandis Apocalypseos suis aeque conveniens Turcarumque incursui iam grassanti accomodatum . . .* (no pl. of pub., 1532).

25 *In Canticum Canticorum Salomonis . . . Explanatio* (Venice, 1585). See *Influence of Prophecy*, pp. 465–7 for refs.

26 *Collectanea in sacram Apocalypsin* (Paris, 1571); see *Influence of Prophecy*, p. 469.

27 *Sopra l'Apocalisse* (Piacenza, 1569); *Opuscula: In Apocalypsim* (Piacenza, 1570); see *Influence of Prophecy*, pp. 469–70.

28 *Interpretatio in Apocalypsin* (Vienna, 1850). For refs. in this paragraph and fuller treatment, see *Influence of Prophecy*, pp. 389–90, 470–2.

29 On Campanella, see *Influence of Prophecy*, pp. 387–9, 451–2, where full refs. are given.

30 *Monarchia Messiae* (Jesi, 1633).

31 Ed. E. Solmi (Modena, 1904).

32 Pub. Amsterdam, 1640.

33 *Aphorismes*, pub. 1635, reprinted by L. Amabile, *Fra Tommaso Campanella ne' castelli di Napoli, in Roma, ed in Parigi* (Naples, 1887), ii, pp. 291 *seq*.

34 F. A. Yates, *The French Academies of the sixteenth century* (London, 1947), p. 292, n. 1, 296, n. 3.

35 Yates, *loc. cit.* (ref. ch. IV, n. 103), p. 12.

36 T. Campanella, *Poesie*, ed. G. Gentile (Bari, 1915), pp. 201–2.

37 *Raccolta di documenti e studi pubblicati dalla R. Commissione Colombiana pel quarto centenario dalla scoperta dell'America* (Rome, 1894), Pt. I, vol. ii, *Scritti di Cristoforo Colombo*, ed. C de Lollis, *Libro de las profecías*, pp. 76–160, especially p. 83.

38 Quoted Phelan, *Millennial Kingdom*, p. 20.

39 Ibid., p. 22; see pp. 19 *seq.* on the apocalyptic dreams of Colombus.

40 On prophetic expectations in early sixteenth-century Spain, see *Influence of Prophecy*, pp. 359–60, 446–7, based on Bataillon, *Erasme*, pp. 55 *seq*.

41 The next three paragraphs are based on Phelan, *op. cit.*, where a full study of Mendieta will be found.

42 Ed. in four vols. by S. Hayhoe, Mexico, 1945.

43 For Mendieta and Cortés, see Phelan, *op. cit.*, ch. III.

44 G. Kubler, *Mexican Architecture of the sixteenth century* (New Haven, 1948), pp. 3–8, stresses the Apostolic significance of the first twelve Franciscan missionaries and illustrates (Fig. 1) a conventual mural of the twelve which recalls the illustration of the Joachite twelve in the third *status* in the Catalan *Breviloquium* (*supra*, n. 54, p. 181).

45 Ibid., ch. VI. *The Indians, Gens Angelicum.*

46 Ibid., p. 79.

47 Ibid., ch. VII. *The Millennial Kingdom in the Age of Discovery.*

48 Ibid., p. 102.

49 Ibid., pp. 102–3.

50 The next four paragraphs are based on C. R. Boxer, (i) *A Great Luso-Brazilian Figure. Padre António Vieira, S. J., 1608–1697.* Fourth Canning House Annual Lecture (1957); (ii) *The Portuguese Seaborne Empire 1412–1825* (London, 1969), ch. XVI, 'Sebastianism, Messianism and Nationalism'; R. Cantel, *Prophetisme.*

51 On messianic expectation and Sebastianism, see Boxer, *op. cit.* (ii); Cantel, *Prophétisme*, ch. II.

52 Unfinished, partially printed at Lisbon, 1718.

53 Also unfinished, still unpub.

54 See Boxer, *op. cit.* (ii), pp. 373–4, on Portuguese Jesuits who accepted messianic beliefs.

55 *Infra*, p. 166. On Lacunza, see A. F. Vaucher, *Une célébrité oubliée. Le P. Manual de Lacunza y Diaz (1731–1801)* (Collonges-sous-Salève, 1941)

56 No doubt the note of messianic mission was struck in many other sixteenth- and seventeenth-century writings. A French example is found in Claude d'Abbeville's *Histoire de la Mission des Pères Capuchins* . . ., published in Paris, 1614, which, although making no direct reference to prophecy, places French conquests in the New World in an apocalyptic context. It is addressed to Louis XIII's Queen in the hope that 'Le Roy Vostre Fils comme l'ange de L'Apocalypse, tenant un pied sur la terre ferme et l'autre sur la Mer' would see the conquest of all savage peoples by grace. The title-page shows the Queen seated below the rays of the sun with her cloak covering kneeling natives. The figure of the angel of Rev. 10.1–2 is developed in the preface, and again, France is appealed to as another Noah to open the Ark of the Church to the little doves who are the poor savages. France is the kingdom of the Sun and of the three Fleurs de Lys d'Or which signify the Trinity. Therefore the Crown of France is chosen for this special messianic destiny.

CHAPTER 6

1 *Supra*, p. 22.

2 M. Flacius Illyricus, *Catalogus Testium Veritatis* (Lyon, 1597), p. 681; J. Wolf, *Lectionum memorabilium et reconditarum centenarii XVI* (Laving, 1600), i, p. 497; J. Foxe, *Rerum in Ecclesia Gestarum Commentarii* (Basle, 1563), p. 57; *Actes and Monumentes* . . . (London, 1563), pp. 70, 135; J. Bale, *The first two parts of the Actes or unchast examples of the English votaryes gathered out of their own legendes and Chronicles* (London, 1551), f. cviiiv.

3 J. Jewel, *A Defence of the Apologee of the Churche of Englande* (London, 1567), p. 434.

4 For example, P. Duplessis-Mornay, *Le Mystère d'inquité* . . . (Saumur, 1611), pp. 325–6; H. Bullinger, *A Hundred Sermons on the Apocalypse* (London, 1561), Preface; R. Abbott, *Antichristi Demonstratio* . . . (London, 1603), p. 62; N. Bernard, *Certain Discourses* (London, 1659), p. 122.

5 E. Stillingfleet, *Discourse on the Idolatry of the Church of Rome* (London, 1672), pp. 238–46. See also J. Bale, *Acta Romanorum Pontificum* . . . (Basle, 1558), p. 441; Foxe, *Actes and Monumentes*, p. 403; Duplessis-Mornay, *op. cit.*, pp. 398–400; E. Leigh, *Felix Consortium* (London, 1663), p. 115.

6 J. Donne, *The Sermons of John Donne*, ed. E. Simpson & G. Potter (Berkeley & Los Angeles, 1956), viii, pp. 264–5.

7   *Eyn wunderliche Weyssagung von dem Babstumb, wie es ihm biz an das endt der welt gehen sol, in figuren oder, gemal begriffen, zu Nürmberg im Cartheuser Closter, und ist seher alt* (Nuremberg, 1527).

8   E. Enders, *Dr Martin Luthers Briefwechsel*, vi, pp. 43, 52; *Corpus Reformatorum*, ed. C. Bretschneider, i (Letters of Melanchthon), p. 565.

9   *An Answer to a Letter of a Jesuit Named Tyrie* (Saint Andrews, 1572), sig. D.vir. I owe this ref. to Mrs K. Firth.

10 Ibid., sig.D.vir-D.viiir, cf. *Expos.*, ff. 190v, 194r, 198v–199r, 200v.

11 Lynne's version, published London, 1548, was dedicated to Edward VI and Edward, Duke of Somerset. It consists of selected pictures, without original captions or text, but with an anti-papal commentary translated, he says, from the German. This does not derive from Osiander's edition, yet Lynne may have been connected with Osiander, since he published an English version of Carion's chronicle with an appendix by J. Funck, Osiander's son-in-law. I owe this ref. to Mr R. Bauchham.

12 *Idolatrie of the last times*, *Works* (Cambridge, 1605), p. 841.

13 See R. Bainton, 'Wylliam Postell and the Netherlands', *Nederlandisch Archief voor Kirkgeschiedenis*, NS, xxiv (1931), pp. 161–7; Bouwsma, *Concordia Mundi*, pp. 19–20, 276.

14 D. Cantimori, *Eretici*, pp. 88 *seq.*, 187–9.

15 Coelius Secundus Curio, *De Amplitudine Beati Regni Dei Dialogi sive Libri Duo* (no pl. of pub., 1554), pp. 42–70.

16 Ibid., p. 60.

17 Cantimori, *Eretici*, pp. 115–19.

18 On Ochino, see Cantimori, *Eretici*, pp. 120–6, 255–6; R. Bainton, *Bernardino Ochino* (Florence, 1940); I. B. Horst, *The Radical Brethren* (Nieuwkoop, 1972), p. 121.

19 F. Pucci, *Omnibus veritatis studiosis divinam ucem charitatemque precatur*, ed. D. Cantimori & E. Feist, *Per la storia degli eretici italiani del secolo XVI in Europa* (*R. Accad. d'Italia. Studi e documenti* 7, Rome, 1937). On Pucci, see Cantimori, *Eretici*, pp. 380–6 and *Influence of Prophecy*, p. 483–4.

20 R. Bainton, *Michel Servet* (Geneva, 1953), pp. 18 *seq.*, referring to (i) *De Trinitatis Erroribus*, pp. 33a, 39a; (ii) *Christianismi Restitutio*, pp. 39, 40.

21 Cantimori, *Eretici*, p. 45.

22 *Christianismi Restitutio* (no pl. of pub., actually Vienne-en-Dauphiné, 1553), pp. 457–62.

23 Quoted A. Friesen, 'Thomas Müntzer and the Old Testament', *Mennonite Quarterly Review*, xlvii (1973), p. 8.

24 See M. M. Smirin, *Die Volksreformation des Th. Münzer u. der Grosse Bauernkrieg* (Berlin, 1950), pp. 134–206, on this problem.

25 Friesen, *loc. cit.*, pp. 13 *seq.*

26 Ibid., p. 14. See also on Herrgott, F. Seibt, *Utopica* (Düsseldorf, 1972), pp. 90–104.

27 P. Wappler, *Thomas Müntzer in Zwickau u. die Zwickauer Propheten.*
 Schriften des Vereins für Reformationsgeschichte, 182 (Gütersloh, 1966),
 pp. 32 *seq.*

28 M. Borrhaus (Cellarius), *In Iesiae prophetae oracula, Messiae servatoris
 mundi, et Ecclesiae sponsae, atque Adversarii eorum mystica descriptione
 referta* (Basle, 1561). See also Friesen, *loc. cit.*, p. 15; Wappler, *op. cit.*, p.
 65.

29 See references in n. 13.

30 On Joris, see R. Bainton, 'David Joris, Wiedertäufer u Kämpfer für
 Toleranz im 16 Jahrhundert', *Archiv für Reformationsgeschichte*, vi
 (Leipzig, 1937), 11–82; Cantimori, *Eretici*, pp. 108 *seq.* G. Williams,
 Radical Reformation, pp. 382 *seq.*

31 On Hoffman, see *Influence of Prophecy*, pp. 491–2, and refs. there given.

32 Ibid., p. 493, on Rothmann.

33 Williams, *Radical Reformation*, pp. 858, 861.

34 On Brocardo, see J. Moltmann, *ZK*, lxxi (1960), pp. 110–29. D. Cantimori, 'Visioni e Spiranze di un Ugonotto Italiano', *Rivista Storica
 Italiana*, lxii (1950), pp. 199–217; *Influence of Prophecy*, pp. 494–499.

35 Cantimori, *loc. cit.*, pp. 203–5.

36 On Ségur-Pardaillon's connection with Brocardo, see Cantimori, *loc. cit.*,
 pp. 202, 214–16.

37 For full references to Brocardo's works as cited in this and the following
 three paragraphs, see *Influence of Prophecy*, pp. 494–9.

38 J. A. Thuanus, *Historia Sui Temporis, Pars Tertia* (Frankfurt, 1614), iii, p.
 896; H. Spondanus, *Continuatio Annalium . . . C. Baronius* (Paris, 1659),
 ii, p. 809.

39 *Les Pléiades, Ou en l'explication des antiques Propheties conférées avec les
 Oracles du célèbre et célébré Nostradamus est traicté du renouvellement des
 siècles, changement des Empires et avancement du nom Chrestien. Avec les
 prouesses, victoires et couronnes promises à nostre magnanime Prince, Henri
 IV roy de France et de Navarre* (Lyons, 1603).

40 Ibid., p. 96.

41 Agrippa d'Aubigné, *OEuvres Complètes*, ed. E. Réaume & de Caussade
 (Paris, 1877), pp. 326–8.

42 Published 1592 by J. Stuckius with a preliminary verse:
 *Carolus ecce tibi redivivus: pellege: dices Henricus nunc est, Carolus ante
 fuit.*

43 See A. Saitta, *Dalla Respublica Christiana agli Stati Uniti di Europa*
 (Rome, 1948), p. 21. *Supra*, p. 140 for Pucci.

44 Ibid.

45 H. Hauser, *François de la Noue 1531–1591* (Paris, 1892), pp. 173–5.

46 F. A. Yates, *Rosicrucian Enlightenment.*

47 *Supra*, p. 108.

48 Preface by John Dee to H. Billingsley, *The Elements of Geometrie of the*

most ancient *Philosopher Euclide of Megara* (London, 1570), f. 2v. I owe this ref. to Mrs G. Lewis.

49 See *Figurae*, p. 299.

50 Yates, *Rosicrucian Enlightenment*, p. 35.

51 Ibid.

52 B. S. Capp, *The Fifth Monarchy Men* (London, 1972), p. 234.

53 On these prophets, see Yates, *Roisicrucian Enlightment*, pp. 158–60; Capp, *op. cit.*, pp. 233–4.

54 Republished London, 1665. See Yates, *Rosicrucian Enlightenment*, p. 158; M. Spinka, *John Amos Comenius That Incomparable Moravian* (Chicago, 1943), p. 83.

55 On Kuhlmann, see W. Dietze, *Quirinus Kuhlmann, Ketzer u. Poet* (Berlin, 1963).

56 *General London Epistle*, p. 52.

57 Horst, *op. cit.* (ref. n. 18), p. 121.

58 Cantimori, *Eretici*, p. 205.

59 Pub. London, 1581. I owe this ref. to Mr R. Bauchham.

60 The Stillingfleet books in Marsh's library, St Patrick's Cathedral, Dublin, include copies of Joachim's *Expos.* and *Lib. Conc.*, the pseudo-Joachimist *Super. Hier.* and *Vaticinia*, in Regiselmo's ed., and the rare seventeenth-century life of Joachim by Gregorio de Laude or Lauro. I owe this information to Mr Warwick Gould.

61 For Bale's prophetic books, see M. Reeves, 'History and Eschatology: Medieval and Early Protestant Thought in Some English and Scottish Writings', *Medievalia et Humanistica*, NS. iv (1973), p. 105; also H. McCusker, *John Bale, Dramatist and Antiquary* (Bryn Mawr, 1942), pp. 35–47.

62 *A Brefe Chronycle* was published in 1544. His summary of Joachimism is actually drawn from the hostile account of Guido of Perpignan (see *Influence of Prophecy*, pp. 69–70, 475, n. 1). When I wrote the latter note I did not know that Bale possessed Guido's work, a fact which makes it almost certain that the Joachimist addition is his.

63 F. A. Yates 'Queen Elizabeth as Astraea', *Journal of the Warburg and Courtauld Institutes*, x (1947), pp. 38, 82.

64 John Dee, *General and Rare Memorials pertayning to the Perfecte Arte of Navigation* (London, 1577), pp. 54–65.

65 *Supra*, p. 150.

66 Pub. London, 1550.

67 *Image*, sigs. E.iv^v, E.vii^v, H.iv^v, K.vii^v, L^r, Lii^r(Pt. 3) Aa. vi^r, Ll. ii^r.

68 *Image*, sig. H.iv^{r-v}.

69 Ibid., sigs. E.vi^r, (Pt. 3) sig. Cc.iv^v.

70 Pub. London, 1587.

71 *Eicasmi*, pp. 108, 144; see also pp. 149–50, 284–5.

72   *A Plaine Discovery of the whole Revelation of St John* ... (Edinburgh, 1593). I owe this ref. to Mrs K. Firth.

73   Ibid., p. 14.

74   T. Brightman, *A Revelation of the Revelation* (Amsterdam, 1615), Preface.

75   Ibid., pp. 181–5.

76   Ibid., p. 337, list including John of Roquetaillade and Arnold of Villanova.

77   Ibid., p. 348.

78   Ibid., p. 499.

79   Ibid., pp. 390–1, 503–4, 528.

80   Ibid., p. 582.

81   Ibid., pp. 121, 966.

82   *A Revelation of the Holy Apocalypse* (London, 1610), p. 43.

83   Ibid., p. 14r.

84   Ibid., pp. 271–3.

85   Ibid., pp. 315–16.

86   Ibid., p. 329.

87   Ibid., p. 339.

88   *Admirable and Notable Prophesies uttered in former times by twenty-four famous Roman Catholicks, concerning the Church of Rome, defection, Tribulation and reformation* (London, 1615).

89   Ibid., p. 7.

90   Ibid., pp. 86–7; see also pp. 149–50. For a similar expectation of a glorious future for England, see R. Bernard, *A Key of Knowledge for the Opening of the Secret Mysteries of St John's Mysticall Revelation* (London, 1617).

91   *The Prophecie of Paulus Grebnerus, concerning these times* (no pl. of pub., no date, but written on 29 May, 1651). The copy used here is Oxford, Bod. Lib., Tanner 225.

92   Ibid., p. 5.

93   Not Amsterdam, as in *Influence of Prophecy*, p. 391. See Yates, *Rosicrucian Enlightenment*, p. 156. Pareus was interested in ecumenism and lectured to Comenius.

94   *Commentary on the Divine Revelation*, tr. E. Arnold (Amsterdam, 1644), p. 440. See *Influence of Prophecy*, pp. 391–2, for full text.

95   M. Fixler, *Milton and the Kingdom of God* (London, 1964), p. 70.

96   *Prophecys concerning the Return of Popery into England, Scotland and Ireland* (London, 1682), see Bod. Lib., MS. Ashmole 546.

97   Capp, *op. cit.* (n. 52), p. 38.

98   Quoted by Fixler, *op. cit.*, p. 125, from Milton, *Complete Prose Works*, ii, pp. 553–4.

99   *Sparkles of Glory or Some Beams of the Morning Star* (London, 1648), p. 52.

100 Ibid., pp. 54–5.

101 Ibid., pp. 37–50.

102 W. Schenk, *The Concern for Social Justice in the Puritan Revolution* (London, 1948), p. 87.

103 *The Testimony of William Erbery, left upon Record for the Saints of Succeeding Ages* (London, 1658), p. 36.

104 Ibid., p. 39.

105 R. Maton, *Israel's Redemption or the Prophetic History of our Saviour's Kingdome on Earth: That is, Of the Church Catholicke and Triumphant* (London, 1642), pp. 5–6, 29–30, 43, 50, 60–5. J. Burroughs, *An Exposition of the Prophesie of Hosea* (London, 1643), i, pp. 80, 131–3, 183–7, writes in a similar vein.

106 J. Brayne, *The New Earth* etc. (London, 1633), p. 92. See also J. Archer, *The Personall Reigne of Christ upon Earth* (London, 1642), pp. 1–30; B. Hubbard, *Sermo Secularis* (London, 1648), pp. 31–2; Nathaniel Homes, *The New World, or the New Reformed Church* (London, 1641), pp. 7–17, 42–59, 74; E. Burroughs, *A Measure of the Times* (London, 1657).

107 W. Dell, *A Plain and Necessary Confutation of divers gross and Antichristian Errors . . .* (London, 1654), pp. 17–18, cf. *Super Hier.*, f. 43v. His translation, paraphrase and extension of this passage are most interesting. I owe this ref. to Mrs G. Lewis.

108 *The Building and Glory of the truly Christian and Spiritual Church . . .* (London, 1646). This recalls a Joachimist idea that the Third Dispensation would be characterized by boys, see Joachim, *Quat. Evang.*, p. 92; *Super Hier.*, f. 1v.

109 Dell, *Building and Glory*, p. 25.

110 Ibid., p. 31.

111 For instance, ideas of progressive illumination are strong in a pamphlet by W. Gonge, *The Progress of Divine Providence* (London, 1645), p. 12, and in the writings of Gerrard Winstanley, see *The Works of Gerrard Winstanley*, ed. G. H. Sabine (New York, 1941), pp. 101–24.

EPILOGUE

1 *Supra*, p. 120.

2 On Lacunza, see ref. *supra*, ch. v, n. 55.

3 Lessing's essay was pub. in 1780. I have used the translation by F. W. Robertson, 3rd ed. (London, 1872), pp. 69–70.

4 Ibid., pp. 70–3.

5 *Nouveau Christianisme* (Paris, 1852), pp. 235–40. I owe this ref. to Professor Norman Cohn.

6 Ibid., pp. 299–346.

7 Ibid., pp. 301–2.

8   *Système du Politique Positive*, iii (Paris, 1853), p. 485. I owe this ref. to Prof. Cohn.

9   *Romola*, ed. G. Biagi (London, 1907), p. 26. I owe this ref. to Mrs D. Bednarowska.

10 Ibid., p. 265.

11 Ibid., p. 10.

12 K. Löwith, *Meaning in History* (Chicago, 1957), pp. 209–10.

13 Ibid., p. 210.

14 F. W. Schelling, *Sämmtliche Werke*, ii, 4 (Stuttgart & Augsburg, 1858), *Philosophie der Offenbarung*, p. 298, n. 1.

15 P. J. Alexander, 'Byzantium and the Migration of Literary Works and Motifs. The Legend of the Last Roman Emperor', *Medievalia et Humanistica*, NS. ii (1971), pp. 47–68.

16 W. B. Yeats, *Early Poems and Stories* (London, 1925), 'The Tables of the Law', pp. 498–516. I owe this ref. to Mr Warwick Gould.

17 *Supra*, p. 152.

18 *Op. cit.*, pp. 465–497.

19 *Supra*, p. 150.

20 Ed. R. L. Herbert, *Modern Artists on Art* (Englewood Cliffs, N.J., undated), pp. 38–40.

21 Ibid., p. 40.

22 C. G. Jung, *Collected Works*, ed. H. Read *et al.*, tr. R. F. Hull, ix, Pt. II (London, 1959), *Aion*, p. 83. I owe this ref. to Mrs M. Wheeler.

23 Ibid., p. 82.

SELECT BIBLIOGRAPHY ON JOACHIM AND HIS WORKS

Abbreviations used in note references are given in brackets.

I
The main works of Joachim

1 *Liber Concordie* (ed. Venice, 1519) (*Lib. Conc.*)
   MSS. Padua, Bibl. Anton., 328, ff. 1–138.
   Rome, Bibl. Corsin., 41. F.2, ff. 1–115.
   Rome, Vatican, Borgh. 190, ff. 5–181.
   Florence, Bibl. Laur., Conv. Soppr. 358, ff. 1–116.
   Florence, Bibl. Laur., Plut. VIII, dextr. x, ff. 1–166.
   Paris, Bibl. Nat., Lat. 10453, ff. 1–91.
   Paris, Bibl. Nat., Lat. 16280, ff. 1–261.
   Bamberg, Staats-Bibl., Msc. Bibl. 152, ff. 1–101.

2 *Expositio in Apocalypsim* (ed. Venice, 1527) (*Expos.*)
   MSS. Rome, Vatican, Chig. A. VIII, 231, ff. 1–104.
   Rome, Bibl. Casanaten., 1411, ff. 1–191.
   Milan, Bibl. Ambros., H. 15, inf. misc., ff. 65–160
   (A longer version of the *Liber Introductorius* of this work)
   MSS. Pavia, Bibl. Univ., Aldini 370, ff. 1–78.
   Rome, Vatican, Reg. Lat. 132, ff. 58–95.
   Paris, Bibl. Nat., Lat. 427, ff. 46–94.
   Paris, Bibl. Nat., Lat. 2142, ff. 103–33.

3 *Psalterium decem chordarum* (ed. Venice, 1527) (*Psalt.*)
   MSS. Padua, Bibl. Anton., 322, ff. 1–42.
   Paris, Bibl. Nat., Lat. 427, ff. 1–45.
   Rome, Vatican, Lat. 5732, ff. 1–36.

4 *Tractatus super Quatuor Evangelia* (ed. E. Buonaiuti, Rome, 1930) (*Quat. Evang.*)
   MSS. Padua, Bibl. Anton., 322, ff. 81–136.
   Dresden, Sächs. Landesbibl., A. 121, ff. 179–221.

5   *Tractatus de Vita S. Benedicti et de Officio Divino secundum eius Doctrinam (Vita)*
(ed. C. Baraut, *Analecta Sacra Tarraconensia*, xxiv (1951)

    MSS. Padua, Bibl. Anton., 322, ff. 141–9. pp. 42–118.
    Rome, Vatican, Lat. 4860, ff. 35–44.

6   *Adversus (or Contra) Judaeos* (ed. A. Frugoni, Rome, 1957) (*Adv. Jud.*)

    MSS. Padua, Bibl. Anton., 322, ff. 57–71.
    Reggio Emilia, Bibl. Semin., R2, ff. 2–11.
    Dresden, Sächs. Landesbibl., A.121, ff. 223–35.
    London, Brit. Mus., Add. 11439, ff. 78–98

7   *Liber Figurarum* (ed. L. Tondelli, M. Reeves, B. Hirsch-Reich, Turin, 1953) (*Lib. Fig.*)

    MSS. Oxford, Corpus Christi Coll., 255A, ff. 4–14.
    Reggio Emilia, Bibl. Semin., R1, ff. 1–20.
    Dresden, Sächs. Landesbibl., A.121, ff. 87–96.

(I have omitted several smaller tracts and sermons, both published and unpublished, and have listed only some of the most important manuscripts)

II
The most important pseudo-Joachimist works

1   *Super Hieremiam Prophetam* (ed. Venice, 1516, 1527; Cologne, 1577) (*Super Hier.*)

2   *Super Esaiam Prophetam* (ed. Venice, 1517) (*Super Esaiam*)

3   *De Oneribus Prophetarum* (ed. O. Holder-Egger, *Neues Archiv*, xxxiii, pp. 139–87) (*De Oneribus*)

4   *Oraculum Cyrilli cum expositione Abbatis Joachim* (*Oraculum Cyrilli*) (ed. P. Puir in Burdach, *Vom Mittelalter*, II, iv, Appendix, pp. 241–327). (full ref. in bibl. to ch. III)

5   *Vaticinia de Summis Pontificibus* (*Vaticinia* or Pope-prophecies) (various sixteenth- and seventeenth-century editions)

6   *Breviloquium super Concordia Novi et Veteris Testamenti* (*Brev.*) (forthcoming edition by H. Lee and M. Reeves)

7   *Expositio magni prophete Joachim in librum beati Cyrilli* or *Libellus de magnis tribulationibus ... compilatus a Theolosphoro de Cusentia* (Telesphorus of Cosenza) (*Libellus*) (ed. Venice, 1516).

III
Selected works on Joachim and Joachimism

E. Buonaiuti, *Gioacchino da Fiore, i tempi, la vita, il messaggio* (Rome, 1931)

A. Crocco, *Gioacchino da Fiore e il Gioachimismo* (Naples, 1976)

F. Foberti, *Gioacchino da Fiore, Nuovi studi critici sull' mistica e la religione in Calabria* (Florence, 1934)

F. Foberti, *Gioacchino da Fiore e il Gioacchinismo antico e moderno* (Padua, 1942)

H. Grundmann, *Studien über Joachim von Floris* (Leipzig, 1927)

H. Grundmann, *Neue Forschungen über Joachim von Floris* (Marburg, 1950)

J. Huck, *Joachim von Floris und die joachitische Literatur* (Freiburg im Breisgau, 1938)

M. Reeves, *The Influence of Prophecy in the Later Middle Ages. A Study in Joachimism* (Oxford, 1969) (*Influence of Prophecy*)

M. Reeves, B. Hirsch-Reich, *The Figurae of Joachim of Fiore* (Oxford, 1972) (*Figurae*)

F. Russo, *Gioacchino da Fiore e le fondazioni florensi in Calabria* (Naples, 1958)

L. Tondelli, *Il Libro delle Figure dell' Abate Gioacchino*, vol. i (2nd ed., Turin, 1953) (*Lib. Fig.* I)

D. West, ed., *Joachim of Fiore in Christian Thought* (New York, 1975)

IV
Select Bibliography relating to separate chapters

CHAPTER 1. See above.

CHAPTER 2.

E. Benz, *Ecclesia Spiritualis* (Stuttgart, 1934)

G. Bondatti, *Gioachinismo e Francescanesimo nel Dugento* (S. Maria degli Angeli, Porziuncola, 1924)

D. Douie, *The Nature and Effect of the Heresy of the Fraticelli* (Manchester, 1932)

E. R. Daniel, *The Franciscan Concept of Mission in the High Middle Ages* (Lexington, Kentucky, 1975)

M. Lambert, *Franciscan Poverty* (London, 1961)

G. Leff, *Heresy in the Later Middle Ages* (Manchester, 1967)

R. Manselli, *La 'Lectura Super Apocalipsim' di Pietro di Giovanni Olivi* (Rome, 1955)

Pou y Marti, *Visionarios, Beguinos y Fraticelos Catalanes* (Vich, 1930) (*Visionarios*)

F. Tocco, *Studii Francescani*. Nuova biblioteca di letteratura, storia ed arte, vol. iii (Naples, 1909) (*SF.*)

J. Ratzinger, *Die Geschichtstheologie die heiligen Bonaventuras* (Munich, 1959) (*Bonaventura*)

B. Tierney, *Origins of Papal Infallibility* 1150–1350 (Leiden, 1972) (*Papal Infallibility*)

CHAPTER 3

J. Bignami-Odier, *Études sur Jean de Roquetaillade* (Paris, 1952) (*Roquetaillade*)

K. Burdach, *Vom Mittelalter Zur Reformation*: I (Berlin, 1913); II, Pt. i (Berlin, 1913); Pt. ii (Berlin, 1928); Pt. iii (Berlin, 1912); Pt. iv (Berlin, 1912); Pt. v (Berlin, 1929) (*Vom Mittelalter*)

N. Cohn, *The Pursuit of the Millennium* (London, 1970) (*Millennium*)

H. Finke, *Aus den Tagen Bonifaz VIII* (Munster, 1902)

F. Kampers, *Die deutsche Kaiseridee* (Munich, 1896)

B. McGinn, 'Apocalypticism in the Middle Ages', *Medieval Studies*, xxxvii (1975), pp. 252–86

M. Reeves, 'Some popular prophecies from the fourteenth to the seventeenth centuries', ed. G. J. Cuming & D. Baker. *Popular Belief and Practice* (Cambridge, 1972), pp. 107–33 (*Popular Prophecies*)

E. Sackur, *Sibyllinische Texte u. Forschungen. Pseudo-Methodius, Adso u. die tiburtinische Sibylle* (Halle, 1898) (*Sibyllinische Texte*)

CHAPTER 4

M. Bataillon, *Érasme et l'Espagne* (Paris, 1937) (*Érasme*)

E. Garin, *La Cultura Filosofica del Rinascimento Italiano* (Florence, 1961) (*La Cultura*)

E. Garin, *Italian Humanism*, tr. P. Munz (Oxford, 1965) (*Italian Humanism*)

F. Secret, *Les Kabbalistes chrétiens de la Renaissance* (Paris, 1964)

D. Weinstein, *Savonarola and Florence: Prophecy and Patriotism in the Renaissance* (Princeton, 1970) (*Savonarola*)

CHAPTER 5

E. Allo, *St Jean. L'Apocalypse* (Paris, 1921) (*St Jean*)

M. Bataillon, *Érasme et l'Espagne* (Paris, 1937) (*Érasme*)

W. Bouwsma, *Concordia Mundi. The career and thought of Guillaume Postel* (Cambridge, 1957) (*Concordia Mundi*)

R. Cantel, *Prophétisme et Messianisme dans l'OEuvre D'Antonio Vieira* (Paris, 1960) (*Prophétisme*)

J. L. Phelan, *The Milennial Kingdom of the Franciscans in the New World. A Study of the Writings of Gerónimo de Mendieta (1525–1604)* (Berkeley & Los Angeles, 1956) (*Milennial Kingdom*)

CHAPTER 6

D. Cantimori, *Eretici italiani del Cinquecento* (Florence, 1939) (*Eretici*)

W. Haller, *Foxe's Book of Martyrs and the Elect Nation* (London, 1963)

C. Hill, *Antichrist in Seventeenth-Century England* (Oxford, 1971)

W. Lamont, *Godly Rule: Politics and Religion 1603–60* (London, 1969)

J. Moltmann, 'Jacob Brocardo als Vorläufer der Reich-Gottes-Theologie und der symbolisch-prophetischen Schriftauslegung des Johann Coccejus', *Zeitschrift für Kirchengeschtichte*, lxxi (1960), pp. 110–29 (*ZK*)

F. Seibt, *Utopica* (Düsseldorf, 1972)

G. Williams, *The Radical Reformation* (Philadelphia, 1962) (*Radical Reformation*)

F. A. Yates, *The Rosicrucian Enlightenment* (London & Boston, 1972) (*Rosicrucian Enlightenment*)

INDEX

Index

205